WHEN THE AK-47s FALL SILENT

WHEN THE AK-47s FALL SILENT

Revolutionaries, Guerrillas, and the Dangers of Peace

Edited and translated by

Timothy C. Brown

HOOVER INSTITUTION PRESS
Stanford University
Stanford, California

www.hoover.org

Hoover Institution Press Publication No. 476
Hoover Institution at Leland Stanford Junior University,
Stanford, California, 94305-6010

First printing 2000
19 18 17 16 15 14 13 12   10 9 8 7 6 5 4 3
Manufactured in the United States of America
The paper used in this publication meets the minimum
Requirements of the American National Standard for
Information Sciences—Permanence of Paper for Printed
Library Materials, ANSI/NISO Z39.48-1992. ♾

Library of Congress Cataloging-in-Publication Data
When the AK-47s fall silent : revolutionaries, guerrillas, and the
dangers of peace / edited and translated by Timothy C. Brown.
    p. cm.—(Hoover Institution Press publication series ; 476)
Includes bibliographical references and index.
ISBN-13: 978-0-8179-9842-4 (pbk. : alk. paper)
ISBN-10: 0-8179-9842-X (pbk. : alk. paper)
1. Nicaragua—History—Revolution, 1979—Personal narratives—Congresses.
2. Insurgency—El Salvador—History—Congresses.   3. Guerrillas—Nicaragua—
Biography—Congresses.   4. Guerrillas—El Salvador—Biography—Congresses.
5. Revolutionaries—Nicaragua—Biography—Congresses.   6. Counterrevolutionaries—
Nicaragua—Biography—Congresses.   7. Conflict management—Central America—
Congresses.   I. Brown, Timothy C. (Timothy Charles), 1938–
F1528.W496   2000
972.84—dc21   00-023505

For Leda, and for all those who choose peace over war, persuasion over coercion, democracy over dictatorship, and individual freedoms over collective dogmas, that their visions may overcome.

CONTENTS

Illustrations

Abbreviations

ACRN	Asociación Cívica Resistencia Nicaragüense. Resistance [Contra] postwar veterans' organization.
AK-47	A Russian-designed automatic assault rifle favored by revolutionaries, guerrillas, and some criminals worldwide. AK stands for Anton Kalashnikov, its designer.
CIAV	Also CIAV/OAS, CIAV/OEA, Comisíon Internacional de Apoyo y Verificacíon, OAS office in Nicaragua responsible for facilitating the Resistance's reinsertion.
DDR	The process of disarmament, demobilization, and reinsertion of an armed group back into civil society.
ERN	Ejército de Resistencia Nicaragüense. See FDN.
FDN	Fuerza Democrática Nicaragüense, the main Resistance [Contra] Army.
FMLN	Frente Faribundo Martí de Liberación Nacional, of El Salvador.
FSLN	Frente Sandinista de Liberación Nacional, of Nicaragua.

FRS   Frente Revolucionario Sandino.
OAS   Organization of American States.
ONUCA   Observadores de las Naciones Unidas en
           Centroamérica, a U.N. military observer force
           responsible for facilitation of several disarmament
           and demobilization operations in Central America.
RN   Resistencia Nicaragüense, used here to designate
           only the armed Resistance and its civilian support
           base. Often also used in the literature to designate the
           parallel external civilian Resistance political
           movement.
YAAD   YATAMA Aiklakla Almok Daknika, Miskito Indian
           veterans' organization
YATAMA   Yapti Tasba Masraka Nana Asla Takanka, the main
           Miskito Indian [Contra] Army.

FOREWORD

An era of bloody struggles, led by armed revolutionaries with AK-47s in hand, which once engulfed our region from the Caribbean Sea to the Panamanian isthmus, with Mexico right in the middle, is coming to an end, and another struggle for justice and freedom but via the ballot box, not out of the barrel of a gun, is beginning. For it to succeed, democratic dialogue must replace the din of battle. This book begins that dialogue.

Those who speak here are among those who once pulled the triggers of their AK-47s, causing the din of combat so loudly heard on the battlefields of yesterday's revolutions. Today they are participants in democracy. The essays collected here initiate an open dialogue among many who once thought of each other as mortal enemies but who, when brought together, discovered they all had been struggling for much the same thing: justice in unjust lands, freedom where there was none, prosperity where far too many were poor, democracy where dictatorship held sway. It is entirely fitting that this dialogue on Central America, Mexico, and the Caribbean, bringing together as it does so many onetime enemies, began in Mexico, in the ancient city of Puebla at the heart of the ancestral lands of the Nahua and beneath the shadow of that most majestic of volcanoes, Popocatepetl, because it was from Puebla more than a thousand years ago our mutual forefathers set out to settle the lands over which Central America's recent conflicts were fought—Guatemala, El Salvador, Nicaragua, Honduras, and Costa Rica.

It is also especially fitting that these former foes in Central America's wars should join one another under the auspices of a North American think tank, the Hoover Institution on War, Revolution and Peace, dedicated to studying just such problems as theirs as part of its renewed efforts in Latin America: to discuss why they once fought so fiercely and to try to better understand the dawning era of democracy in which each is now an active participant. Although historically much has divided Mexico and Central America from the United States, all those whose voices are heard here believe ardently that peace is far better than war, that freedom is infinitely preferable to tyranny, and that democracy is always preferable to dictatorship. Central America's wars were fought precisely because none of these blessings was truly available to the common folk. Today peace, freedom, and democracy are all within our grasp. To achieve them, ancient problems must be resolved. Yesterday's conflicts were responses to real grievances, and until these grievances are resolved our goals cannot be achieved. I also believe that the best route to achieving them is through democracy.

One need not pass judgment on the exceptionally varied ideologies of the former revolutionaries and guerrillas who participated in this study, or on the sometimes excruciatingly painful actions they took, to be heartened by having activists of such diverse backgrounds sit down together to discuss not just their pasts but also their futures. It is especially heartening that they did so in the presence and with the support of international peacemakers dedicated to facilitating their dialogue. Those who speak here speak of lives lived over an immense range. Those lives reflect personal commitments and experiences covering the entire twentieth century, all of America from the United States to Panama, and each of its liberation struggles. They range from the voice of a second-generation Mexican revolutionary, and second-generation friend, whose family roots run deep from within both the Mexican Revolution and Augusto Cesar Sandino's anti-imperialist war to the Sandinista revolution in Nicaragua to a simple Nicaraguan mountain peasant whose life story spans the same century and many of the same events but from a vastly different perspective. Yet both voices ring true.

It is also not necessary either to endorse or to criticize any of those who speak here to recommend strongly that one listen to these voices. Each has much to say of great value to anyone trying to understand why our region slid into the abyss of war and who is now dedicated to helping it through its painful transition from war to peace. They all speak of how the problems of closed systems and unfair distributions of income and power pushed them over the abyss and into armed struggles, and all warn that we must henceforth heed the will of the masses and respond to those who have been marginalized for too long, lest this sad and violent story repeat itself.

Of special interest are three essays included here. One is by a woman, a female combatant, a comando of the Nicaraguan Contras who speaks not just for herself but as a voice from among one of our traditionally most marginalized groups, women. Regardless of what one thinks of her cause, her story is an inspiration because it says so much about the ability and willingness of women to play key roles alongside men in efforts to change their worlds. A second is by a Miskito Indian. Again, and regardless of how one views his cause, his story is both a warning and an inspiration, a warning that in the modern democratic world the too long marginalized Indians of the Americas—and here Mexico need take special note—must henceforth be heard but that, if heeded, they can become responsible players on the national scene. The third is actually a set of several essays by simple peasants who fought on all sides of the region's conflicts. Their struggles say to everyone, whether left or right, rich or poor, urban or rural, "We the peasants can no longer be ignored. We, too, must be heard." Together, these essays constitute a clear warning that unless ways are found to include such groups—women, Indians, peasants, and any others who have too long been excluded—our dreams of a peaceful, free, and democratic future may well remain just that, dreams. To realize them, the too long marginalized must henceforth be included.

Finally, and of very special note, is a final set of essays by international peacemakers. One, a United Nations general, warns us that peace is more than the mere absence of war. It is not enough for those once at war to lay down their AK-47s and be disarmed. They must also be brought into the new democratic world as full participants. A second, by a former American ambassador to Colombia, forewarns that unless this is done and done well, war can take on a life of its own. Finally, and optimistically, an Organization of American States peacemaker relates a tale of victory snatched from the jaws of defeat, of how he learned to help build peace where once there was only war not from learned scholars or public servants in faraway places, but by finally learning to listen to the simple peasants and workers, the Indians and women, in short the common folk who are the real victims of the violence inherent in armed conflicts. By reversing the traditional approach, he discovered that the people really do know best.

For me, perhaps the most important lesson to draw from this study is encapsulated in the title of one of its essays, by the former military commander of El Salvador's Faribundo Martí Liberation Front: "The Very Best Strategy Is to Avoid War." The second is that this is best accomplished through open and free dialogue among all segments of a society and that this is best done from within a free and democratic system. The final lesson is that with peace and prosperity the ultimate prizes, we should all become peacemakers, not warmakers. The Hoover Institution and the editor, Timothy C. Brown, are commended for initiating this dialogue; what they have produced is commended to the reading of all those committed to peace with justice. May this be only the beginning.

Cuauhtémoc Cárdenas
Coalition Candidate for President of Mexico, 2000
Former Mayor of Mexico City
Mexico City, November 28, 1999

Acknowledgments

This book is the product of many more persons than can be fully thanked here by name, although I am deeply indebted to all of them. But some played special roles, first and foremost among them John Raisian and Charles Palm, director and deputy director, respectively, of the Hoover Institution, without whose help, both moral and material, this study quite simply would not have been possible. Hoover's Bill Ratliff also provided invaluable suggestions and, when most needed, a sympathetic ear. To them should be added Enrique Cardenas and above all Paul Rich of Puebla, Mexico's Universidad de Las Americas, who graciously hosted the first-ever meetings between revolutionaries and guerrillas on which this study is based despite a veritable flood of unusual requests and demands I made on them. To them must be added the contributors themselves, from the former revolutionaries who cast off lifelong clandestine habits to speak candidly in public to the guerrillas who sat down with once mortal enemies. Plutarco Hernández was particularly instrumental in convincing his revolutionary colleagues to participate, as was Oscar Sobalv-arro with the guerrillas. Also, my warmest thanks to Sergio Cara-magna and the OAS for their invaluable help, without which nei-ther Sandino's bodyguard nor *Tigrillo* would appear, and to Ambassador Frechette and General Douglas, both of whom inter-rupted exceptionally busy schedules to participate. Finally, I must both thank and apologize to my long-suffering wife, our children, and our children's children, without whose indulgence of their too often moody and cantankerous husband, father, and grandfather, even with all the other help acknowledged above, this book would never have seen the light of day. Only with them did it become reality.

1

"¡HIJO DE PUTA! WHY DID WE EVER FIGHT?"

It was not your typical academic panel. True, the setting was delightful, the warmly decorated main auditorium of Mexico's most elite private university. But the host, the Universidad de Las Américas (UDLA) in Puebla, Mexico, had felt called on quietly to beef up security, so there were additional police waiting in the wings, just in case. Many in the audience were visibly nervous, asking one another if it was safe to be there. Even the panelists I had brought together were worried lest violence break out, and several asked me as organizer and moderator, only half jokingly, if I was sure their fellow panelists had left their AK-47s at home. The event was the first ever face-to-face encounter between former radical revolutionaries and Nicaraguan Contra guerrillas, between leaders of Nicaragua's original Sandinista National Liberation Front (FSLN), El Salvador's Faribundo Martí Liberation Front (FMLN) and the Mexican revolutionaries who had supported them, and equally prominent though less well-known commanders of two of Nicaragua's democratic Resistance Contra armies, the Fuerza Democrática Nicaragüense (FDN) and the Miskito Indian Yapti Tasba Masraka Nana Asla Takanka (YA-TAMA).

The fears were understandable because all the panelists were veterans of very violent conflicts and, until just recently, had been mortal enemies fighting on opposite sides of exceedingly bloody wars. But they need not have worried. Immediately after the first two sessions, three former top Contras, *Comandantes Rubén* (after Nicaraguan poet Rubén Dario) and *Tigrillo* (Wildcat) of the FDN and *Blass* (after an historic Miskito Indian hero) of the Miskito Indian Resistance, rushed up to me to say: "*¡Hijo de puta!* Son of a b————! We were really worried when you invited us because we thought you were dropping us into a nest of Sandinistas. But they're more Contras than we are!"

They wanted to talk longer, but the international and Mexican press were swarming around us, and all three were quickly drawn away for interviews. As soon as they went off to talk with journalists, the other three panelists and a Mexican revolutionary who was with them surrounded me: *Fermán Cienfuegos* of El Salvador's FMLN, *Comandantes Marcial* and *Martínez* of the FSLN, and "Pepe" Puente, a second-generation Mexican Marxist revolutionary. *Fermán Cienfuegos* summed up their reaction: "*¡Hijo de puta!* Son of a b————! Why did we ever fight one another? They think just like we do. If we had known who they really were, there never would have been any wars!"

Both reactions were perhaps a bit tinted by the emotions of the moment, but they were essentially accurate. Whether revolutionary or guerrilla, all the panelists had in common deep commitments to the well-being of their countrymen, an earlier willingness to put their lives on the line in support of their convictions, and hard-earned new convictions that Central America's wars were both unnecessary and unnecessarily bloody. All still remain committed to the struggle to resolve their region's myriad problems, but they are now dedicated to doing to do so via the ballot box, not out of the barrels of their AK-47s.

This book is divided into three parts. Each of the twelve participants speaks for himself or herself only. Part I, "Revolutionaries," and part II, "Guerrillas," are more descriptive than prescriptive. Part III, "The Dangers of Peace," is more prescriptive and is especially valuable in that it suggests field-tested models for peace-makers to follow.

Part I contains five essays or autobiographical commentaries by former revolutionaries whose personal experiences span Central America's twentieth-century conflicts, from the rebellion of Sandino in the 1920s to the resolution of the war in El Salvador in the mid-1990s. Part II presents commentaries by four guerrillas of the Nicaraguan Resistance, including one who is a bridge between the Sandinistas and the Contras; a female comando (as Contra combatants called themselves);[1] an indigenous force commander; and the last chief of staff of the Contras. Part III features three international public servants who have dedicated their lives to trying to resolve conflicts: an American ambassador, a Canadian general with the United Nations (U.N.), and a peacemaker from the Organization of American States (OAS).

Three of those whose views are presented in this book were not actually panelists at Puebla: one because he was over ninety years old and frail, one because the U.S. Immigration Service refused to issue her a timely travel document, and one because he was not yet ready to go public. But their comments are at least as valuable as those by panelists who did appear. Chapter 2 is the remarkable story of a radical Mexican revolutionary, José Obidio "Pepe" Puente León, and is told here in detail for the first time. He and his family have for generations played key, if almost entirely unknown, roles in half a dozen revolutionary movements, from Nicaragua's original Sandino uprising to Fidel Castro's march to the Sierra Maestra of Cuba to more recent armed conflicts in Nicaragua, El Salvador, Guatemala, and Honduras. Puente's essay begins the book because he is a living organic link between the Mexican Revolution, the original Sandino's resistance to the American Marines, Castro's Cuban Revolution, Cuban and Soviet involvement in Latin America's revolutions during the cold war, both the 1963–1979 anti-Somoza Sandinista uprising and the 1979–1990 Sandinista socialist revolution, and unsuccessful radical attempts at revolutions in El Salvador, Honduras, and Guatemala. Don Alejandro Pérez Bustamante, whose story is told in chapter 3, was the personal bodyguard to legendary Nicaraguan general Augústo César Sandino; it was to him that the namesake of Nicaragua's revolutionary movement entrusted his very life. Decades later, he was a Resistance (Contra) *correo*, or clandestine network chief, to whom hundreds of Nicaraguan Contra comandos entrusted their own lives.

Chapters 4 through 6 are by top radical guerrilla leaders. Alejandro Martínez was a conservative anti-Somoza combatant in the 1940s, fought in numerous guerrilla campaigns, became a senior field commander for the Sandinistas, was pushed aside when he objected to the post-Somoza socialist revolution, and then became an anti-Sandinista commander and the first choice of the Central Intelligence Agency (CIA) in 1980 to head up the Contra movement.[2] Plutarco Hernández was a lifelong revolutionary and a national director of the Sandinista Front for more than a decade; he was a principal architect of that Front's clandestine training, recruitment, and communications systems inside Nicaragua during the war against Somoza. But he too turned against the Sandinista Revolution after 1979. In 1998 he was Costa Rica's ambassador to Russia. *Fermán Cienfuegos*, the author of chapter 6, was the military commander of El Salvador's radical FMLN movement for two decades. *Cienfuegos* is Hernández's first cousin.

Part II begins with a legendary peasant guerrilla leader, Encarnacíon Baldivia, *Tigrillo,* who was first an anti-Somoza combat leader, then a founding leader of the peasant-generated Milicias Populares Anti-Sandinistas (MILPAS) guerrilla movement that was the precursor to the Contras. In 1998 he was a Liberal Party peasant leader. He is followed by a second founding leader of the MILPAS, Oscar Sobalvarro Garcia, *Rubén*, who went on to become the last chief of staff of the main Contra army, the FDN, and president of their postwar veterans' organization, the Asociación Cívica Resistencia Nicaragüense (ACRN). The final two guerrillas are Saris Pérez, *Angélica María*, a woman comando and ranger, and Salomón Osorno Coleman, *Comandante Blass*, the chief of staff of the Miskito Indian Resistance's YATAMA army. When added together, the nine former revolutionaries and guerrillas whose thoughts are collected here have almost 250 years' experience at revolution and guerrilla warfare.

Part III changes the focus from one of insider descriptions and commentaries by armed participants in Latin America's recent wars to one centered on efforts to help resolve both these conflicts and their underlying social conditions. The last three essayists draw lessons from the wars that the first nine fought. The former United States ambassador to Colombia, Myles Robert René Frechette, describes the ongoing and exceedingly bloody revolutionary conflicts in that country. At first blush his contribution may seem out of place. But readers are asked to keep it clearly in mind when reading the next two because the purpose here is not merely to describe what happened in the past but to suggest how we can do better in the future.

Ambassador Frechette's essay is followed by the contribution of Canadian major general Ian Douglas, the original commander of the U.N. International (military) Observer Force in Central America (ONUCA), who discusses the process of disarming a guerrilla force, lessons learned by the U.N. in Central America, and why he believes ONUCA failed in its larger mission. Although disarmament was technically successful, Douglas has since become convinced that it is only the first step in a much more complex process and that in the larger sense his mission failed because the U.N., which depended on public discourse rather than dispassionate analysis for its information, was badly misled as to the real identity of those with whom it dealt and the roots of the conflict they were supposed to help end.[3]

In terms of broad implications, the final contribution, by Sergio Caramagna, the representative of the secretary general of the OAS in Nicaragua in 1997–1999, is of exceptional interest. It deals with the process of reinserting former guerrillas and their families back into civil society and is the product of nine years' hands-on experience trying to bring peace to Nicaragua's countryside well after the Contras laid down their AK-47s. As did General Douglas, Caramagna also found that his mission initially failed because its design was based on wartime propaganda images that did not reflect reality. But, unlike ONUCA, the OAS stayed long enough to correct its mistakes by learning who the people they were assigned to help really were and by successfully shifting its emphasis from treating them as maligned "objects" to dealing with them as human "subjects," which allowed it to abandon its original propaganda-based programs that failed in favor of reality-based efforts that worked. Drawing on these new and successful reality-based efforts, Caramagna provides an exceptional and probably unique first-draft manual for peacemakers based on the lessons learned from the experience.

In many ways this work has been a labor of love, since my own experience in Central America dates back to my youth many years ago. After five wars, ten years as a Marine, twenty-seven years in diplomatic service, and eight years in academia, I remain fascinated by the region. Even more, I consider all the panelists personal friends. I have known *Comandante Marcial*, former Sandinista national director Plutarco Hernández, for more than forty years, all the Contras and General Douglas and Sergio Caramagna for over a decade, and Ambassador Frechette since he was my boss in the 1970s. My friendships with *Fermán Cienfuegos* and "Pepe" Puente are more recent. But all twelve have helped me better understand what happened in Central America and, even more important, each has demonstrated commitment to ending revolutionary violence in Latin America by silencing the region's AK-47s and then continuing the struggle to right the region's historical wrongs, but via the ballot box, not out of the barrel of a gun.

Those well versed in the standard historical versions of the events discussed by these participants will quickly find that what they say happened often differs sharply from the conventional wisdom. For example, Pepe Puente says his father and PEMEX paid Fidel Castro's bills in Mexico; Alejandro Martínez says he saw missiles in Cuba after the Cuban missile crisis; *Fermán Cienfuegos* says the FMLN helped finance the Sandinista revolution; several say Carter not Reagan first offered the Contras covert paramilitary aid; and so forth. It should be kept in mind that while the *bona fides* of each participant were thoroughly confirmed, and I made considerable effort to document when possible their assertions, these are personal narratives not scholarly treatises. These then are their stories, which are well worth listening to.

PART I

Revolutionaries

2

JOSÉ OBIDIO "PEPE" PUENTE LEÓN, THE LIVING LINK

A BIOGRAPHICAL SKETCH

José Obidio "Pepe" Puente León was born in Tamualipas, Mexico. At the tender age of twelve, Puente's father met and fell under the spell of Nicaraguan rebel General Augústo César Sandino, beginning a personal lifelong commitment to revolution and to creating an organic link between his family and Nicaragua. His father later became a lifelong senior official of Mexico's Sindicato de Trabajadores de Petróleo de la República Mexicana (STPRM). In 1954 "Pepe's" father introduced him to both the real leader of Nicaragua's Sandinista revolutionary movement, Noél Guerrero Santiago, and the founders of the Cuban Revolution.[1] "Pepe" went on to become a key link between the Cuban and Soviet embassies in Mexico City and the Sandinista movement, but he was closest to the original Sandinista revolutionaries and took his distance from the better known Nine Comandantos who took control of the movement after July 1979 and then led Nicaragua's unsuccessful 1979–1990 socialist revolution. In 1998 he was an aide to Mexico City Mayor Cuauhtémoc Cárdenas, leader of Mexico's Partido Revolucionario Democratico (PRD) and son of former President Lázaro Cárdenas. Here for the first time Puente speaks publicly about his journey from radical revolutionary to participant in the democratic process.

□ □ □

THE ROAD FROM SANDINO TO
SANDINISMO, AND BACK

José Obidio "Pepe" Puente León (as told to the editor)[2]

Truth above all else. What I say here is both difficult and dangerous but is the truth as I know it based on my lifelong personal
participation in revolutionary movements in the Americas, especially the two most important ones, those of Cuba and Nicaragua.
For me, at the times of their inceptions, prosecutions, and triumphs, they were two of the world's most historically beautiful
attempts at revolution and earned themselves the sympathies of
peoples and governments throughout the world.[3] Yet after their
triumphs, both went sour.

All my revolutionary life I was a Marxist–Leninist and acted
accordingly. But since ending my participation in violent revolutions, I have begun analyzing my experiences, especially my mistakes, and now realize that when I was younger I was too carried
away by the currents of the historical moment. A convinced
Marxist–Leninist never hesitates to act, either politically or by engaging in armed conflict if the conditions of the moment seem
appropriate, and I was certainly a Marxist child of the moment.
But many years have passed and I am no longer afraid to tell my
story, nor do I fear the consequences.

The names of my children demonstrate how dedicated I was
to world revolution, and even the house I live in has a profound
revolutionary history because for many years it was the principal
safe house in Mexico City of the Sandinista revolution. All six of
my children are named after revolutionary heroes. The first, Eva
Fidelia, after Fidel Castro, was born when I still admired him; my
second, Lenin Obidio, after Lenin; my third, Illia, after Lenin's
father; my fourth, Sandino Stalin; my fifth, Engels Marx; and my
sixth, Stokely Mao, born during a period when I was flirting with
Maoism and also a great admirer of the American Black Power

movement and its leader, Stokely Carmichael. A full-wall mural in my living room depicts these and my other heroes. At the top center is a medallion of Marx and Engels. Below them, starting on the left to the right, are Lenin, then Stalin, followed by Mao Tse Tung, Sandino, Fidel Castro, and "Che" Guevara. Stokely Carmichael is in an Africa-shaped tree above Sandino. Nicaragua and Bolivia, which had active revolutionary movements when it was painted, are highlighted on a map insert, as is the United States, which is exploding.[4]

Being the Son of a Son of Sandino

To understand how I became such a dedicated Marxist revolutionary, first you must understand my family background, especially my father. My family home is in the town of Ciudad Madero near Veracrúz. My father was born nearby and at the age of eight began working as a water boy for a foreign oil company owned by a British corporation, carrying water to the workers and for the radiators of motors in buckets hung from the ends of a long pole on ropes. In those days there were no laws or rules protecting workers, and it wasn't at all unusual for someone his age to work in the oil fields. But he was ambitious, and evenings after work he kept studying until he earned his elementary school certificate, and then went on to earn a certificate as a secretary.

One of the most popular men in the oil fields where my father worked was a Nicaraguan by the name of Augústo César Sandino. In fact, as far as many of the Mexican workers were concerned, he was the most important man in the area because he had worked there once before, then gone back to Nicaragua to fight for his country, then come back, and made it no secret he was preparing to go back a second time. Sandino not only made no secret of his plans but also took advantage of two favorable conditions. First, there was a great deal of animosity against Americans among the people of the Veracrúz area at the time because, just a few years before, American Marines had occupied the region by force, and it was against the American Marines in

Nicaragua that Sandino was preparing to fight. And second, there was deep unhappiness among the workers with their foreign bosses, British, Dutch, German, and others, all of whom exploited them unmercifully. So anyone planning to tweak the noses of the imperialists was a hero, and Sandino tapped readily both these sources of unhappiness.

For many of the same reasons Sandino also garnered the sympathies of many Mexican officials and local politicians, who also believed strongly in the struggle against imperialism. His ideas were as popular with them as with the workers, and his reputation grew by word of mouth, often at public events which many of these leaders attended, dances and fiestas, at which one of the most popular forms of entertainment was the singing of popular songs or recitation of poems, many of them in support of Sandino and his struggle. My father often told me how, when he was only twelve years old, he himself met Sandino and, though just a child, began helping collect money to meet Sandino's goal of $5,000, which he said he needed to go back to Nicaragua. During his time in the oil fields Sandino sold gasoline and cooking gas and traveled extensively as part of his job. My father remembered him as well-educated, very ideological, and very popular even with management, because he spoke English and served them as an interpreter and was also able to gain of the confidence of the workers because he was popular among them.

An important but little-known source of support for Sandino also came from the region's Masonic lodges, which hosted many of the dances and fiestas in their halls, in part because Sandino himself was a Mason, as was my father later on. Sandino also caught the eye of two other Masons, then Governor Emilio Pórtes Gil and General Lázaro Cárdenas, then military commander in Veracrúz, both later presidents of Mexico in their own rights. Pórtes Gil decided to support Sandino and his cause and began to channel government money and other help to him, including providing him with transport back to Nicaragua. Cárdenas, as military zone commander in Veracrúz, had personal contact with Sandino but would not have provided that kind of help without the approval of the governor. But because of this support, the government gave Sandino arms from its arsenals and assigned army officers to him as advisors.[5] Lázaro Cárdenas was probably the officer in charge. Even after Sandino returned to Nicaragua and began fighting the American Marines, Mexico apparently continued to ship him arms and recruits through Tampíco, transporting them as well as arms purchased by sympathizers in the United States to him.[6] Many private citizens also did what they could to support Sandino, and money was sent to him from sympathizers within several of the oil companies.

My father told me several Mexicans who went to fight alongside Sandino were killed in combat, including some army soldiers, and I later met several who had been with him, including Andrés Garcia Salgado and Francisco Cortéz, and talked to them about their experiences. They confirmed that many Mexicans had fought alongside Sandino, including officers of the Mexican army, and even some troops, and that several Mexican army soldiers had died in combat against the American Marines. Knowing how Mexicans felt about the United States Marines during that period, I have no doubts they were telling the truth.

It was at this time that my father became politically radicalized, which led later to his joining the Communist Party. As he grew into a teenager, he became conscious of the class differences between the foreigners managing Mexico's oil industry and the Mexicans doing the work and was one of the first oil field workers to organize a labor union by pulling together the existing mutual aid societies of several of the oil companies. He went on to become secretary-general of the Sindicato de Trabajadores de Petróleo de la Republica Mexicana [STPRM], Mexico's national oil worker's union, in the 1940s for a short while and continued in the Communist Party and as a union leader for the rest of his life.

I grew up in this Communist Party–labor union environment and spent as much time as I could with my father in union halls, in organizing sessions, absorbing his ideas. Until 1945 my father's communism was no problem. But then the government of Mexico passed into the hands of a more conservative president, Miguel

Alemán, who moved against the STPRM and specifically against my father. He had earned Alemán's personal enmity when, in 1945, he ordered the members of his Ciudad Madero STPRM Local not to vote for the PRI [Partido Revolucionario Institucional] and the government party lost the election there, the only municipality they lost in all of Mexico. Once president, Alemán ordered the army into the STPRM's union halls, and my father and those who followed him were kicked out. By then I already considered myself a Marxist and remember being very happy when the same year the Soviet Union took over Berlin and Eastern Europe. Imagine! By the age of ten I was already a Stalinist.

From 1945 until 1950 my father's situation was difficult. Then it got worse. In 1950 the PRI split, and a retired general, Enrique Guzmán, supported by Lázaro Cárdenas and several other generals, ran against it in the national elections. My father was their candidate for congress from Ciudad Madero, and I was active in his campaign. I was working in the early mornings delivering milk and selling newspapers and put up posters of my father as I went on my rounds. But my father lost and was pushed even further aside for a while. But still he remained very active in the union and the oil fields and retained a great deal of influence. After a while he began working on union and oil industry programs in Mexico City, including running training programs, while I finished my education at a private high school.

Noél Guerrero Santiago, the Original Sandinista

After I graduated from high school I wanted to study engineering at the Universidad Nacionál Autónoma de México [UNAM], so my father brought me to Mexico City, where he introduced me to his friends from the oil world as he tried to set me up. One of his closest contacts was an advisor on union affairs to the STPRM and other major Mexican labor unions who turned out to be a lifelong Marxist–Leninist Nicaraguan by the name of Noél Guerrero Santiago. At the time, Guerrero was close to Mexico's top labor union leader, Vicente Lombardo Toledano. Just a few days after I met him in the offices of STPRM Local 34 in Mexico City, my father received a call, I believe it was from Lombardo Toledano, saying Guerrero had been arrested by Mexican immigration and was in a jail on Avenida Miguel Schultz and asking my father to go see him, which we did immediately.[7]

Fidel, "Che," and Other Cuban Revolutionaries

To our surprise, on our first visit Guerrero introduced us to some Cubans who were also being held there, led by Fidel Castro and including Fidel's brother Raúl, Ernesto "Che" Guevara, Ramiro Valdéz, Juanito Almeida, Camilo Cienfuegos, and several others. They had been detained by the police at a guerrilla training camp on the slopes of Popocatepetl Volcano near Mexico City close to a village called Amecameca. There was apparently no connection between the arrest of Guerrero and the detentions of Fidel and his group. Guerrero's problem was basically a matter of immigration. Castro's was far more serious because the Cubans had been carrying arms without permission, were clearly involved in preparing for an armed conflict, and were accused of violating Mexico's sovereignty. But both problems were resolved in the typical Mexican manner, by having powerful friends intervene on their behalf, not least Lázaro Cárdenas and Vicente Lombardo Toledano, two of the most powerful men in Mexico.[8] Many Mexicans of the time were quite sympathetic to Castro because of his earlier assault on Cuba's Moncada Barracks, so even though he had been engaged in what normally would have been an inexcusable violation of Mexican territory, they were able to intervene to free him. But it took almost two months. So while they waited in jail my father and I visited them often. Classes at UNAM didn't start until February and I had little else to do, so even when my father couldn't make it I went to see them almost every day, especially Castro's group, and took them fresh fruit and vegetables my father bought for them.

One visit stands out in my mind above the rest, when Fidel told us he was organizing an expedition to go to Cuba to fight against the Batista dictatorship and had been given a boat, the *Granma*,[9] by his brother-in-law, a Mexican engineer married to Fidel's sister Emma, who still lives in Los Pedregales, a very nice district of Mexico City. But both its motor and hull were in bad shape, and Fidel asked my father if he could repair the motor for him. Noél Guerrero urged him strongly to do so, but my father was cautious and checked first with a number of his communist friends, all of whom said Castro was one of them and should be supported. So my father and I went down to Tampíco and borrowed a truck from Petróleos Mexicanos [PEMEX], went to the *Granma* and took the motor out ourselves, loaded it into the truck and took it to the shop of a friend in Tampíco, Luís Sígri, who owned a company where it could be overhauled, Talleres Electromecánicos on Avenida Tamualipas. It was a large motor and fairly expensive to repair, but Sígri did the work and my father arranged for all the costs to be charged to PEMEX, where he was then deputy director of maintenance and warehouse operations. I would never say my father stole anything, but he did "recuperate" the costs of fixing that motor. We then took it back down to the *Granma*, which was tied up at Santiago de la Peña in Túxpan, and put it back in. While we had been doing the motor, another friend, also a Marxist and labor activist by the name of Sr. Decado, had repaired the hull, so once we finished the *Granma* was ready for Castro to use.

When Castro and his men got out of jail they went to live in the home of a woman named María Antonia, who provided them with room and board, paid for by my father from STPRM union funds. They also went back to training for war, this time with Mexican government blessings. It was arranged for them to be helped by a retired Mexican army general, and they were also given more than enough money to live well. I used to go see them at María Antonia's house, which was in a fairly nice part of town at 49 Calle Amparo, next to the Social Security building, and sometimes went out on the town with them. Castro's men lived it up like good Cubans, going out almost every night drinking. They also had a very good cook from Cuba, Zabalú, who made sure they ate well at home, too.[10]

One of the key networks helping Castro and other Latin American revolutionaries in Mexico at that time was controlled by another Nicaraguan, Edelbérto Tórres Espinosa, a lifelong Marxist–Leninist who ran a sort of salon for revolutionaries in Mexico City. I consider Edelbérto Tórres Espinosa the real godfather of the Sandinista revolution.[11] He was especially close to "Che" Guevara, who had been with him in Guatemala a few years earlier when Tórres had been an advisor to then President Arévalo until Arévalo was overthrown by a CIA-backed coup. While in Guatemala, Tórres had been quite close to the Alianza Popular Revolucionaria Americana movement there,[12] one of whose activists was a young girl named Gilda Gadéa. "Che" met her in Tórres's home, where they fell in love and were later married. After Tórres fled Guatemala they and other Latin American revolutionaries created a sort of revolutionary salon around him and his family. During my own visits to Tórres's home there were always lots of Nicaraguans and others around, all talking about revolutions and armed actions. But whether Cuban, Nicaraguan, Guatemalan, Peruvian, or whatever, they all mixed together and thought not in terms of nationalities but of ideology and beliefs. What I also remember was that my father continued to pay the expenses for many of them. For example, he paid all the expenses for Fidel Castro and his group while they were in Mexico City preparing their revolution and years later continued to do the same for Nicaraguans organizing their own revolution against Somoza.

Castro to the Sierra Maestra

As the time came closer for Castro to launch his operation, Fidel moved his men down to a region near Ciudad Madero, possibly because its terrain is so much like that of Cuba and because it was nearer to where they planned to embark. I had become fascinated and went down as often as possible to see them when they were in town taking breaks. They loved to carouse late into the night, and I often ended up paying off their cantina bills. They drank amazing quantities of beer and ran up large tabs at a number of local bars, most of which my father paid off from union or PEMEX funds, although in a couple of cases local communists helped by writing off some of them. As the time came closer for them to leave I tried to convince Fidel to let me go with them to Cuba, but he put me off, probably because I was still very young and also not trained as a guerrilla.

In 1956, Fidel sailed in the *Granma* and until 1959 was in the Sierra Maestra mountains of Cuba. I am still proud that he arrived thanks to the repairs my father and I made to its motor. From the time Castro arrived in Cuba until the success of the revolution, my father and I did everything we could to help him from here. I myself became a clandestine *correo*, or courier, for the 26th of July Movement in Mexico and often had contact with other clandestine couriers, especially those coming from the United States bringing money and other support for Castro's guerrillas.

We also did other things to help Castro while he was in the mountains. In 1957 my father formed the first of many Mexican José Martí societies, in Ciudad Madero. It had an office, a library, and most importantly a propaganda section. Many of the top political activists in Mexico spoke there often and helped us collect money to buy arms and other supplies for Castro. We also received some arms directly from Mexican army arsenals, which were opened up for us by senior officials, and from the police, who were also quite sympathetic. After we had collected up some arms, we would meet in our home or the José Martí Society offices with the captains of ships going back and forth to Cuba from Veracrúz or Tampíco, and arrange for them to be shipped to Castro. We also helped volunteers get to Cuba through Mexico. I particularly remember that a lot of Americans came through our area en route to join Castro, some in groups as large as eight or ten, and that they usually brought their weapons with them.

The Triumph of the Cuban Revolution

Needless to say, when the dictator Batista fell we were euphoric and considered it a major internationalist triumph for Marxism–Leninism and revolutionary struggle in Latin America. It took Fidel eight days to arrive in Havana after Batista fell, but soon after that he sent for my father, who went to Havana on the 20th or 21st of January of 1959 and was to stay for many years as a senior advisor helping develop a system of labor unions. He ran training programs, gave lectures on television, and traveled to union halls throughout the country. I joined him in April 1960. Tickets were cheap and the planes almost empty because people had already begun to fear what was happening in Cuba. My own feelings were very different because I felt a great kinship for Fidel. To me, while a fellow communist, Fidel was a fairly humane one, not a rabid hard-liner like his brother Raúl or "Che," and that made a difference. Until the day I went to Cuba I maintained contact with the Nicaraguans gathered around Tórres and remember that we all believed the Cuban Revolution would quickly be followed by others elsewhere. There was also a sudden increase in small revolutionary groups, especially in Central America, where Nicaragua's Somoza was the principal target because everyone considered him ripe for revolution.

Actually, the first two Central American revolutions began even before Castro's efforts, one in Guatemala led by Marco Antonio Yon Sosa and a largely Conservative guerrilla movement in Nicaragua's Segovian mountains called the Sandino Revolutionary Front [FRS]. The FRS's main effort had been made in 1956, led by a former general who had been with the original Sandino, Ramón "Moncho" Raudales, but they had been largely destroyed by Somoza's Guardia Nacional. Still, a few FRS guerrillas did escape and went deep into the mountains, where they remained active.[13]

The Assassination of Somoza

That same year, 1956, the first Somoza dictator, Anastacio "Tacho" Somoza Garcia, was assassinated. Most people believe

Somoza's assassination was the work of a single student, Rigoberto López Pérez. But Tomás Borge insisted to me during several long conversations at my home that it was actually the result of a plot. At the time Borge was a student activist, and he and another student, Edwin Castro, planned it along with López, who was an excellent dancer. They all knew that Somoza, although himself too overweight to dance much, loved to watch others do so, so the plan was to find an opportunity for López to distract Somoza by dancing before him with one of their prettiest female student activists to get as close as possible to the dictator. As soon as he was close enough, Edwin Castro and Borge would cut off the electricity and López would shoot Somoza with a pistol he had smuggled into the dance hall. In the end both Edwin Castro and Borge failed to perform their parts of the mission, but López succeeded anyway. I had always heard that López had acted alone, and at first did not believe Borge. But when I asked other top Sandinistas, they confirmed his story. The plot didn't go as planned, but it was still successful.

The reaction of the Nicaraguan Guardia Nacional, commanded by Tacho's son, Anastacio "Tachito" Somoza Debayle, a West Point graduate, was ferocious, and many of the most visibly active radical students had to flee the country. But there were others infiltrated into positions where they were less obvious, including some inside the Guardia Nacional itself, who stayed on and continued to work toward revolution. It was about this time that the image of Sandino emerged as the main symbol of opposition to the dictatorship. Among the most important leaders of the opposition then who were to go on to form the Sandinista Front were Carlos Fonseca Amador and Francisco "Chico" Buitrago. Carlos was very much the Marxist and in 1958 was invited by the Russians to an international student festival in Moscow.[14] Some think he stayed to study there, but he did not, although he did write a book about his visit.[15]

Becoming an Active Revolutionary

While with my father in Havana in 1960, I worked on a number of revolutionary projects, cut sugarcane, helped him with his

A rare photograph of Carlos Fonseca Amador, a founder of Nicaragua's Sandinista Liberation Front, with his natural mother, María Fonseca, in Matagalpa in 1958, when he was twenty-two years old. Fonseca's father was Fausto Amador, the principal administrator of the agricultural properties of the Somozas. Contrary to their customary order, which puts patronym first, then matronym, Carlos Fonseca chose to put his father's surname second. Private collection.

work organizing unions, and even helped organize several Committees for the Defense of the Revolution [CDS]. I remember that we went from meeting to meeting constantly and I found it all fascinating. But after about four months, I decided to go back to Mexico to continue my work there, only to find that while it had been easy to go to Cuba it was not so easy to get back. The Mexican airlines kept saying there was no space, even though that wasn't true. My father also wanted to go back for a short visit and found it hard to get reservations. So we decided to go ask our good friend "Che" Guevara, then president of the Cuban Central Bank, for help and went to see him.

While we were waiting in Guevara's antechamber, Noél Guerrero, the man we had visited so often while he was in jail in Mexico, unexpectedly appeared. We were delighted to see him, even more when it turned out that Guerrero had become even closer to "Che" than we were. Almost the moment he arrived, we were ushered into "Che" 's office. Guerrero had some sort of document in his hands "Che" was anxious to see. But they finished their business quickly and we all began talking about revolutionary activities in other countries. It was the first time I had seen "Che" since 1956, but he remembered me well, and my father had seen him several times since arriving in Cuba. As the conversation became more and more animated, right in front of "Che," Guerrero asked me if I wanted to join another revolutionary movement in Nicaragua. My answer was an immediate "Yes!" My father and "Che" told Guerrero they wanted to go, too. It was a moment of great revolutionary enthusiasm. Among others who later said they, too, wanted to go were Camilo Cienfuegos and Tamara Bunke,[16] and "Che" really did try to join us. But Fidel told him he was needed more in Cuba, so he stayed. Had he gone, history might have changed.

Of course, neither my father nor "Che" actually became guerrillas in the Nicaraguan revolution. But I did. I was twenty-three years old, had graduated from UNAM, and had no other responsibilities, so I became a full-time revolutionary trying to overthrow the Somoza government. My connection to Nicaragua was especially deep because of my father's closeness to General Sandino's earlier revolution. "Che" did manage to get us reservations and even gave us tickets, and when we got back to Mexico I immediately started to work for the movement, which as yet didn't even have a name.

My first task was to select and prepare a safe house for our use. I rented an apartment at 164 Calle Chola in Colonia Narvárte. My father went back to Ciudad Madero to arrange for money to pay the rent, buy cots, and generally prepare the apartment as a way station for Nicaraguan guerrillas going back and forth to Cuba. The first to arrived was "Chico" Buitrago, who was to become my closest friend. That was in late 1960. As a recall, "Chico" received three months' training in Cuba and then came back through en route back to Central America. Second to arrive was Carlos Fonseca Amador, then just another guerrilla, albeit with more experience than most. Carlos also arrived from Nicaragua as did, in quick succession, Ivan "Chéle" Sanchez, Ricardo "El Diezcito" Duarte, and Faustino "El Cúje" Ruíz. They were quickly followed by three more Nicaraguans who became leaders of the revolution, Orlando Juan Quintana, Silvio Mayorga, and Tomás Borge. A few did not come from Nicaragua. Dr. Manuel Andara, for example, came from Ensenada, Mexico, to join us.[17] Regardless of where they came from, it was my job to provide them with a place to stay in Mexico City and to help them travel to and from Cuba. Most of the money was provided by my father, who paid for their tickets to Mexico from wherever. I worked under the direction of Edelbérto Tórres. He managed the operation, my father paid its costs, I did the leg work.

The Sons of Sandino Join the Revolution

We were not the first Nicaraguan revolutionary group to organize. Another had been active against Somoza since 1954 and was much more advanced than we were in their efforts to organize guerrilla warfare inside Nicaragua. But when we became the best source of Cuban and other foreign support, its then leader Edén Pastora decided to join with us. He didn't have too many men, but those he had were well-trained and experienced guerrillas who knew the terrain inside Nicaragua much better than we did. Two of the best were Heriberto Rodríguez, who had been active since 1956, and Pedro Pablo Ríos from Ocotál. When Pastora decided to join with us, the guerrillas he brought into our movement turned out to be the best we had. They were the true sons of Ramón "Moncho" Raudales of the original Sandino's army. Carlos Fonseca Amador himself had been a guerrilla in Pastora's Rigoberto López Pérez column, which was led by a former Somoza Guardia Nacional soldier named Julio Alonso, and had been wounded at a disastrous 1959 battle they fought and lost at El Chaparrál. Another former Pastora guerrilla, Santos López, was my commander when I received my own baptism of fire at Bocay, but that was later.

Usually I would meet our people as they flew into Mexico City. Since at first I didn't know most of them personally, we used a system of hand signals to identify one another. A few times I had to go all the way to Tapachula on the Mexico–Guatemala border to meet someone, which was an especially long trip as there was no road all the way. I went by bus to Tonolá and then caught the train for Tapachula. We then took the train back to Tonolá and bus to Mexico City. It was also my job to make sure all those traveling had visas both for Mexico and Cuba, which was not usually a problem. In the case of Cuba, the Cuban Embassy in Mexico City arranged visas quickly for all our guerrilla recruits transiting to Havana and also provided them with tickets. As things progressed, I became the movement's principal liaison officer with the Cuban Embassy in Mexico and came to know those stationed there fairly well. My original working contact was with a first secretary named Orlando Rodríguez, but many others followed.

Preparing for Action

Once enough of our men had been trained and came back, we began arranging to start guerrilla operations inside Nicaragua. I was responsible for handling the money to pay our expenses for this as well, money that came from several sources, in particular Tórres and the Cubans. We decided to establish first an advance base on the Patuca River in Honduras. It was a long trip there from Mexico, especially since there was no road to the Patuca, so we would first go to Tegucigalpa, then to San Pedro Sula, then to Puerto Lempira, and finally overland through the Mosquitia to the Patuca. The Honduran government was well aware of our activities and in fact supported us this time. The president, General Villeda Morales, detested Somoza and agreed to help us, so we were not only able to operate freely inside Honduras, but we also received support from the Honduran armed forces. We bought arms from them, and they delivered them to us at our Patuca River base. We paid, they delivered, which would not have been possible without Villeda Morales's approval.

To provide for an urban center to support our operations along the Patuca I went to Tegucigalpa to find another safe house, which was especially important for comrades who were coming back from Cuba. I found a good one in Comayagüela, the twin city of Tegucigalpa, next to the Ticabus station.[18] The family was sympathetic to our movement and provided us with sleeping space and cooking and laundry services and cleaned up when we needed it. I then went back to Mexico City to accompany Noél Guerrero down to Honduras so he could take charge of our efforts from there.

The trip back was a real adventure. We went piled into a tiny Renault 5 owned by Dr. Roberto Garda Rodríguez, who drove all the way. In addition to Guerrero and myself, the wife of "Chico" Buitrago, Estelita, and my daughter Illia also went with us, making for a very full Renault. We drove overland via San Cristobal de Las Casas and through the highlands Maya towns of Guatemala down to El Salvador and then up to Tegucigalpa, where we went directly to the safe house.

From that point on Noél Guerrero controlled everything, both our money and us, with an iron fist. But we didn't mind. We thought of him as our maximum leader, and nicknamed him *El Patriárca*, the Patriarch. He began giving us concentrated courses in revolutionary discipline, Marxism, and clandestine compartmentalization. We absorbed it all easily because of our youthful energy and our certainty that we would find it even easier than Castro had to overthrow the dictatorship in Nicaragua. I was among the few who had not been trained in Cuba, since at that time, unlike later, Castro was being very careful not to train Mexi-

Dic. 5 de 1962.

Sr. Nicéforo Pérez Cardenas.

S . Ismael Hernández Alcalá.

México. Df.

Estimados compañeros:

Espero que se encuentren bien y que sigan fortalecidos en sus luchas sindicales.

El objeto de la presente es pedirles encarecidamente una ultima e importante ayuda económica para bien de nuestros propósitos.

En este sentido hemos enviado un amigo que pondrá esta carta en manos de Uds.

Las ayudas que Uds. nos dieron cuando yo estuve por allí han resultado de mucho aprovecho y el agradecimiento de todos nosotros es sincero. Ahora los molestamos de nuevo y estamos seguros que nuestro compañero no se vendrá con las manos vacías.

El compañero hablará con Uds. y les suplico tratarlo como si fuera yo mismo.

Es poco lo que hay que decirles en una carta y sobre todo cuando el dinero se interpone y juega indudablemente su papel importante en la primera escena del drama.

Les ruego saludarme a Pedro, Avelino y demás amigos.

Fraternalmente.

Signed letter of December 2, 1962, from Noél Guerrero Santiago to two contributors requesting funds. Guerrero was exceptionally security-minded, and this is the only known example of a letter signed by him. Private collection.

cans there but instead was arranging for them to take their training elsewhere, especially in Russia, North Korea, and Libya, and in the Middle East by the Palestine Liberation Organization. But I had not been one of them, either. Actually the few experienced guerrillas with our group were not Marxists at all but from the Fuerza Revolucionario Sandino (FRS). Among them were Harold and Alejandro Martínez.[19] We also began infiltrating people into Nicaragua, among them Carlos Fonseca, Borge, "Chico" Buitrago, and José Benito Escobar and his brother Inocencio. A sister of the Escobars' worked at a store in central Managua called the Tienda El Néne, which served as our post office during 1961 and 1962.

How the Sandinista Front Got Its Name

At first our movement had no name. But by the middle of 1961 it became obvious we needed one to differentiate ourselves from others. Most people believe the Frente Sandinista de Liberación Nacional [FSLN] was named in Tegucigalpa, Honduras, on July 23, 1961, but that is not true.[20] In reality, even at that early date the Cubans were concerned with divisiveness inside our movement and decided to take many of us to Havana to try to straighten things out. I was one of them. Most of us were young students and, although we didn't have serious problems with Noel Guerrero, we were concerned with some of the others in our group, including "Che" Peña, Tamara Bunke's boyfriend at the time, who was very close to "Che" Guevara and often tried to order us around.

We went to the safe house the Cubans provided in Havana for our full-time use, a basement apartment six or seven steps down from the road on Calle 23 near the Havana Riviera Hotel.[21] Among the things we discussed was what to name our movement. Noél Guerrero proposed we call it the Frente Nicaragüense de Liberacion [FNL], and Silvio Mayorga suggested Frente Revolucionario Sandino [FRS], the name of the earlier anti-Somoza rebel group led by General Raudales to which the Martínez brothers had belonged. But by then Carlos Fonseca Amador had begun to emerge as our natural leader, not the least because he was both well informed and charismatic. So when he kept insisting on Frente Sandinista de Liberación Nacional the younger members of the group, including me, backed him. His suggestion was finally unanimously adopted, although I later found out his defeat made Guerrero an enemy of Fonseca. Of those who attended the meeting only three are still alive, myself, Tomás Borge, who later became a top *comandante*, and Guerrero. We put out a story that the meeting took place in Tegucigalpa, in part to cover up the crucial role the Cubans played and in part to make the decision seem more nationalistic. But the FSLN was named at that meeting in Havana under Cuban auspices. The version claiming it took place in Tegucigalpa was just a cover story.[22]

Our First Disaster

Reinforced by Pastora's group, our newly named FSLN felt strong enough to organize its first incursion. The plan was for those of us in Honduras to join up with a second group of twenty-five to thirty trained guerrillas under the command of Rafael Somarriba, who had been prepared in Cuba and would come directly from there to Nicaragua by ship. We would meet near the Atlantic mouth of the Rio Coco (Coco River), where he would give us some arms he was bringing. Somarriba left Cuba well enough, but he and all of his men and the arms disappeared completely. We never did learn what happened to them. With the failure of Somarriba's forces to arrive, we were unable to take any armed action, so we went back to Tegucigalpa and the drawing boards.

Throughout 1962 we continued to prepare the groundwork for an eventual revolutionary effort inside Nicaragua, concentrating on building up civilian support structures and establishing weapons and medical caches in the Rio Coco area, especially near Bocay, Bocaycito, Quilalí, and along the upper part of the river.[23] But the Cubans became angry and started pulling back. I'm still not sure why, but I do remember the first secretary of the Cuban

Embassy, Orlando Rodríguez, yelling at me when I tried to argue that we needed help because we were ready to go: "Really? You're no better than a bunch of corrupt prostitutes in a whorehouse. Why should we help you?" To say the least I was shocked. My own guess was that the Cubans had begun wondering about some of our leadership. In any case the Cuban Embassy then cut us off completely, and our only support for a while came from the Russians and Edelbérto Tórres, until Pan American Airlines came to our rescue.

Pan American Airlines to the Rescue

Several years earlier Pan American had allowed Tórres to be taken from one of their airplanes by Somoza's police as it was transiting through Managua. After an international outcry, he had been freed and had filed a lawsuit for damages. The lawsuit had recently been settled in his favor, and Pan American had paid him. So in addition to regular monthly payments of $4,000 from the Russians that reached us through Tórres, he himself also gave us money out of his settlement, which was between $300,000 and $400,000. It seemed especially ironic to us that an American company ended up paying many of the expenses of our Marxist movement. My father also continued to cover our basic expenses out of funds he "recuperated" from the oil workers' union and PEMEX. We did not engage in more forceful forms of "recuperation" such as kidnapping, war taxes, or bank robberies, the approach developed later by the Salvadoran Faribundo Martí Liberation Front (FMLN.)

We managed to enlist some other help as well by engaging in what we laughingly called "revolutionary seductions." Ivan "Chele" Sánchez, a Ladino from an elite family from Granada, was especially good at this. Among those he seduced were the daughter of a Honduran diplomat and a stewardess from Transportes Aereos Controamericanos (TACA) airlines, both of whom then helped us smuggle guns and other arms into Honduras to supplement those we bought from the armed forces. The diplomat's daughter brought us diplomatic bags full of hand grenades and submachine guns, while the stewardess was especially helpful in taking things directly into Managua, as TACA was one of few airlines that went there directly from Tegucigalpa. Carlos Fonseca sometimes got upset about our girl chasing, and would tell us: "*Jodidos*. Look at the legs of the revolution, not women." But in matters of sex, unlike revolution, we paid him little mind.

Our Second Disaster

Suddenly in May 1963 Guerrero said we were to go into Nicaragua, so eighty-eight of us left Tegucigalpa and our Patuca River base for the border. But when we reached the border, much to our surprise, Guerrero divided us into two groups and ordered each to go to an area we had not prepared and where we had neither support structures nor supply caches. To top off the surprises, Guerrero also told me and Dr. Andara we were not to go with either group but had to accompany him back to Mexico City, reducing the eighty-eight man guerrilla force to eighty-six. I was so furious tears actually came to my eyes. But I had no choice because I was under revolutionary discipline. "Chico" Buitrago was also angry because we were to be separated, but there was nothing either of us could do about it. Tomás Borge was not among either group, having just been expelled for lack of discipline by Rigoberto López Crúz, *Pablo Úbeda*. By dividing those who went in into two groups and sending each to an unprepared area, Guerrero sealed their fates. But I did not know that at the time.[24]

As ordered, I went back to Mexico with Guerrero and began once again to work collecting money to support those in the field. There was considerable enthusiasm in Mexico City among our sympathizers, and Edelbérto Tórres collected $40,000; at my father's behest Joaquín Hernández Galicia, *El Quíno*, secretary general of the STPRM, gave me another $10,000; and Andara went to Cuba and came back with another $10,000, altogether $60,000. I gave it all to Guerrero.

At first we heard very little about what was going on inside

Nicaragua. But in August we began reading strange press reports suggesting things were not going well. Guerrero assured me and others that they were just propaganda, even one reporting that Ricardo "El Diezcito" Duarte and my best friend "Chico" Buitrago had been killed. He even took me and my daughter Illia to visit "Chico" 's wife Estelita, who was pregnant, and reassured her her husband was alive. When we arrived back at my house, Guerrero said to me: "I have to go somewhere." That was the last time I ever saw him or the $60,000. And by then "Chico" was long dead.

Desperation

Suddenly our movement was in deep trouble, our leader missing, and our treasury empty. Desperate, and thinking Guerrero must have gone to Tegucigalpa without telling me, I went there looking for him. But no one there had seen him either. A few of our supporters were still in Tegucigalpa and told me one of the two groups was still operating around Bocay under Orlando Juan Quintana, so I headed south to join them. It took me about ten days to work myself inside Nicaragua to where they were. When I told them we were broke and Guerrero was missing, the atmosphere turned very somber. Still we decided to try to take some sort of guerrilla action in hopes we could spark a wider uprising and decided to capture the small Segovia town of Wiwilí, which was garrisoned by an entire platoon of Somoza's Guardia Nacional. Our intention was to wipe them out completely, and had we been able to do so it would have been a major psychological blow to the Somoza government and its forces. But we failed.

We arrived just outside Wiwilí at about 4:00 one morning and began deploying to attack. The Guardia had a lookout post on a platform about two meters high near where we were, which we had expected. What we had not expected was to find little children playing below it at that hour of the morning. With them there Quintana delayed the order to attack because he was unwilling to risk their lives. But they stayed and stayed until at about

5:00 a.m., an hour after we arrived, we were discovered by the Guardia, and a fire fight broke out. Silvio Mayorga was wounded immediately but Bayardo Altamirano pulled him to safety, and we managed to withdraw under fire from our positions. But the battle turned out to be a death sentence for most of us. Guardia reinforcement quickly arrived and began sending out reconnaissance patrols. They were very successful, and only fifteen of us survived. I was among the few who escaped.

As I fled, I got lost in the mountains for more than thirty-three days. To this day I have no idea of where I found the strength to keep going alone and under constant threat. But I finally managed to make it to the Honduran border, crossed over, and made it to our Comayagüela safe house, where the woman running it lent me enough money to get back to Mexico.[25] I finally got back in November and immediately went to see Edelbérto Tórres, whom I hadn't seen since the decision was made for us to go inside because Noél Guerrero had forbidden contact with him "for secur-

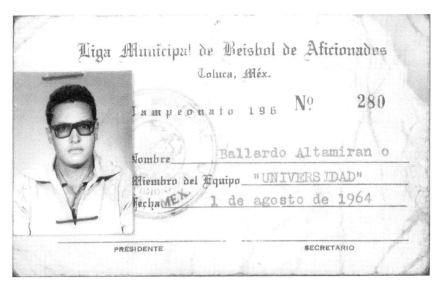

Counterfeit ID document of Bayardo Altamirano, for use during his revolutionary activities in Mexico. During Nicaragua's 1979–1990 socialist revolution, Altamirano was a top aide to Tomás Borge. Private collection.

ity reasons." When I told Tórres what happened, he was shocked and said, "All is lost. Why didn't you tell me? I thought Carlos Fonseca was running things, not Guerrero. We all know Guerrero is bad news."

We had been badly handled and sent into Nicaragua to engage in stupid actions that were militarily absurd and allowed the Somoza National Guard to wipe out both our groups. When we retreated, we abandoned everything, our supporters, our weapons and medicine caches, everything, and we really had not even had any serious battles because we had remained purely on the defenses. And yet only fifteen of us had survived. I didn't realize it at the time, but the Bocay disaster would eventually help change my thinking. But not just then. There was still a revolution to fight.

Starting Again

Back in Mexico I reorganized our operations so at least those who had survived would have a place to sleep and eat. In addition to our fifteen survivors, the Honduran army had detained twelve of our peasant supporters who had fled from the zones as well and expelled them to Mexico. Tórres had them under his wing but needed somewhere for them to stay. The old safe house was much too small for twenty-seven people, so I started looking for another. I also began trying to reestablish contact with our people inside Nicaragua, especially in the Managua area.

Carlos Fonseca was still inside at the time, as were several others, including Victor "El Mejicáno" Tirado, another Mexican who had joined us early on.[26] Suddenly, both were picked up by the Nicaraguan security services. We were afraid Somoza would have them killed. But when he was arrested Tirado claimed his real name was Francisco Ortega, a Mexican citizen, and demanded to see the Mexican ambassador, who intervened somewhat reluctantly on his behalf. Still, as a consequence Tirado's treatment improved considerably, and the threat to Carlos receded. A few months later both were expelled.

In late January 1965 Tórres called and told me Carlos was in Tapachula on the Guatemala–Mexico border. My father gave me some money to go meet him and escort him back to Mexico City. When I arrived Carlos was living in the back room of the home of a Mason and being supported by the Masonic Lodge there. It took some time to arrange our return to Mexico City, and while we waited he told me a fascinating story. After he was expelled from Nicaragua he had been moved from military jail to jail all the way to Guatemala, where the army high command issued orders to kill him. But while he was in his Guatemalan jail he had several long conversations with his warden, who became so interested Fonseca managed to convert him to revolutionary thinking. So instead of being killed, Carlos was sent to the border so he could get back to Mexico and our movement. The warden was Major Luís Augusto Túrcios Lima, who went on to lead one of Guatemala's principal guerrilla operations.

Back in Mexico City the others were reunited and hungry but at least still alive at our new safe house on Avenida Alvaro Obregón in an apartment much bigger than the earlier one and that had a narrow entrance for better security and a rug store on the ground floor to help cover our comings and goings. But after he greeted them, for security reasons I took Fonseca to a different safe house, this one on Calle Guanajuato.

Financially we were in bad shape. Not only had Guerrero and our treasury disappeared, but both the Cubans and the Russians became reluctant to help us after our defeat, and the Nicaraguan exile community was unhappy over how we had lost the money they had collected for us earlier. We began trying to regenerate our support among Mexican politicians and social figures but were barely surviving. Thanks yet again to my father, at least we could pay the rent and buy food, clothing, and other necessities, but we needed a better source of income. So we turned to capitalism.

Revolutionary Capitalism

With the Cubans, Russians, and Nicaraguan exile community reluctant to help, I began casting about for some way to make more money. Since I did have an engineering degree, I decided with Fonseca's blessings to start a small business, which I named JOPSA, after my own initials [José Obidio Puente, Sociedad Anónima]. My father provided the initial capital, and I bought a Dodge Coronet station wagon. To my amazement the business went very well indeed, not the least because my workers were all Sandinista comrades, two of whom, Pablo Úbeda and Silvio Mayorga, were my foremen.[27] It was amazing how much money we began to make because all JOPSA's workers were trusted comrades who neither asked for nor received salaries or insurance and because my father began steering business our way from his friends in the oil industry. We soon became the largest builder of gasoline stations in Mexico City. Imagine. Almost all the gas stations built in the city during a number of years were built by Sandinistas. I remember that while we neither paid salaries nor provided insurance, we did have lots of money and enjoyed life immensely, going out to restaurants, to the Plaza Garibaldi for mariachi music, and so on. The first stage of our Sandinista revolution had ended in the defeats at Bocay and Bocaycito, but our newfound "capitalist" prosperity, thanks to our construction business in Mexico City, marked the beginning of the second stage.

Amnesty Restarts the Revolution

When in 1966 Somoza declared an amnesty for all those who had participated in the earlier guerrilla efforts, our response was to begin reinfiltrating comrades back into Nicaragua, and the Cubans responded by again providing us with help. With activities picking up once more, Carlos Fonseca, by then our undisputed leader, agreed we had again outgrown our quarters and needed a bigger place, so we bought a house with JOPSA funds. It's still my

The Cubans provided clandestine courier services to the Sandinistas, as shown by this calling card of Mario Gill of Cuba's Prensa Latina Special Operations Department in Mexico City. On the back of Gill's calling card are listed twelve clandestine mail pouches delivered by him to "Pepe" Jiménez (Puente) in 1965, three from Nicaragua (N), five from Costa Rica (CR), and four others. Private collection.

LABORATORIO
DE LA
CLINICA BELEM
REVILLAGIGEDO 108-101   Dr. M. PACHECO A.

Fecha____111/31/65____Nombre

Sr. Carlos Fonseca Amador.

Grupo sanguíneo ____"A"____
"POSITIVO"
Rh (D)

LABORATORIO
DE LA
CLINICA BELEM
REVILLAGIGEDO 108-101   Dr. M. PACHECO A.

Fecha____111/31/65____Nombre

St. María Hayde Teran Navas.

Grupo sanguíneo ____"B"____
" POSITIVO "
Rh (D)

Despite his intensive revolutionary life, Carlos Fonseca
Amador still found time to marry. These blood tests
were done March 31, 1965, in preparation for his
Mexico City marriage to María Haydé Teran Navas
who, with their son Carlos, now lives in Nicaragua.
Blood type A + is not uncommon in Nicaragua. Private
collection.

home. We all moved into it together, including my wife, our grow-ing family, and all the top Sandinistas in Mexico. Even Estelita Buitrago, the widow of my friend "Chico," lived here.

From then on for several years the profits from JOPSA fi-nanced many of our revolutionary activities. We were so busy that as the company's guerrilla/workers left to go back into Nicaragua, JOPSA ran short of workers, so Carlos and I decided we had to start "exploiting the proletariat," and began hiring Mexican workers. We were in an extraordinarily good position to do so safely, without worrying about worker honesty or efficiency, be-cause enough Sandinista comrades remained in Mexico City so that all JOPSA's foremen were revolutionaries and extremely loyal. Among those who stayed for a while were Victor Tirado and Pablo Úbeda. With comrades as foremen, extremely low overhead, and all our key personnel living in the same house, profits were so high we were able to fund several Front operations completely. After discussion with Carlos, I even furnished the ground floor of the house with top-of-the-line furniture from the Chippendale Galleries. Carlos may have been a Marxist, but he understood salesmanship and knew that having a well-furnished home to which we could invite clients could greatly increase busi-ness. In the end JOPSA became so large we had a fleet of seventeen trucks plus other vehicles and were able to provide Carlos with all the financial support he needed to run several operations. From 1965 until 1979 the home in which I still live was the center of Sandinista Front activities in Mexico City, and for much of that period JOPSA remained an important source of financial support. I ran the business; Carlos Fonseca ran the revolution and used to tell me constantly: "Remember. You are my Engels."

Disaster Strikes Again, Chinese Style

By late 1966 we had reestablished ourselves inside Nicaragua and were ready for new revolutionary efforts. I was also working at reestablishing our relationships with Cuba, but it was taking time. But in the interim we had found a new sponsor, the People's

Republic of China [PRC]. I don't remember who took the initiative, but after our defeat in the Bocay and return to Mexico City we made contact with the PRC's trade office in Mexico City, and officials there invited us to come in and describe to them what had happened. I went with Pablo Úbeda to their offices with maps of our operations and the routes we had used. We also explained to them our support structure and contacts among the peasants. The Chinese decided to provide us with support and did so quickly, giving us lots of money to buy arms and inviting us to China for training. Based on recommendations by Pablo Úbeda, an experienced rural guerrilla, and our new sponsors, we changed the geographic focus of our efforts to the area of Pancasán in the mountains of Matagalpa. Our preparations for a new effort went forward quickly, perhaps too quickly. In August 1967 Somoza detected our new networks and, as soon as he spotted our headquarters, launched a fierce attack that wiped out almost everyone there. Our most important losses were Pablo Úbeda and Silvio Mayorga, both of whom were killed. Needless to say, that cut our efforts short. The Chinese also pulled back.

Carlos and Costa Rica

Carlos Fonseca was in Managua at the time but wasn't captured, and we still had important networks in the cities and smaller urban areas, particularly among students, labor unions, and some intellectuals, so our other activities continued. The year 1968 was very quiet for us. Carlos traveled constantly between Nicaragua, Costa Rica, and Mexico, trying to prepare for yet another effort, while I continued as contact between the Front and its supporters, constantly looking for money and propagandizing. Then, in 1969, Carlos was arrested in Costa Rica in connection with a bank robbery and put in a jail in the town of Alajuela near San José. It looked like our third effort at revolution inside Nicaragua was also turning sour. Then things got worse.

We decided to mount an operation to get Carlos out of jail, and Plutarco Hernández took charge of it.[28] Among his men were

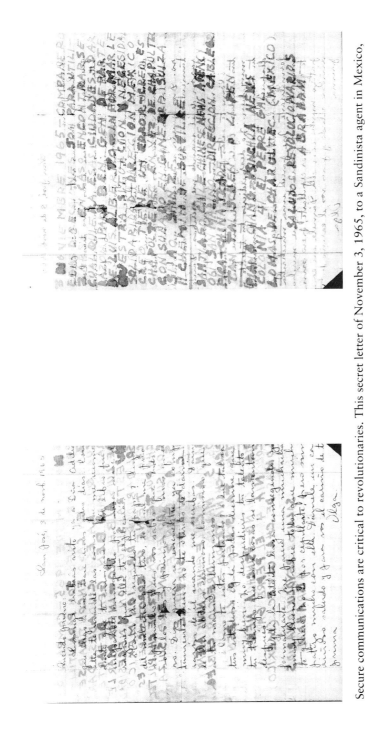

Secure communications are critical to revolutionaries. This secret letter of November 3, 1965, to a Sandinista agent in Mexico, confirms the relationship between the Sandinistas and the intelligence services of the People's Republic of China. Side one is innocuous, but side two, written in lemon juice and later developed with steam, identifies three Chinese intelligence contacts in Geneva, Switzerland (Shao Shinze, Chinese Consulate), Santiago, Chile (Tan Tai Schen or Li Pen, Chinese News Agency), and Mexico City (Piang Chang, Hsinchau News). The Sandinista agent is told to identify himself as Luís Alberto and ask for Ben Gen. Private collection.

Germán Pomáres Ordóñez, *El Danto*,[29] Humberto Ortega, and Rúfo Marín, the son of the Rúfo Marín who had been with Sandino in the 1920s. Plutarco's comando did manage to get Carlos out of the jail, but only under a hail of fire from Costa Rican Guardia Civil guards, and within hours all those involved except *El Danto* were captured. The only one wounded was Humberto Ortega, who received a slight wound in his hand. The escape of *El Danto* was the single bright spot, since he was a major peasant leader and very good in the mountains as a guerrilla. But now not only Carlos but also Plutarco Hernández, Humberto Ortega, Rúfo Marín, and several others were in jail, this time in the Central Penitentiary in San Jose.

Our First Air Hijacking

There was nothing for it but to organize yet another operation to try to get them out. Carlos Rafael Agüero, the nephew of Fernando Agüero,[30] a leading Nicaraguan politician, was assigned to head it up. But the most important persons during its preparation were actually Plutarco's parents, Doña "Chelita" and Don "Nago," who took charge of communications with those inside prison, taking them food, clothing, and secret communications on almost a daily basis.[31] In October 1970, Agüero's team managed to hijack an airplane owned by United Fruit in which a number of top American businessmen were traveling. Several Latin American presidents were at an OAS meeting at the time, and through them we negotiated freeing the hostages in exchange for Carlos, Plutarco, Rúfo Marín, Humberto Ortega, and others. When they were released, the Costa Rican public treated them like heroes, with people lining the highway all way from the penitentiary to the airport. The Mexican government sent an airplane to fly them back to Mexico City, where Tórres and I met them.

In Mexico the group was again received like heroes, and we were all euphoric. The first day we went to one of my favorite restaurants, La Fonda del Recuerdo, where I introduced them to Toritos and Antojitos Veracruzanos, tequila with tomato juice and Tabasco sauce, and Veracruz-style hors d'oeuvres. My father and Edelbérto Tórres went with us as we traveled around Mexico City in one of JOPSA's new station wagons followed by two carloads of Mexican security officers, and all of them, including the security officers, joined us at the restaurant and had as much fun as we did. JOPSA footed all the bills. The next day we bought the men new clothes, since theirs were in bad shape, went to the Plaza Garibaldi to listen to mariachi music, which like all good Central Americans they loved, then ended up once again at La Fonda.

At first I was told President of Mexico Díaz Ordáz wanted to meet the group personally after the hubbub died down. But the United States, Nicaragua, and Costa Rica began pressing for their return to Costa Rica, so we had to do something quickly before the pressures became too much. In 1967 I had managed to meet with the Cuban officials in Mexico in charge of liaison with us and had then been invited to Havana to meet with the intelligence officers responsible for liaison with revolutionary groups throughout Latin America. I took a full report of our activities with me, which was well received and earned me access to a number of top officials of the Communist Party, who also gave me a warm welcome. This was followed up in 1968 by the Cubans, who sent the FSLN an official invitation through the Cuban ambassador to Mexico, Joaquín Hernández Armas, to attend the tenth anniversary of the revolution. I went as the Front's representative. While there I was able to meet with a number of top Cubans, including a short meeting with Fidel that laid the groundwork for a positive response from Cuba to our situation. Castro had pretended throughout the operation that he had not been involved, but in reality he was its author.[32] So when we decided to go quickly to Cuba it was easy. On their third day in Mexico I simply collected up their passports and sent them to the Cuban Embassy. They were returned October 29, and we went to Havana the next day. In Havana I had opportunities to talk again with Fidel and his brother Raúl, as well as with Ramiro Valdéz, Juanito Almeida, and other Cuban leaders.

When I left Havana a little while later to go back to Mexico,

Carlos asked me for two things: to send him $5,000 for expenses and to go to Costa Rica to pick up some personal items he had left behind. The $5,000 was easy. Back in Mexico City I simply drew the money from JOPSA funds and sent it to him in cash in the Cuban diplomatic pouch. But the trip to Costa Rica made me nervous. I knew the country well enough, but we had just been involved there in an attack on a Costa Rican jail and then an airline hijacking. Still I went, first making contact with Plutarco's parents, who put me up at their home and gave me all the help I needed.

Much to my surprise there really was no problem. I easily got hold of Carlos Fonseca's things, which filled two big suitcases, and had no trouble flying back to Mexico City. But I was still afraid that there either the American CIA or the Nicaraguans would try to intercept me at the airport, especially since I knew arriving passengers were under photographic surveillance by Mexican officials, who shared their take with the CIA station there. So I took some evasive actions and went first to one hotel, where I had arranged to be met by one of JOPSA's cars and taken to a second. After moving around several more times for a few days, I decided it was safe and went home with Carlos's belongings, which I took to him a few weeks later when I made another trip to Havana. I then spent all of January in Havana with him and the others there, including Edén Pastora, Plutarco, and Humberto Ortega, and met Humberto's brother Daniel for the first time.

The Incompetence of "Che" as a Theoretician

When I think back about how we suffered disaster after disaster, I realize that all of our efforts to try to create what were known as *focos guerrilleros*, or guerrilla concentrations, were led by people from outside the regions where we tried to create them, and every one of them failed. The idea was invented by "Che" Guevara before he himself ever actually tried to create one and proved to be possibly the greatest tactical error ever made by those of us trying to start revolutions. Everyone, including us, who tried to follow "Che" 's model failed miserably. Not once did an attempt to apply his model in the field result in an effective uprising. That is because to be successful a guerrilla must take advantage of existing conditions, not try to invent new ones. A revolutionary can perhaps polish preexisting conditions a little, but he can never create the conditions for a revolution. Guerrillas are also entirely dependent on the local populace to survive, and when they are outsiders with strange ideas and accents they can rarely gain enough sympathy on their own to be safe and effective. When the right conditions do not exist, they invariably fail. It was a lesson "Che" himself was to learn too late several years later in Bolivia.

How We Finally Got It Right, Just Before It Went Permanently Wrong

At that point the Cubans offered us greatly increased assistance, an offer we promptly accepted. Our main Cuban liaison officer in Havana at the time, with whom I met many times, was Amado Padrón.[33] While picking up Carlos's things in San José I had taken the opportunity to meet with a number of our people, several of whom came out of Nicaragua to see me, and we reestablished the system by which they could travel to and from Cuba via Mexico. Dozens of comrades began coming out of San José and Managua to Cuba for guerrilla training. Many also went on to North Korea, Russia, or other places for advanced courses. Carlos Fonseca and Plutarco were among those who went to North Korea.[34] It was a very busy period, but we had time for our friends, including Plutarco's parents Doña "Chelita" and Don "Nago," who went to Havana during this period to spend several months with him.

A short while later Plutarco and Carlos Agüero went on a trip to Russia and Western Europe, only to suddenly appear in Mexico at my home, having arrived by ship from Spain to Veracrúz. They stayed with me for several weeks preparing to go back to Nicaragua, and at this point Plutarco took the name Comandante Marcial. His job back inside Nicaragua was to head up all our efforts to build a system of clandestine communications and to recruit and train new guerrilla operatives. He was also put in command of our first small armed action, and given the temporary codename Comandante Cero, the name we gave to the commander of any major actions, which made him, not Edén Pastora, our first Comandante Cero. I continued as international liaison for the Front in Mexico and elsewhere. Among my principal activities, I was the main clandestine courier carrying messages to and from the Front's scattered leaders as they arrived in Cuban or Russian diplomatic pouches.

How the Ordinary Nine Came to be the Top Nine

But even as our efforts progressed, divisions appeared within our ranks. The main cause of these was Humberto Ortega's constant efforts to push Carlos Fonseca aside and seize leadership for himself. It became so bad that there were three separate factions represented in Cuba and Mexico City. That part of our history is fairly well covered in several books, but one incident is of special interest. In 1978 I received a telephone call at my home from Amado Padrón from Havana, who said he was calling on behalf of Fidel Castro. Padrón asked me to choose three persons from each of the three principal factions that had emerged within our ranks and send them to Havana, where the Cubans wanted to try to reduce the tensions between them. By then the revolution was well under way, and all its real leaders were inside Nicaragua and couldn't come out, so I did the next best thing and called three from each faction from among those outside Nicaragua and not participating in actual revolutionary fighting and sent them to Havana via Mérida, Yucatán, in a small airplane I leased for them. Much to my amazement, far from simply getting together representatives of the three factions to try to reduce the tensions between them, Castro made them our new national directorate, without even consulting with the real leaders of our Front. That is the real origin of the Nine Comandantes, who later became the famous Nine Directors of Nicaragua's 1979–1990 revolution. I could easily have gone myself and become one of them. But I was extremely busy with what seemed like more important business. Besides, I never imagined Castro was going to name a new directorate himself, so I just sent them on their way. Only later would I find out just how disastrous this would turn out to be.

El Salvador's FMLN Finances the FSLN

Even as the Nine were being named by Castro we were working hard to push the revolution forward inside Nicaragua. But despite growing support, money remained one of our major problems. I saw a possible solution. I was also in contact with Plutarco's first cousin, Eduardo Sancho Castañeda, Comandante Fermán Cienfuegos, the military commander of the FMLN in El Salvador. Unlike us, the FMLN understood from the beginning the importance of finances and engaged in a very active program of "recuperating" money through robbing banks, kidnapping for ransom, and collecting revolutionary war taxes, so they had a great deal of capital.

Fermán used to come to Mexico City regularly and I had gotten to know him quite well, especially thanks to Plutarco, so during one of his visits I suggested that the FMLN lend us some money. He agreed, and within a month brought $5 million to me in Mexico City in cash and gave it to me for the use of the FSLN. Plutarco, the man among us he most trusted, carried it to San José, Costa Rica, where he delivered it to Humberto Ortega.[35] Later Fermán brought even more cash, which we also sent down, until the total reached at least $15 million.[36] I was surprised later to find out that out of the first $5 million Humberto Ortega had given only a half million to each of the other two factions and kept $4 million for his own. By 1978 I was convinced history was going our way, especially because some of the most important figures in Costa Rica, including then President Rodrigo Carazo Odio and former president José Figueres, were among our strongest supporters, we were receiving a large flow of arms through Panama with the help of Panamanian president Omar Torrijos,[37] and we had large training camps and were operating freely along the Costa Rica–Nicaragua border.

But not everything went so well. Daniel Ortega, Tomás Borge, and several others had been captured in Nicaragua and were in Somoza's jails. So we organized another special operation, this one led by Edén Pastora, whose commando captured the Palacio de Gobierno in Managua in August of 1978, leading to their release and expulsion from Nicaragua. As leader of the action, Pastora became our third Comandante Cero. Daniel Ortega came through Mexico en route back to Havana. But Borge was in bad shape and stayed in my home in Mexico City for eight months while he was recovering.

By managing the millions sent us by the FMLN, Humberto Ortega became very powerful within the movement. He traveled constantly between Havana and Costa Rica but spent most of his time in Havana until Fidel Castro personally warned him that if he didn't start spending more time nearer the forces in action, Edén Pastora was going to take over the Front. From then on he mostly stayed in San José. Pastora, now commander of our Southern Front on the Costa Rica–Nicaraguan border, spent most of his time with the troops, not in San José, so the threat to Humberto's ambitions did not materialize.

While, needless to say, the FMLN's dollars were of great importance, our activities grew so fast that even that was not enough, so I spent much of my time collecting more, much of it in Mexico. Carlos Sansores Pérez of the PRI began occasionally to give me help in quantities that averaged around $100,000, and friends in the Ministerio de Gobernación also arranged to give me some funds. Small amounts also flowed in from Venezuela, Colombia, and other Latin American countries and from donors in the United States and Europe. But even these did not cover the greater part of our costs, so Cuba made up the difference.

Comes the Revolution

It's surprising how even something you've been working toward all your life can suddenly catch you unawares. That is what happened to me. As part of our efforts to organize international political support, Carlos Andrés Pérez, then president of Venezuela, organized a World Congress for us in Caracas in July 1979. Sympathizers came to it from all over, Spain, France, Greece, the Arab countries, seemingly everywhere. The congress had just ended and I was in the air flying to Bogotá to begin a trip throughout South America when the news reported that Somoza had fled Nicaragua and our forces were marching into Managua. Plutarco was with me, and we went back to Mexico City as quickly as possible, where Carlos Sansorez Pérez gave me an armored Ford automobile and arranged for an airplane to take it and us to Managua. To our surprise, when we arrived the country was already in the hands of the Nine I had sent to Havana. But I had been close to most of them for many years, so I was very hopeful. My son Lenin Obidio was already there as the chief bodyguard of Tomás Borge, so we spent a lot of time at Borge's house. At first I planned to stay for quite a while, like my father had done when Castro invited him to Havana in 1959. But I was also shocked by a number of the things that were going on, not the least how the Nine were pushing aside those who had really fought the revolution, among them Plutarco Hernández and even Edén Pastora, in favor of people who had made very little personal sacrifice in the cause.

The final break came over, of all things, a song. At dinner one evening Borge told me part of the proposed Sandinista national anthem labeled the Americans "enemies of mankind." I was not an admirer of the American system but felt there was a great difference between the people and their government. Besides, it made no sense deliberately to antagonize the United States no matter how one felt, and I strongly recommended it be taken out. Borge said he agreed with me and would try to do something. Instead,

Order of August 28, 1979, from the new Sandinista minister of the interior Tomás Borge to the Germán Pomáres Complex to issue a special ID card to Lenin Obidio Puente. Private collection. In a November 1999 telephone interview, Lenin Puente confirmed to me that he was at the time chief of Borge's personal bodyguard and driver of the armored Ford donated by Carlos Sansores Pérez of Mexico to the victorious Sandinistas, which was being used by Borge. A Panamanian and a Korean completed Borge's team of bodyguards. In *The Patient*, p. 188, Borge claims barely to know "Pepe" Puente and seeks to discredit him but does not mention Lenin.

he denounced me to the other eight. After that happened, I talked to my son and we both decided to leave Managua and go back to Mexico. Borge seemed surprised and tried to convince my son to stay, but Lenin said he would not stay without me, so Borge then offered me a major post in the government, perhaps a vice ministry. But I had fought for a cause, not spoils of office, and refused.

Back to the Ideas of the Real Sandino

Back in Mexico, even though bitterly disappointed that my revolution had been captured by a small group of former comrades who had not themselves really fought for it, for more than

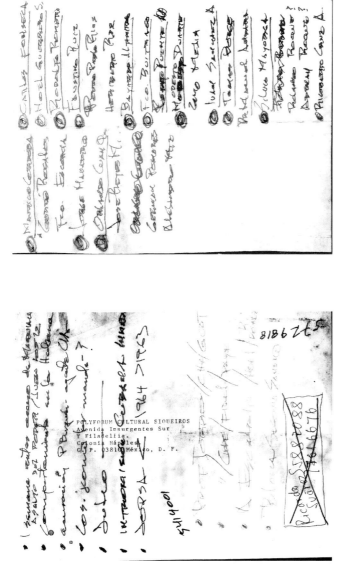

Notes taken by "Pepe" Puente during a discussion of the history of the FSLN among top Sandinista leaders in Managua in late 1979 confirm the key roles played by various actors listing, in order, Fonseca and Guerrero, and then Puente, Altamirano, "Chico" Buitrago, and Germán Pomáres (*El Danto*). Topics discussed included "comportamiento hacia La Habana" (stance toward Havana), "involucramiento Cuba en la Revolución" (Cuban involvement in the revolution), and JOPSA, 1964/63. Pencilled notes on bottom read: Prof [Edelbérto] Tórres/Che [Guevara/Guat[emala]; ditto [Torres/Che[Guevara/Fidel [Castro]/Pepe [Puente]; Escalafon [rank order]/Noél [Guerrero]/R. Domez [unknown]; Blanca Segovia Sandino [Augústo César Sandino's daughter]. Private collection.

a decade I kept my peace. As things in Nicaragua under their management went from bad to worse, it became harder and harder to keep quiet, but I did so. It was especially hard in 1990, when the Nine lost everything for which I had sacrificed for so many decades of my life. But now, at the end of the century, the times have changed so dramatically I have decided to speak out.

When I was younger, as with so many Marxist–Leninist revolutionaries, I was very dogmatic and lived in a narrow world. In my case I also saw life through the commitments my father had taught me and acted with the discipline my mother instilled in me. Today I realize that the truth is what is most important, and it is now my duty to advance my beliefs not with arms but through the democratic process. I am still deeply concerned with social injustice and the suffering caused by dictators and still believe it was my duty to help overthrow the Somoza dictatorship. But it is now my duty to tell the truth about other things, which is especially hard for someone who led a clandestine life since childhood.

Now I realized just how many mistakes we made, especially our use of violence. Perhaps I still half-believe we may have been right at the time, given the historic conditions, but certainly today violence is not the way to achieve social justice. And even in those days we went about it wrong, misled by "Che" Guevara's concept of the guerrilla *foco*, which was not the right way to proceed because instead of creating the conditions for revolution all we really did was provoke local skirmishes against a false enemy, the army, without ever threatening the political power of a government itself. Even if violence was justified in the past, it cannot be justified today. Today it is possible to participate openly in the democratic process to obtain social justice, and that is what I am doing, working with Cuauhtémoc Cárdenas, the son of one of my father's strongest supporters, Lázaro Cárdenas, to bring real democracy to Mexico. I continue to believe Mexico does not have a just government and that it is the responsibility of all of us to try to work to make things better for the people. Today that is best done with ballots, not bullets.

3

ALEJANDRO PÉREZ BUSTAMANTE, SANDINO'S BODYGUARD

A BIOGRAPHICAL SKETCH

During the Constitutional War in Nicaragua, "Don Alejandro," Alejandro Pérez Bustamante, was a personal bodyguard to legendary Nicaraguan guerrilla General Augústo César Sandino. He also served him as an occasional civilian operative during his later war against the U.S. Marines. Whereas José Obidio Puente was linked through his father to Sandino, Don Alejandro himself lived for several years on a daily basis with Sandino, so his impressions of Sandino and his vision for Nicaragua are firsthand. A peasant from the region in which Sandino fought his major wars, Don Alejandro's farm, where this autobiographical essay was recorded, lies on the upper slopes of El Súngano (sometimes spelled El Zúngano) mountain, just across a narrow mountain valley from the much more famous El Chipote mountain where Sandino had his headquarters.

At first glance Don Alejandro, as he is affectionately called by all those who know him, seems a rather ordinary, albeit somewhat aged and unusually sturdy, peasant farmer. But it takes just a few minutes to realize he is anything but ordinary. He first met

Sandino while both were working at the San Albino mines on the Rio El Jícaro in the Department of Nueva Segovia.[1] Their second meeting took place after Sandino robbed the mine safe to pay for raising a small guerrilla band at the beginning of what is known as the *Guerra Constitucionalista*. (Sandino's more famous campaign against the American Marines came later.) Don Alejandro joined Sandino, becoming his personal aide and bodyguard, stayed for the remainder of that campaign, and was with him when he laid down his arms. When Sandino then left for Mexico, Don Alejandro went with him, first to Mexico City, then Tampíco, and finally Mérida, Yucatán, where he took responsibility for collecting the Mexican government subsidies that paid Sandino's expenses. Shortly thereafter, and before Sandino went back to Nicaragua, he returned to Nicaragua and his farm via Venezuela and Colombia. He did not rejoin the ranks of Sandino's soldiers during the campaign against the Marines, but was in Ocotal when a Marine–Sandino battle took place, during which he saved the life of the original Rúfo Marín, father of the Rúfo Marín mentioned by "Pepe" Puente in the preceding chapter.

Decades later, Don Alejandro became a *Juez de Mesta*, or local magistrate, a position he held during the Sandinista campaign against Somoza. The *Jueces* were prime targets of the Sandinistas during their 1970s war against Somoza, and, according to Plutarco Hernández, more than 300 were executed. But Don Alejandro was left alone. After their victory, the Sandinistas pressured him for support. When he resisted, the army fired on his home, killing his wife and pushing him into active opposition as a *jefe de correos*, or local support network director, for the Contra Resistance movement. Today he is *comarca cacique*, or chief, of the peasants of El Súngano.

Some readers may note that the timing of Sandino's movements, as told by Don Alejandro, does not fully coincide with other historical versions. In particular, his insistence that Sandino visited Mexico twice is new. Given Don Alejandro's personal knowledge of these events, no attempt has been made to reconcile his with the other narratives.

□ □ □

"SANDINO WOULD HAVE BEEN A CONTRA"

Alejandro Pérez Bustamante,
(as told to the editor)[2]

Thank you for coming to my farm. I always like to talk with visitors, and you are not the first one to come here. I've even had American congressmen come see me. Maybe they find my story interesting. They always seem to want to start with my family, so I'll do that first. I'm from a peasant family. My father was Benvenuto Pérez Banegas, from Honduras, the town of Yuscaran. My mother was Segunda Bustamante, a Nicaraguan from Totogalpa near here. When they met, my father had come to this part of Nicaragua just to bum around, the way men do. He was wandering around Santa María when he met my mother in Somoto, fell for her, married her, and brought her to this area. Both my parents were Catholics, of course, as everyone was in those days in the mountains, and both were very poor. I was conceived, born, and raised right around here (El Súngano).[3] My father was a laborer on farms around this area, which is how he earned the beans he put on our table when he was around, which wasn't all the time. When he was here my father worked on the Hacienda La Gotera, not too far from El Súngano, and my mother died here.

When I was a little boy we moved around some. I remember we lived a while in a place called El Morado, not too far from here. My father never went to school, and neither did my mother. In those days there weren't any schools in these mountains to go to, so I never went, either, and still I don't know how to read and write, although I did learn a little from some of my friends, like how to sign my name, but not much else. But that was all I ever learned about writing.

I was married to Máxima Sevilla for more than thirty years, but only in a civil ceremony. I had several brothers, four as I remember, and ten children of my own with Máxima, five girls and five boys. Four are still alive. They were all peasants and farm laborers like me. Except when I was away at war, I worked up in these mountains for other people or on my own farm and still work on what little land the Communists left me, the same as my father, except that he never did well enough to have his own farm. When I was a little boy, it was the time of President Zeláya. My parents were fairly light-skinned, almost European looking, and both spoke Spanish.

If I have a hometown, it's Quilalí. I have about thirty-five grandchildren and seven great-grandchildren, so I have been well blessed with family. I will probably have a few more grandchildren and great-grandchildren before I pass away. That's the way it is.

I don't really remember either the date or year when I was born, but I'm well over ninety years old now. You have to remember that I was born well before the war between [Emiliano] Chamorro and José Zeláya. When Chamorro and Zeláya had their war, all of the documents in the civil registry were destroyed, so I don't have a birth certificate or anything like that, nor do most of the people who were born around here in those years. When the first war started between Sandino and the Conservatives I was just a little kid like my great-grandchildren are now, just hanging around the house with my mother or taking day jobs on farms around here, and was still a kid when I went into Sandino's army, just seventeen years old. My mother was pretty poor when I was small, but between what I was able to earn working on other farms and with Sandino, I managed to support her after my father disappeared. We didn't have our own milpa in those days, but instead we worked for other people.[4] When I joined Sandino he hadn't even broken with Somoza yet. It was his Constitutional War, the one between the Conservatives and Liberals, not the second one between him and Somoza and the Marines.

In those days the area around here didn't amount to very much. Quilalí was the biggest town, and it only had its six or seven houses.[5] As you can see, there are a lot of mountains around here, and it's still pretty poor. At that time my mother was moving from house to house working as a servant, trying to keep us together and feed her family. After a while she came up into this area here looking for a place to work and live. At that time if you were a peasant you just came up, found a piece of land, and began farming it. Once in a while she or one of us kids would go down to Quilalí, just look around at the little shops they had, and maybe buy a few little things. We would take down coffee, cones of sugar, beans, corn, whatever we could produce that people in town might buy so we could get a little money in order to buy things we needed ourselves but couldn't make. My mother usually couldn't do this herself because she was almost always busy working in someone else's house to make a little bit of money to buy food for us. We were basically raised on the sweat of our mother, and I remember being hungry most of the time.

At the time the first Sandino war started I had been going around here and there looking for jobs. The first time I met General Sandino I was working as a laborer in the mines at San Albino.[6] It was the first time I had left the area around Quilalí. Up until then I had been just a peasant farm boy. I didn't know anything of all about what was going on in Nicaragua in those days. There weren't any radios or newspapers, and we couldn't have read them if there had been. Besides, we were really not very interested in goings-on a long ways away, so I hadn't heard anything at all about the war between Liberals and Conservatives or anything like that. I certainly didn't have any idea about going to war myself or joining anything like Sandino's army. I had just gone up to the mines looking for a job. There was work pretty much for everybody in the mines, so it wasn't too hard for me to get my job.

But while I was working at the mine I did meet Sandino. He was working as a clerk in the offices, and I was just a sixteen-year-old worker. But there weren't all that many people working there, and besides he was friendly, so I did meet him. His job was as a bookkeeper, and he was keeping the accounts for the main office of the mine. I didn't really get to know him very well then, since he was working in a different part of the mine, and I didn't stay very long. Besides, he was only there for a short time himself while I was working there and disappeared just twenty-two days after I arrived. I stayed just a few more days myself and then came home to my mother's. It was just ten days after I got back home that the war in this part of Nicaragua exploded.

When I first met Sandino up at the mines, I had no idea he was a military officer or even interested in military things. It was only later when I got to know him fairly well, after he had become a guerrilla around this area and I joined him, that I found that out. When I first met him he just seemed like a civilian and acted and dressed like one. I remember that he was fairly nice personally and that he had just come from Mexico.[7] I remember that. As I remember he had learned how to do the work he was doing at the mines while he was in Mexico and had been working at San Albino for about a month before I got there. About twenty days after he disappeared, he began his guerrilla operations. I realized later that the main reason he was at the mines was probably so he could look over the operation in order to rob the place. That certainly was what he did a little while later, although I had come back home before he attacked the mine.

At first when I came home I just went back to working as a day laborer, and for while I didn't hear anything at all about what Sandino was doing. When I did hear he was at war, I decided to visit him to see what was going on, so I went to see him at his camp on El Chipote, the mountain just across the way from here. That was just after he had been involved in a small battle at El Jícaro just north of here with the soldiers of the Conservatives. He had started his war with just a few men with a handful of hunting weapons, shotguns and the like. When I met him that second time, he was with some of them. That was just a little bit after I had left San Albino. It wasn't even fifteen days from the time he robbed the mine and disappeared to the time things exploded up here in the mountains. I decided then and there to stay with him and did so, and followed him down off the mountain soon after that because the Conservatives were pulling back from the little towns up in this region. So we came down and went over to Wiwilí, which is another small town not far from here.[8] When we got to Wiwilí, Sandino put me in charge of making sure he had enough to eat and made me his personal assistant and took a liking to me. Although he sent quite a few of his men off to other places, I stayed with him.

Among the men with Sandino that time as guerrillas was Cirilo Morán, his second in command, who was short and fairly dark-skinned. He was Sandino's closest collaborator at that time, but I never did know where he was from. He was already a grown man by then. He was quite nice to me actually, although we didn't have all that much to do with each other. Camilo Guillen was also with him. He was sort of blond and solidly built. He had a fairly good education as I recall. I used to talk to both of them occasionally, since among those of us with Sandino at the time we treated each other almost as if we were brothers. Rúfo Marín was also there. He was much taller and solidly built, with a dark complexion. He was the son of Don Pio Marín, who was well known around here. I remember that Rúfo Marín was rather quiet. They, of course, were all older men, and I was just a kid. I remember some of the others were with him as well, Carmen Tórres, for example. Tórres was already an older man, and even talked like an old man. There was also Florencio Silva, who was also light-complexioned. He was one of the people with Zeláya in the old days.

Sandino was always friendly with all of us, which is what you'd expect from someone trying to organize a new army.[9] You have to remember that in those days Sandino's army was just in the process of getting organized. Originally there were only about twenty of us. But by the time we got to Wiwilí there were about thirty. During our time around Wiwilí we only had a few small battles. One of the first was back in El Jícaro. In our first three or four small battles, we didn't have anyone killed or wounded. We had shootouts with Conservatives at La Ceiba in Sábana Grande, in the cemetery at El Jícaro, and in a few other places, and also ambushed a Conservative named Alfonso Vivas, who had been going around the region robbing people, taking things from them, and acting very badly. He was a fairly bloody person and was also a Conservative general from Managua.

After we had been fighting up here in the mountains for a while, I went with Sandino down to the Atlantic Coast. He had already arranged with General [José María] Moncada in Mexico to meet in Puerto Cabezas, and Moncada sent him a message saying that he was ready to have the meeting. Moncada had offered Sandino some weapons, so Sandino said to us that his big interest was going down to pick them up. When we went down to the Atlantic Coast we traveled down the river (the Rio Coco) in canoes, and the only people we saw were some Sumu Indians and later some Miskitos. There were only six of us in the group that went down to the Atlantic Coast, but quite a few people joined us after we got there, and we grew until we had about forty people with us altogether.

But when we got to Puerto Cabezas, Moncada didn't give the general all the guns he was expecting. Instead he just gave him forty Con-Cons, which were old single-shot bolt-action Mexican-made rifles. Up until then the only arms we had were a few older pistols and some Mauser rifles. The Mausers, and a few Remingtons we had, were all pretty old, too. They had been around for quite a while and really weren't good enough for our needs. Sandino was very unhappy. We were also pretty short of other things. Up until then we had eaten pretty much whatever was available or what the peasants gave us. We didn't have uniforms, just our regular clothing, including our shoes, which were usually the peasant kind of rubber boots that we still wear around here.[10] At least Moncada gave us some food before we left. From the Atlantic Coast we came back up here to the mountains, and then we did have a few battles, but actually not too many here in the Segovias. The most important ones were to be later, down around Jinotega and further toward the Pacific.

I continued with Sandino from then on as his personal aide and did whatever needed to be done. One of the things I did was to herd his mules for him. I also began acting as his personal bodyguard. In some ways it was just like being a servant. I remember that Sandino was always very easy to get along with and, as a result, everybody around him liked him regardless of who they were. But then he was a very well-educated man.

After we came back with the rifles from the Atlantic Coast our first major move was down into Chontales, Boaco, and thereabouts. Chontales was where we had our first really serious battles, and there we did lose some men. I was there for the first big battle myself. Moncada had come over to the area, and the army had pulled back as a result. It was General Moncada who was attacking, and we went down and joined him in a base known as Las Mercedes. They already had some army troops surrounded nearby when Sandino arrived. Sandino had invented a bomb known as a *cuero de guatusa* that we would throw at the enemy like grenades. We moved right up to the front lines and attacked, yelling "Viva Sandino." As soon as the army soldiers heard us yelling and screaming, they took off. I remember hearing the soldiers yelling: "Sandino's coming with his *cueros de guatusa*," which were really just bags made out of pigskins that we filled with explosives and whatever else we could find; we would put a fuse in and light it just before we threw them. The soldiers ran all the way to a place where we surrounded them and had them under siege for about fifteen days. I remember that some of them died curled up like they were in their mother's womb. They weren't able to get food or even water. The only thing they had was air. That was when the war ended between the Conservatives and the Liberals, and the American minister showed up to make peace.

By then Sandino had named me his first assistant, which really meant I was his chief bodyguard. Actually, he needed a bodyguard mostly just to keep people from bothering him. It wasn't that he had many people to fear. But he was very open with people, and it was important not to let just anybody who wanted to walk up to him. After the battle, Moncada agreed to lay down his arms. Sandino also laid down most of his arms, too, although he did hide a few after some of his soldiers found out Moncada had made a secret deal with the American minister. From there he went off to Diriamba to see his mother, and I went with him. After that Sandino and a number of us came back up into this area. By then I was twenty-one years old. I went looking for a job, but there wasn't work available anywhere around here. So when he decided to go to Mexico, I went with him.

I remember he went by car and it was really a long trip. First we went to Mexico City and then back down to where he had been before on the coast. He was hoping to get some Mexican support to come back, but there were a lot of problems with that, I guess. I used to hear him and his officers talking a lot about that. We moved from place to place, and after a long time wound up in Mérida, down on the Yucatán, where we stayed at a hotel for a long time. I used to get packets of money from some government people to pay for our food and things, and they paid for the hotel, too. Finally, I got the chance to take a trip to see Venezuela and Colombia, and I left him. Later I came back here, and he came back, too. I was still a big believer in him, but I didn't rejoin him as a soldier during the time he was fighting against the American Marines as a guerrilla. But I did give him some other help.

I was involved in one battle that is fairly famous, at the town of Ocotal. That battle took place after General Sandino had gone back to Mexico and then come back again and was the first important fight between him and the Marines. I went to Ocotal before the battle as a supporter of Sandino and was staying in a house of "Nacho" Santillón when Sandino attacked. I wasn't armed but was in touch with his people. The battles started at 2:00 in the morning. Rúfo Marín, whom I knew from my time with Sandino in the mountains and during the battles in Chontales, came into Ocotal with the attacking force until he was wounded very near the house I was staying in. It was a two-story house, and during the battle I was hiding upstairs. Marín's men had established his headquarters just across the way from me. Sandino's main army and the Marines had been shooting at each other since about 2:00 a.m., and the Marines, just like I was, were in a two-story house nearby.[11] Most of the time I spent hiding up against the wall of one house or another, moving from one to another through their patios. From several of them I could see Sandino's soldiers moving back and forth because there was a lot of shooting going on. Rúfo Marín was in command of them. During the early part of the attack he actually came to the house where I was, and we had a chance to say hello and exchange a few words. He told me I should be very careful because the situation was dangerous.

A couple of hours later, when I was running from one house to another, I saw Rúfo fall. He had been shot, so I ran out together with another civilian, grabbed him, and pulled him into the house I was in, called the Casa Francesa (the French House) I suppose because the family that lived there had originally come from France. Rúfo was pretty badly wounded. I did what I could to help him.

After the battle in Ocotal, Sandino kept fighting, but I came back here and went to work on the hacienda of the Duartes or on my own farm and stayed here during most of the war with the Yankees. There were a few small battles around here, including sometimes when the Marine airplanes bombed the mountains over there (pointing to El Chipote). I went back to visiting Quilalí to sell things just like I had before. It was still just a little town, but in those days there was also a small group of American Marines there. I didn't have anything to do with them, although once in a while I might see them and remember that finally they went away. I remember hearing some battles in the distance, too. But I had long since left Sandino's forces and wasn't involved in any of them.

From that time until fairly recently there really weren't any battles around here. But there were some during the war between the Contras and the Sandinistas. The Sandinistas even attacked my house! When the Sandinistas took over Nicaragua they tried to get me to support them publicly because they knew I had been Sandino's chief bodyguard. But they weren't anything at all like my general and I refused. At first they tried to persuade me by sending people to my house to argue with me. When that didn't work, they threatened to take my land away from me. But that just made me more unhappy with them. Finally, some Sandinistas came and arrested me and took me down to their place in Quilalí, where they held me while they tried to convince me that I had to cooperate with them or else. But they were Communists and General Sandino had been a Liberal and not anything like them. In fact, he had thrown the Communists out of his army. The Sandinistas were also almost all from the cities down on the Pacific, not peasants like the people who had supported Sandino up here in the mountains. The Sandinistas were also taking our land and our crops away from us when they could and trying to get us to join their organizations, all of which we didn't like. The more I resisted, the angrier the Sandinistas became, until finally they went from just talking to me to torturing me. I still carry on my upper right arm this scar left by a bayonet one of them stuck into me trying to get me to join up with their side (points to scar). But in the end they let me go, and I went home, coming up here to my house on El Súngano. But that wasn't the end of it. After I got home, Sandinista soldiers from their base in Quilalí fired mortars at my house. They hit my house and killed my wife of thirty years. I still have the shell casing from one of their mortar bombs that didn't explode well [points it out].

I had never believed in them but hadn't been prepared in the beginning to fight against them despite what they were doing. But after that I became a supporter of the *chilotes*.[12] General Sandino was my hero, and I remember him as an honorable and very gentle man who was careful with the peasants and who was fighting for Nicaragua. He was very religious and a Catholic, and certainly not a Communist. I remember when he ran the Communists out of his army. In fact, if Sandino had been alive during the Sandinista revolution, he would have been a Contra himself. He would never have done what they did to the peasants or invited foreigners like the Cubans into our mountains to run our country for us the way the Sandinistas did.

Even my experiences with Somoza were much better than those with Sandinistas. Mostly, he just left us alone, which was fine with us. Until the Sandinistas started fighting him in the mountains, he didn't even have many soldiers or police up here, and those that were here were pretty much people like us and acted fairly well. Even when the Sandinistas were up here in the mountains themselves fighting against Somoza, his people always treated us well and never caused any problems for me or my neighbors. It was only when the Sandinistas took over that we began to have problems because their ideas were so strange and made the peasants very angry. By then I had become an old man but was very well known, and many people came to me to ask what Sandino would have done. I always told them exactly what I said before. If Sandino were here he would help us fight against the Sandinistas. Today I am happy just to stay on my farm surrounded by children, my grandchildren, and my great-grandchildren. The government can come help with some things, like schools and medicine. But mostly we would rather just be left alone.

4

Alejandro Martínez Sáenz, *Comandante Martínez*

A BIOGRAPHICAL SKETCH

Contrary to conventional wisdom, many Latin American revolutionaries have been moderates or even conservatives. From a Nicaraguan Conservative family, *Comandante Martínez,* born in 1928, became an anti-Somoza activist at his father's side, and as a consequence he and his family were forced into exile in Costa Rica, where Alejandro later became a citizen and has lived since, except when he was at war. In 1944 he engaged in his first anti-Somoza guerrilla actions; in 1948 he fought as a member of the revolutionary forces that put José "Pepe" Figueres in Costa Rica's Presidential Palace; in 1956 he joined the anti-Somoza forces of former Sandino General Ramón Raudales and was with him when he was killed in combat. After Raudáles's death Martínez stayed inside Nicaragua for another year as a guerrilla with a small remnant of the group, but went to Cuba fifteen days after Castro's triumph, only to fall under a political cloud there and remain until 1971. Finally allowed to leave in 1972, in 1974 he again joined an anti-Somoza force and was a senior FSLN field commander until 1979, when he broke with the Front. From 1979 to 1990 he was an anti-Sandinista guerrilla leader. In 1980 the CIA tried to recruit him, but he declined. Today he is a reserve colonel in the Costa Rican Guardia Civil.

□ □ □

CONSERVATIVE, REVOLUTIONARY, AND GUERRILLA

Alejandro Martínez Sáenz (as told to the editor)

It is hard to believe I'm now more than seventy years old and spent fifty of those years fighting Nicaraguan dictatorships, first Somoza for thirty-four years and then the Communists that captured our movement in 1979. My family is from Rivas. My father was a Conservative member in the National Assembly during the presidency of the first Somoza, Anastacio "Tacho" Somoza Garcia, and a close cousin of Violeta Barrios de Chamorro, who was president from 1990 to 1996. My mother was the daughter of General Sáenz, well known in my country's history. My father, who was educated in San Francisco and served in the U.S. Army during World War II, taught me it is important to fight for democracy, a lesson I have never forgotten.

Nicaragua was hardly a democracy while I was a student, so I began studying its past conflicts to see what might be done. The most important historical example I found was that of General Augústo César Sandino, and I read every book and article I could find about him. Since some did not circulate in Nicaragua, several were brought to me from Mexico by friends and relatives. I also spent hours listening to stories about Sandino and his struggle, many told by my relatives who had been with him, and became convinced that we too would have to launch an armed struggle if we were to become democratic.

Becoming a Conservative Revolutionary

I began my own struggle while only fourteen years old, when my father and I both became involved with efforts by General Hurtado to overthrow Somoza. As a consequence my father took us into exile in Costa Rica. That was in 1939. Once in Costa Rica my father supported several expeditions against Somoza, including one by General Alfredo Noguera Gómez in 1944 in which I was also involved, and so it went. From 1944 on I continued to be involved in revolutionary movements, including the 1948 war in Costa Rica that put José Figueres in power, during which I served with General Antonio Salaveri at Villamil in what was known as the Virgen de Los Angeles Company.[1] We fought twice, once at La Congreja against Carlos Luís Fállas and then in the decisive battle of the war at El Tejar. There were sixty of us in that battle, most from the Caribbean Legion. We ourselves were not part of the Caribbean Legion, but we did coordinate our operations with them. The legion had been organized in Mexico as an alliance to liberate the entire Caribbean and Central America of dictators, with Somoza a key target. Among its leaders were Spanish Republican generals Vasconcelos and Alberto Bayo. Bayo went on to be a top advisor to Fidel Castro. There were Nicaraguans, Cubans, Hondurans, Guatemalans, Mexicans, and a number from the Dominican Republic in its ranks.

The very next year, in 1949, I became a guerrilla for the first time when I went with General Raudales on an invasion attempt, becoming one of his officers. We first went to Mexico, which was always supportive of revolutionary movements like ours, met with Lázaro Cárdenas, and asked for help, which he gave us. I remember Cárdenas telling us he was very conscious of the situation in Nicaragua because the liberation of Central America was dependent on what happened there. We then went on to Guatemala, where we received even more help from President Arévalo. In fact Arévalo became very close with Raudales and committed himself fully to our cause. I also came to know him well and still have the copy of his famous book *The Shark and the Sardines* that he autographed and gave me.

Arévalo provided almost all the arms for our invasion, bolt-action Springfields and Mausers, two 30-caliber water-cooled machine guns, some pistols, and ammunition. He also gave us other assistance. Just before we left to invade Nicaragua, we were briefed by some Guatemalan army officers, and we left Guatemala in a government DC-3, planning to land in the Segovias. But the Guardia had been tipped off and was waiting for us. We tried to land three times but failed and finally went back to Guatemala. My next involvement came in 1955, when some Calderonistas[2] prepared by Somoza at El Chipote tried to invade Costa Rica. I joined Figueres as a company commander and fought the invaders in Santa Rosa.

With Raudales

In 1958 I was informed that Raudales was organizing another expedition against Somoza from Honduras, and again I joined him. We established a forward base on the Patuca River on the Honduran side east of Danlí from which we would infiltrate into Nicaragua through the mountains toward Wiwilí. We began by creating support bases among the peasants and building secret weapons caches and medical depots in order to establish a main operations base east of Wiwilí on the mountain of Kilambé. It's a very difficult mountain, and we were never entirely successful. Our supply lines were extremely weak, and we lived off the land. Altogether we had about 250 men. At least during that campaign, unlike in 1954, we made it into Nicaragua. I commanded Raudales's scout platoon. Our first combat was a skirmish with six Guardia who quickly retreated. Then Raudales sent us on a mission to El Chipote. En route we ambushed a company of Guardia at San Pablo Hill. Altogether we had three skirmishes before the final battle at Los Encinos near the Yalí River, where the attacking force was the Guardia's Company K, led by one of Somoza's best officers. We ambushed them, and at first they were unable to dislodge us. But reinforcements arrived, and we came under air attack by Mustangs. Raudales was hit in the lower face, and we had lost our only doctor so were unable to give him proper medical treatment. He bled to death six hours later. That was one of the saddest nights of my life. He had been a great man. After Raudales was killed most of the force withdrew, but a few of us stayed in the mountains.

In the Mountains

It was during my year in the Segovian mountains after Raudales was killed that I learned several important lessons, including the absolute need of having networks among the peasants. There were never more than about twenty-five or thirty of us, most the sons of men who had been with Sandino, and we were entirely dependent on their peasant families. Once when we came into a small settlement all the women were crying, and I discovered they were terrified the army would take reprisals because we had been there. They taught me the high price revolutions can exact, even from those not fighting. I also learned the value of timely intelligence information.

Somoza used local magistrates as his eyes and ears in the mountains. They kept him informed about how many of us there were, what kind of arms we had, how we were in terms of supplies and medicines, and so forth, until I finally noticed that every time a local magistrate saw us, about thirty minutes later we had the Guardia after us. Once I figured that out, we decided to push the magistrates out of the regions. Our tactics were fairly simple. We would capture a magistrate and assemble the peasants of the neighborhood. If they said he was a good person we gave him two or three hours to leave for the nearest town. But if he had been involved in such things as killing peasants, we executed him. Actually, we shot only five or six. But that was enough.

Another group of rebels existed under a former Guardia officer by the name of Somarriba, the leader of a small group of dissident officers who had tried to stage a coup against Somoza during the presidency of Somoza's puppet Argüello. He trusted the Hondurans to help him. But in fact they kept Somoza informed of what we were doing, so when his group finally went inside in 1959, by which time I was in a Cuban jail, the Guardia was waiting. It was as a consequence of his misplaced trust that the battle of El Chaparrál took place later in June 1959 on the Nicaragua–Honduras border not too far from Danlí in which my brother Harold and Carlos Fonseca Amador, the founder of the FSLN, were wounded. My brother was left for dead on the battlefield but was saved by a peasant, as was Carlos Fonseca.

Two of the men killed at El Chaparrál were personal aides to "Che" Guevara, both of whom I knew personally, Rogelio Silva and another whose name I forget. They had been sent by Castro to fight and act as advisors and were attempting to create what Guevara called a guerrilla *foco*. But with most of their men killed at El Chaparrál the attempt ended. Some have said the battle took place in Honduras, but actually it took place in Nicaragua. The Honduran army just picked up those who survived.

There was also another rebel movement about that time that left Cuba in fishing boats and sailed to the Atlantic coast of Honduras just north of Nicaragua. It was led by a Dr. Palma and a Sr. Romero, both of whom have since died. They took a large load of arms to Honduras but never went into battle. After about forty days of doing nothing they were discovered and returned to Cuba. The arms were being carried to another Marxist organization, the Sandino Liberation Front [FSL], but never arrived. But I wasn't around for either of these events because my own life had taken a bizarre turn.

To Cuba and Jail

A year after we went to the mountains, and before El Chaparrál, we heard about the successful Cuban Revolution and were euphoric over Castro's victory. We decided to send a delegation to Cuba via Mexico to seek his help, and I was among those selected. We were assisted by a man named Laurralde, a 26th of July Movement officer in Mexico who had earlier helped us get some arms after Faustino Pérez, one of Castro's men from the yacht *Granma*, put us in touch with him. He arranged for us to travel via Guatemala on Cuban identity documents, and when we arrived in Havana, Laurralde said that we were Cubans and they waved us through. We were even met at José Martí Airport by some senior Cuban officials, including Teodoro Machado.

At first in Cuba everything seemed almost ideal, until eight days later when we first met with Fidel and Raúl Castro and discovered that both were Marxist–Leninists. It was a shock to find that, although in public their speeches were all about democracy, in private their thinking was pure Marxist. Both Fidel and Raúl said during that meeting that the only possible way to have a successful revolution was to fight against the Yankee imperialists and the West, just as Sandino had. But I knew Sandino had been a nationalist and believed in a very different kind of revolution from the one Fidel and Raúl Castro told us in private they intended to stage. He had clashed repeatedly in Mexico with Marxists trying to capture his movement, and again in Nicaragua when he expelled Faribundo Martí and others for plotting behind his back. He had even ordered a Marxist, Dr. Terencio, shot because of the plot. So I said to Fidel that Sandino had not only not been a Communist, but he had fought against Communism. That was a nearly fatal mistake.

When we first arrived we had found many traditional enemies of Costa Rican democracy already there supporting the revolution, people like Carlos Luís Fallas and others we had fought in other places. They considered us enemies, and my remarks to the Castros gave them an opportunity to denounce me. Fifteen days after our meeting, Cuban military intelligence came to my house and arrested me on the accusation of being a counterrevolutionary. I was to be a political prisoner for four years.

While I was in La Cabaña prison,[3] the Cubans applied both physical and psychological torture and falsely accused me of being a CIA agent.[4] But that was not true. Their real problem was that I was an authentic Sandino Sandinista, not just a Marxist–Leninist calling himself one, of the original generation that had followed directly behind Sandino and a founder of the original anti-Somoza movement to take his name, the Sandino Revolutionary Front [FRS]. Every day the prison warden would call out several names of prisoners who were led into a courtyard we could clearly see from our cells and shot by firing squad. About eighteen months after I arrived, my name was called. I was lined up before the stake, tied to it, and faced by a firing squad of six guards with AK-47s. I did not ask for mercy and refused to wear a mask. The officer in charge gave the "ready, aim, fire" orders, but they did not shoot. I'm not quite sure why. It's hard to explain how you feel when you're in front of firing squad with your life passing before your eyes. From La Cabaña's execution wall I was taken directly to a military "hospital," where I was subjected to additional interrogation for six months. But I couldn't tell them anything because I didn't know anything. So finally they took me back to prison. It's not that there were no CIA agents in Cuba. It's just that I was not one of them. I did meet one who was a prisoner with me. I only knew him by his code name, *Gasolina*. In fact he survived and is now living secretly in Miami, where I saw him a few years ago. He was a communicator and operated a radio on a fishing boat, and he was later released in some sort of deal.

An Agronomist under Island Arrest

After four years they finally released me from La Cabaña and took me to a sugar plantation to work. I was out of jail but still not free to leave Cuba. Once there I received a message from Faustino Pérez, who had just been appointed director of Cuba's Institute for Drainage Engineering. Because he had been on the *Granma* and had helped save "Che" Guevara's life when he was wounded during Castro's first battle, Faustino was considered a true Hero of the Revolution. We had become friends in Mexico, and I had seen him in Cuba before I was jailed, and he knew I was an agronomist. The message said Pérez had been seriously wounded and asked me to visit him at home, where I found he had been shot during an assassination attempt by orthodox Communists in the intelligence services. When Castro found out the attempt had failed, he was concerned with what the political impact of the story might be if it got out, so he found Pérez his new job, one appropriate to a Hero of the Revolution but far from real power.

When Pérez recovered he invited me back to his house for a second visit, and when I arrived he signaled to me to be silent and pointed outside. I was surprised that a Hero of the Revolution was afraid his conversations were being intercepted in his own home. Outside he told me "I am not a Communist but I am a Fidelista and intend to see the revolution through" and offered me a position at his institute, which had all sorts of international technicians, Russians, Bulgarians, East Germans, and many others. Of course I accepted. The revolution's leaders were trying to run everything from Havana, which made for some strange orders. Once I worked on a project in Oriente Province under orders to plant bananas in a region where bananas had never grown before. We planted six hundred acres, but they didn't produce two pounds of bananas.

Russian Missiles after the Missile Crisis

Probably the most interesting experience I had while with Pérez was in 1966 when we were sent out to solve a problem with some water wells at a military base named Managua.[5] I was interested because the capital of my country was also named Managua. When the base commander found out I was Nicaraguan, he invited me to tour the base and at one point took me down into some very large tunnels with big doors on the outside that led to some very large circular silos covered by camouflaged round doors. We used special elevators to get into the area. The silos contained gigantic rockets. I was very scared when I saw them because, having already been accused once of being a CIA agent, I feared that if the intelligence services found I had been inside such a secret place I might disappear, never to be seen again. There were four or five missiles, each in a separate silo, with a large gallery beneath and a lot of technicians moving around in electric vehicles. That's how big it was. This was after the famous Cuban missile crisis, when supposedly all the Russian missiles had been taken out, and I said so to the commander. He laughed and said, "No. These are the famous etceteras that were left behind." I suppose because I was close to one of the Heroes of the Revolution he assumed I was totally trustworthy. He said they were Cuba's guarantee that there would be no American invasion, because as long as they had the rockets, if the Americans invaded 15–20 million Americans would die.[6]

Leaving Cuba

While I was at the institute I met and married a Cuban woman with whom I have two children. A few years later, when my wife became very sick, Faustino Pérez intervened on my behalf with Fidel when he came to the institute to award some diplomas. After the ceremony Pérez called me over and said to Fidel: "I want you to meet a comrade of ours. He was in prison for many years and was tortured while in the La Cabaña." Fidel reacted forcefully and said: "We never torture prisoners here," at which point I answered: "That's not true, comrade. Come look at my scars. You're being misled by your people. If you will come with me to the prison I will show you what is happening." Fidel, noticing from my accent that I was not Cuban, asked where I was from. "I'm a Nicaraguan who had been fighting against Somoza and came here in 1959 looking for help from the revolution to continue my struggle but instead was put in jail and have since been held here against my will." Fidel told me to write him a report, which I did. I still have a copy of it. He also asked what I wanted to do. When I told him I wanted to take my wife with our children to Costa Rica for medical attention, Fidel gave me a card to take to Celia Sánchez, his confidential aide.

When I met Celia Sánchez I found out one of her brothers had been a prisoner with me in La Cabaña and had been shot. When I told her I had seen her brother executed she began to cry and asked me to write a description of how her brother died, which I did and took back to her. As she read it she began to cry again. When she finished, she gave me a note authorizing passports, for my wife and two children. Celia Sánchez committed suicide not too long after that. My wife died before we could leave. But, in any case, since we already had passports, the Cubans expelled me and my children, but to Chile, not Costa Rica. It took me eight months to get us home to Costa Rica. That was in 1972. At first I just stayed with family, recovering.

Back to My Own Revolution

In 1974 I was contacted by yet another anti-Somoza revolutionary movement that was part of the FSLN, and, despite my experiences, since I was still very much anti-Somoza, I joined them. By then the Marxists inside the Sandinista movement had become quite strong, and my idea was to try to counter their growing strength. I remember meeting here in Costa Rica with some of the other non-Marxists who had been with me in earlier wars against Somoza and warning them they should make certain that when we overthrew Somoza the Communists did not take control. We had to do that by capturing the vanguard from the Marxists but were unsuccessful. Even so I began organizing and inserting small groups of guerrillas into Nicaragua. Their first missions were to create support bases among the peasants as far north as Chontales, because without such support it's not really possible to have a guerrilla movement. I went in myself perhaps a dozen times.

At first the people were afraid. But during 1975 and 1976 we were able to create larger and larger support areas. Whenever I returned to Costa Rica we would meet in safe houses to discuss the places where we had been most successful in order to identify where we could put larger guerrilla units. They had to be areas where they could eat and where we had cached at least a few weapons and some medicine. Finding arms, medicines, and some supplies wasn't as difficult as you might think. For example, in Costa Rica government security officers helped with weapons. Others helped with ammunition, food, shoes. It was a very well-organized operation. We were not a regular army so we had fewer needs. While we didn't have official help, the Costa Rican government was sympathetic and looked the other way. It had been a very long process. But from 1975 on, during the government of the third Somoza, we began having more success.

From 1977 through 1979 I was almost continuously in combat and often commanded patrols that penetrated fairly deeply into Nicaragua. One of the most interesting was a reconnaissance in force against Rivas, my hometown. There were fifty-five men in the unit, which was to be led by Plutarco Hernández. But he broke his arm just before we left, and I led the patrol instead. We went to the border disguised as a special unit sent by the Costa Rican president and changed our identities after we were inside. With so few men we hardly expected to hold any positions and in fact did not intend even to enter the town. But it was thirty kilometers from the border to Rivas, and we were surprised that the Guardia never stopped us, even though the terrain is quite open, so we marched right in until we reached the central plaza. There were Guardia right on the plaza, but even they didn't challenge us. The only thing I could imagine was that since we were dressed in olive green uniforms they simply assumed we were another Guardia unit. Anyhow, we deployed in front of the cathedral, and I gave the order to open fire, at which point the Guardia scattered. After a short while we withdrew back into Costa Rica, again without problems.

I was involved in a number of skirmishes and battles along the sector of the border that was our responsibility. We would cross over from Costa Rica into Nicaragua, attack a Guardia position, and then go back into Costa Rica where the Nicaraguans could not follow us. We did that dozens of times. That way we tied down about three companies of the Guardia, perhaps 600 soldiers. They had to defend the entire border, while we could attack where we wanted, and so they needed lots more troops than we did. It was only later after we had become stronger and the Guardia weaker that we began to hold positions. By then we were essentially a conventional army.

From Revolutionaries to Regular Army

During the final year of the war against Somoza our army changed from a guerrilla force into a conventional army thanks to several countries. Costa Rica gave us bases, support, and freedom of movement on its territory. Panama provided us a channel of arms and ammunition.[7] Venezuela and Colombia sent arms, especially FAL rifles. But the most important of all was the United States, which assured our victory by withdrawing its political and military help from Somoza while at the same time turning a blind eye to the involvement of Panama, Costa Rica, and above all Cuba.

At the time I was commander of Base 12, near the headquarters of the Southern Front on the Costa Rica–Nicaragua border just across from Cárdenas. I was also a member of the general staff. Our army became large enough in 1977–1978 to convert from guerrilla to more or less conventional warfare. By then the front had hundreds of well-trained soldiers in Costa Rica, and several thousand recruited and organized inside Nicaragua. Those in Costa Rica were in eighteen different bases spread along the entire border with Nicaragua and divided into several groups. Each of the three "tendencies" had what was in effect its own force, and there was also an international brigade. We also had special units in safe houses in San José. One of the most active was only two blocks from the American Embassy. My own unit was entirely Nicaraguan, but there were many internationalists in others, usually men who had been trained as guerrillas in Cuba. In addition Cuba sent small special forces units to fight and had advisors inside Nicaragua. I did not see him personally but heard that General Ochoa, then Castro's favorite, came to Costa Rica several times. The Cubans numbered about two or three hundred and, on at least two occasions, went into combat directly against the Nicaraguan Guardia.

The situation changed even more when in 1978 the three political "tendencies" in our movement were pulled together by Castro. I was not involved because I could not go back to Havana where everything was being arranged, and I was also afraid that the end result would be as negative as it turned out. From then on it was a very difficult war for us. We were fighting Somoza but knew the Marxists inside our movement were supported by the Cubans and quite capable of stealing the revolution from us.

The Marxists Steal the Revolution, Thanks to the United States

Just before the triumph of the revolution I was in command of the small but strategically important position at Cárdenas but fearing more and more that the Communists were going to steal power as soon as Somoza fell. In early 1979 we actually began organizing to fight them if that happened. About that time Edén Pastora brought a political commissar to my base, a Mexican by the name of Montenegro, but I refused to accept him. It was then that I realized what was going to happen and in May 1979 called a press conference and denounced the threat of a Communist takeover to the international and local press.[8] I held Cárdenas until the end of the war and continued to warn against the danger of a Communist capture of our movement. I made contact with the United States Embassy in San José and told them of my concerns and also spoke personally with "Pepe" Figueres. He shared my concerns but at first did nothing. In addition I contacted the Venezuela Military Mission then working with the Sandinista southern front and warned them also that the Marxists were going to steal the revolution. But none of them took any actions.

Toward the end, command of the army passed to the political directorate of the FSLN. Some people have since said we did not know that they were Communists, but we knew perfectly well. I had known most of them for many years, and we had been in Cuba together. There was absolutely no question about their political preferences. I myself was involved in much of their training and remember how much Marxist political indoctrination they received and how enthusiastically they embraced it.

We did not win the war against Somoza. American President

Jimmy Carter won the war for us. The Americans were also very well acquainted with the political leadership of the FSLN and the politics of its members, so why they supported them even though they knew they were Communists has always been a mystery to me. We were evenly matched with the Guardia until Carter changed the balance in our favor by withdrawing political legitimacy from Somoza and, more important, by cutting off Somoza's ammunition supplies. Until then we were not winning the war. Although I understand some American government officials have later said they did not realize the leadership of the Sandinista Front was Marxist–Leninist, there is simply no way that could possibly be true. They were much too well informed. The leaders of the Front, especially the Communists, traveled all the time to Havana, to international Communist youth meetings in places like Vienna and throughout Europe, to Russia, and often even to the United States to make contact with American Marxists there. It simply is not believable that American intelligence did not know who they were or what they were doing.

If nothing else they must have known after I made public announcements following my capture of Cárdenas. I made public announcements to the press, contacted the American Embassy, contacted the Venezuelan Military Mission, and talked to former president of Costa Rica Figueres, who agreed with me. If not before, certainly by then the American government had to know the dangers posed by the Communists, inside the Sandinista Front. And that was three months before the fall of Somoza in May of 1979, when I began saying publicly that the Sandinista Front was going to be captured by the Communists who were going to establish a dictatorship and then threaten all of Central America. We sent messages to the press and we brought journalists to our camps and I talked to them; we did everything we could to sound a warning to try to keep our triumph from being stolen. I even talked with the American liaison officers in the area, since what we were doing in Costa Rica was no secret. I even had OAS observers come to my camps, so there was no doubt in their minds we were operating inside Costa Rica. One of my officers also

made contact with Costa Rican intelligence operatives we knew
were working with the Americans and with the American Embassy in San José.[9]

After we occupied Cárdenas we became even more convinced
the Marxists were going to try to steal our revolution, so we
began preparing the peasants quickly and trying to organize a
support base should we have to go back to war. I tried for three
months until, during one battle while I was leading my assault
troops, I was hit by two bullets fired from inside my own unit
from no more than twenty-five feet away. That made it obvious
to me that the Marxist Sandinistas had already decided to try to
eliminate me physically if possible. I captured one of the rifles
used and took it with me to Costa Rica, where Costa Rican
Guardia Civil Colonel Sánchez Monester, an expert in ballistics,
confirmed that it was the same FAL from which one of the bullets
that wounded me had been fired. That made it obvious that at
least two of my own soldiers had shot at me. We were advancing
toward the enemy at the time and the bullets came from behind
me. I was in Costa Rica briefly for treatment but kept fully informed of what was happening since, after all, I was a member of
the general staff.

After the Sandinistas occupied Managua they ordered Leonel
Poveda to take a column and move against me and disarm my
troops. But Poveda refused, saying that I was a good commander
and comrade, so they sent another commander. But we captured
his forward element of sixteen men and sent them back to him in
their underwear, barefoot. That was my first battle against the
Communists, just thirty-five days after the triumph of the revolution. The only politician who realized how badly things were
going was José "Pepe" Figueres, who asked the Venezuelans to
equip 500 men for me and help fly us to a small airfield we had
prepared inside Nicaragua. They tried. But when we took in the
first supplies a battle broke out, and we were caught between
Lake Nicaragua and the Costa Rican border by the Sandinistas.
When we ran out of ammunition, we retreated back into Costa
Rica, and what we feared happened.

México, D. F.
18 de Diciembre de 1965.-

Compañero:

Voy aclarar muchas cuestiones de importancia esperando se den cuenta de lo que voy a decir.-

El C. Gilberto le ha de ver contado como andan las cosas en relación a los señores prestamistas, por eso está de más explicar punto por punto; lo único que me queda es que cumplan las indicaciones que el C. Gilberto les dio, para que así no se pierda esta fuente de ingresos. Si Uds. hacen todo tal como se dice aquí la ayuda no faltará, más si en cambio no lo cumplen ayuda no habrá. El trabajo de investigación debe hacerse como los señores prestamistas lo indican, y las indicaciones se las dio el C. Gilberto, no crean que cuando nosotros les decimos que hagan esto y lo otro es obra nuestra, no, si les indicamos que hay que hacer es porque lo señores prestamistas asi nos lo han indicado, Bueno sobre esto Uds. tiene demasiados datos. Espero que ahora si nos vamos a poner de acuerdo en esa clase de trabajo, pero no es malo volverlo a recordárselos.-

Con respecto a los muchachos que van a viajar a la feria de Enero, acabo de recibir un cablegrama de Virgilio en donde me pone que Uds. tiene listo a los viajeros. Voy hacerles unas recomendaciones para que no se encuentren con dificultades.- Si ellos llegan después del 25 de este mes se van a encontrar con que don José ni yo estaremos en la capital, pero si salen como el 21 se encontraran todavía con don José, Más si no estamos ninguno de los dos que el Dr. Orlando o Pepe los ponga en contacto con la Embajada de la Isla, o si no que acudan a las oficinas del Movimiento de Liberación Nacional que estan en república del Salvador, ya que esta organización es la encargada de las invitaciones. No se si llegaría el delegado que los iba a invitar, mas si llegó creo que él les ha de ver dado algunas indicaciones para ponerse en contacto con ellos aquí, pero como yo no se si llegó, por eso es que les doy esas indicaciones para en caso de que haya problemas, y se las doy también por que yo no voy a encontrarme en esta ciudad. Ahora, si el Sr. que llegó a invitarlos les dio todas la orientaciones necesarias mucho mejor, pero sino lo que tiene que hacer es que a los C. que van a viajar a la Isla vengan con suficiente dinero, tant para estarse aquí lonecesario para arreglar sus papeles como para viajar a laIsla, esto se los digo por que no se como fue la invitación que les hicieron. Son indicaciones que no salen sobrando, acabo de hablar por tel fono a la oficina del Sr. que llegó a invitarlos y me dijeron que todavía se encontraba fuera del país, y como no lo voy a poder ver, por eso una vez mas, les digo que les hago esas indicaciones.- *Dinero aquí no hay. Los pre tamistas onquen de vocociones, o demos deque ocoban de dan*

El C. que viaje debe de ir bien preparado para que expongan de una manera concreta los problemas de nosotros y del pueblo, es decir, que por primera vez se diga resumir la voz del movimiento revolucionario nicaraguense en el ambito internacional, Que se hagan en contacto con todas las personalidaes que van a asistir y que su voz sea una de las que ocupen bue nos lugares. Sobre Uds. ya sabrán como hacerle.-

Letter of December 18, 1965, from Humberto Ortega, later Commanding General of the Sandinista People's Army, to Carlos Fonseca Amador, sent to Fonseca in an envelope (on facing page, along with second page of letter) addressed to *Valentín*, Fonseca's code-name at the time. Despite the heading, it was reportedly written in Havana. In it Ortega speaks on behalf of the Cubans, identified as "los prestamistas" (the money-lenders), about the visit of one Comrade Gilberto (apparently DGI) and warns Fonseca in paragraph two: "If you do exactly as he says you will receive assistance. If not, you will receive nothing." In paragraph three, Ortega tells Fonseca how to contact "La embajada de la isla" (Cuban Embassy) in Mexico City and identifies "El Ingeniero" ("Pepe Puente") as a top Sandinista-Cuban contact there. For a supposed subordinate, the tone is surprisingly imperious. Private collection.

En lo dicho anterior con respecto de que yo no me encontraré aquí es - por lo siguiente:

Cuando reciban esta carta ya habré salido rumbo a Europa, voy a lo que - Uds, ya saben, no se sabe que tiempo se estará pero se hará lo posible por estar el menos. Salgo este domingo 19 en la tarde. Cuando regrese pondré u telegrama diciendoles que ya estoy de regreso. Por eso es que cuando -- vengan los viajeros no me encontrarán aquí, pero ya tiene algunas explica-- ciones sobre eso. Ojala que todo salga bien, voy bien preparado y creo que sabré ponerme a la altura de mi deber como revolucionario.- Cuando regrese prepararé mi viaje para estar con Uds.-

Quiero agregar unos puntos mas con respecto al trabajo de organización, lo concretaré:

El punto fundamental para llevar a cabo un buen trabajo revolucionario es contar con una buena organización. Si nosotros logramos superar todas - nuestras fallas, tengan la seguridad que dejaremos muy atras al Partido y - esto nos dará a nosotros mas prestigio. Nosotros estamos en capacidad de ha cerlo y vamos a demostrarlo con los hechos que lo haremos. Demostrar a los demás partidos que nosotros somos los únicos en llevar el trabajo revolu-- cionario adelante, para que nos tomen en cuenta. Si esto no se hace por fal ta de dinero, hagamos lo posible con contar con nuestros propios esfuerzos que es mas honroso y mas meritorio. No se olviden lo primero es contar con una buena organización y creo que lo podemos hacer.-

El compañero que lleva esta que me la entregará al Ingeniero, es un com pañero que trabaja con nosotros aquí en México, es de confianza, si Uds. - quieren pueden platicar con él. Virgilio lo conoce, pueden pedirle datos a - él. Es conveniente que cuando él se regrese pueden mandar alguna carta --- o al una que otra cosa, que el ingeniero sirva de enlace para que lo vean, esto es si Uds. quieren. Yo por mi parte estaré de acuerdo. Alberto tam-- bien lo conoce.-

Que pasen un Feliz Año Nuevo. Saludes a todos. Reciban un fuerte abra- zo revolucionario de

Humberto

CORREO AEREO · VIA AIR MAIL

The Cuban Role

The important thing to keep in mind is that from 1962 on everything the FSLN did in terms of revolutionary activities was actually run by the Cubans from Havana. They organized everything, with "Che" Guevara and Manuel Piñiero trying to run it all in accord with "Che"'s theory of *focos*. And everything they organized failed. They failed at Pancasán, they failed on the Atlantic Coast, they failed in the Segovias. The people they sent to tell the Nicaraguans how to fight their guerrilla wars were little more than travel agents who flew in and out via Mexico from Havana, and the Nine who became the revolution's Marxist political leaders after 1979 spent most of their time between then and July 1979 flying in and out of safe places to Cuba looking for money and comfort. In Havana they were treated like minor royalty, surrounded by girls and living in nice houses. For them revolution was the good life, and few ever seriously risked their lives. They were purely opportunists. The people who did the actual fighting inside Nicaragua clashed repeatedly not just with Somoza but also with the Marxist Sandinistas.

The First CIA Contact: 1980

By late 1979 I was again involved in armed raids against the Sandinistas from Costa Rica, working in small groups. A year later, in December 1980, the CIA contacted me.[10] Two Americans and an Argentine military officer came to see me in San José. The Argentine said he was from army intelligence. The Americans said the United States wanted me to take command of a new anti-Sandinista movement and invited me to Washington, D.C., to meet with other officials. They said the United States had decided to provide paramilitary support to some anti-Sandinista Nicaraguans, and I was their first choice as leader because I was a nationalist and anti-Marxist but not a Somocista and had both a clean record and military experience.

I went almost immediately to Washington, D.C., as a guest of the American government, and I remember it was 25 degrees when I arrived and I was freezing.[11] One of the American officers met me when I arrived, accompanied by a young lady whose name I don't remember. They put me in the L'Enfant Plaza Hotel and would come by to take me to a safe house, a private home in Georgetown, for meetings.[12] I met with officers from the Department of State, the CIA, the Pentagon, and the White House, eight or ten Americans altogether.[13] Among other things, we discussed strategies. One we considered was to organize small propaganda teams to infiltrate Nicaragua to engage in destabilization activities. We also discussed the establishment of both a northern and a southern front, with the northern in Honduras and the southern in Costa Rica (see appendix).

They offered to give us all the resources and arms needed but in return wanted to impose a general staff that was almost exclusively former Guardia and to direct the war from Washington, conditions I was not prepared to accept. One of the American officers had forewarned me in Costa Rica that this was what the Americans and Argentines were going to do and had even given me their names. The best of the Guardia they proposed was a Major Manzano, but most had bad records. I was not opposed to the Guardia as such. They also had the right to fight for their country. But my basic fear was that any war directed from Washington would end up as badly as all the other wars directed from Washington had, and I also considered having Somocistas in top positions a political error of major proportions. I stayed in Washington ten days. But when I decided not to accept, I came back to Costa Rica and returned to my other anti-Sandinista activities.

To War Once More, This Time Against the Sandinistas

By early 1982 we had quite a few men making raids in and out of Nicaragua, and there was another group of anti-Sandinista fighters in the north that had been organized in Guatemala in 1979, mostly former Somoza Guardia and known as the Legión 15 de Septiembre. Their main idea was to regain power, but the revolution was a reality and it simply was not possible to go back to the Nicaragua of Somoza. Still, we were prepared to cooperate. There were also other groups in the south, mostly former Terceristas who had been pushed out by the Marxists and had stayed behind in Costa Rica. In 1982 I joined the new Southern Front forming in Costa Rica, although I thought it a mistake to select Edén Pastora, who had just defected from the Sandinistas, as its leader because of his personality. Actually, the choice of leader was between me, my brother Harold, or Pastora. But if Pastora had not been named it would have caused a division immediately, so we gave way. We fought many battles against the Sandinistas. I myself went into Nicaragua several times, once all the way to the Segovias to meet with peasants who were fighting. Sometimes we had to fight our way in, especially when we entered at Barra Colorada at the mouth of the San Juan River, where you need special boats and pilots so you don't capsize. We also had to be alert for Nicaraguan patrol boats and observation airplanes.

One little-known but important battle we fought took place in 1982 when we captured the Sandinistas' military positions at Peñas Blancas with a force of almost 200 men. By then the Sandinistas had dug in and even planted mine fields, but we crossed the border almost five kilometers away from their positions and then attacked them from the rear. We destroyed their fortifications at La Agúja, near Sapoá. In fact the ruins are still there. The battle lasted for hours, with both sides using fairly modern weapons. The Sandinistas even used two or possibly three Russian tanks but still lost quite a few men. We lost three.

How we obtained our arms was interesting. Even before Somoza fell, a number of Costa Rican liaison officers who had been working with the Sandinistas had become deeply disillusioned.[14] When they left in July of 1979, the Sandinistas did not take all of their weapons with them. Since the Costa Rican government had helped move the arms through Costa Rica to attack Somoza, these Costa Rican officers knew where they were. In a few cases they had even hidden arms instead of delivering them, so we ended up using arms that had been given to the FSLN against them. The best were M-16s, but we also obtained about a hundred and fifty AK-47s and some Chinese RPGs (rocket-propelled grenades) with plenty of ammunition, and quite a few Bastones Chinos, a kind of rocket launcher.

After Pastóra took charge of the Southern Front, we became heavily infiltrated by the Sandinistas. Even Pastóra's personal secretary turned out to be a Sandinista agent. In the end, the Southern Front failed to live up to its potential. It was not for lack of men or support. We had more volunteers than arms and were receiving substantial help from the United States, from $800,000 to $1 million a month, plus weapons and air drops. We actually took over many of the bases once used by the Sandinista Front to overthrow Somoza, especially along the San Juan River. Some were even Costa Rican Guardia Civil bases they abandoned so we could use them. We had 1,200 men operating inside Nicaragua. The Southern Front failed because of Pastóra and his CIA patrons.

One thing I noticed that seemed very curious was that after Pastora's Southern Front was created, the Sandinista army didn't really seem to want to fight very hard against us. I speculated this might be because they were more interested in defeating the northern front where there were former Guardia, whereas in the south were people who had fought against Somoza. Even so, some of the toughest fighting took place in Nueva Guinea, in a sort of "peasants' land reform reserve" created by the first Somoza, a very large area that was highly sympathetic to the Somozas. There were many other areas where it was very hard just to subsist, places deep in the jungle that have many diseases against which we had few defenses—dengue fever, malaria, jungle leprosy—and millions of mosquitoes. There are even poisonous worms, all of which can make life miserable. During the war against the Sandinistas I spent most of my time either in San Carlos or in San José. I tried to go inside as much possible but was constantly being called back. In our war, the troops mostly stayed inside permanently while the commanders moved back and forth.

Losing the War, and the Peace

But the war itself failed because of outsiders. Toward the end the attitudes of the Costa Rican and other Central Americans and of the United States changed. From 1988 on, we were no longer welcomed allies. The Americans here in Costa Rica at the time explained they had serious internal problems in the United States due to Iran–Contra, Oliver North, and other things. They began to withdraw their help. That is what ended our struggle.

Even today (September 1997) I estimate there are still about 2,000 former Resistance fighters still armed inside Nicaragua. By no means did all disarm in 1990. They have no choice. Because the law does not reach the peasants, and our peace agreements have not been respected, our people must protect themselves. Some of those still armed live in what are known as *witácas*, small plots of land hidden in narrow valleys where they grow basic food for themselves like sweet potatoes and corn and can fish and hunt. They are often very well organized among themselves. A few have gone into banditry, but most have not.

Closing Comments

One final comment. Based on a lifetime of experience as a revolutionary, I am now convinced the most important thing is peace. To attain the dreams of General Sandino we need real peace, democracy, and help for the poorest regions of the country. With peace, democracy, and help the peasants of the Segovias can make Nicaragua rich because they are very hard-working people with rich soils to till. They can make Nicaragua the breadbasket of Central America. The tradition of marginalizing and mistreating them must end. Now they must be treated right, not given over to foreign or domestic exploitation. My own dream is to create a foundation to help the Indians and the Segovian peasants resolve their problem. If this is done, Nicaragua can become a positive example, not just for Central America but for the world.

5

PLUTARCO ELIÁS HERNÁNDEZ SANCHO, *COMANDANTE MARCIAL*

A BIOGRAPHICAL SKETCH

Born in San José, Costa Rica, Plutarco Hernández was raised in a revolutionary home by parents who themselves played important roles in several radical movements. His revolutionary credentials are impeccable. In fact he was a revolutionary before he could read and write, carrying clandestine messages in his shoes at the tender age of four to a San José safe house of the Cubans who were later to form that country's 26th of July Movement.[1] As a high school student he founded Costa Rica's Socialist Youth Movement and was rewarded by being invited to the 1963 World Youth Festival in Havana, where he met Fidel Castro for the first time. Hernández studied at Patrice Lumumba University in Moscow and then spent a year in specialized guerrilla leadership training at Campamento Cero east of Havana and another six months in a special guerrilla commanders' course in North Korea, personally supervised by Kim Il. Using the nom de guerre *Comandante Marcial,* he then secretly entered Nicaragua to become the chief of internal clandestine training for the Sandinista Front. He ended his wartime experience as a key commander of the FSLN's Southern Front during the final push to overthrow Somoza. Until July 1979, when Nicaragua's revolution transmogrified from a united front fighting the Somoza dictatorship into a socialist revolution, Plutarco Hernández was as prominent as any of those who are more famous for having staged that country's revolution, and he was especially close to the Sandinista Front's founder, Carlos Fonseca Amador. Jirón's *Quién es Quién en Nicaragua* (Who's who of Nicaragua) dedicates six pages to his biography, more than to either Daniel or Humberto Ortega, and calls him the most important single dissenter against the FSLN.[2] Pushed out of the FSLN's leadership by the Nine, Plutarco abandoned revolutionary activism. In 1997 he was a senior campaign aide to now Costa Rican President Miguel Rodríguez, who, after his victory, named him ambassador to the Russian Federation and the newly independent states.

□ □ □

REFLECTIONS ON THE PAST: MY JOURNEY FROM REVOLUTION TO DEMOCRACY

Plutarco Elías Hernández Sancho

The forum at which this paper is presented is a historic event. It is the first ever to bring together former revolutionaries and guerrilla fighters of several of the armed movements that were active in Central America during the cold war, and peacemakers from international organizations concerned with the transition from war to peace in Latin America. I wish therefore to extend my warmest appreciation to the University of the Americas, which provided its campus in Puebla, Mexico, as the venue for this unique encounter; its sponsor, the Hoover Institution of Stanford University; and especially to its organizer, Timothy Brown, whom I have personally known for several decades as a tireless student of the problems of Latin America in our times. I believe it is also highly significant that some of the most important public figures in Mexico, including former President Miguel de la Madríd and Mexico City mayor Cuauhtémoc Cárdenas, have expressed personal interest in and support for this gathering. And finally, I wish also to express my appreciation and congratulations to my fellow panelists, who, despite past differences, were willing to set them aside and come together for the first time to discuss the problems of the transition from war to peace in our historically troubled region. It is through such meetings that those of us who were at one time, and for so many years, armed opponents at war against one another will learn how to be peaceful protagonists in the modern Latin American revolution that is creating a new world of peace, economic opportunities, and participatory democracy in our once war-torn region.

A Personal Approach Centered on Nicaragua

Rather than present an academic commentary, what I wish to do instead is to discuss both past conflicts and future opportunities in Central America from a personal and more subjective perspective. Because I spent so many years of my life as a revolutionary activist, including almost fifteen as a national director of Nicaragua's Sandinista National Liberation Front and as a principal architect of its clandestine operations inside Nicaragua against the Somoza regime from 1965 through 1977, most of my comments will be about the Sandinista revolution, why it happened, and why it failed. This is a complex issue to discuss in only a few pages, so I will try to concentrate only on the key points as I see them and, in particular, lessons that can be learned from this experience, in particular how better to proceed into the new era of democracy and open economies in which today the peoples of the world place so much of their faith and hopes for a better tomorrow.

The Consequences of World War II Alliances

Perhaps the best place to begin is at the beginning, with a discussion of some of the historical events I see as having had important influence on events in that small but troubled region known as Central America. The most important took place during the World War II period, especially the politicomilitary alliance between the major Western nations and the Soviet Union in opposition to the Berlin–Tokyo–Rome Axis then seen as a common enemy. It was this alliance that ultimately served both as the point of origin for later events that were to lead to the emergence of a bloc of united social states in eastern Europe and as a catalyst for the creation of political alliances between bourgeois democratic political parties and their socialist and communist counterparts throughout the rest of the world. Such alliances also emerged in Latin America. But given the importance of Western religious values there, to gain acceptance even during this period of alliances it was necessary for the socialist and communist parties to "soften" the term *communist* before they, as Marxists, could effectively penetrate into the political life of the region. It might be helpful to describe how this was accomplished.

Softening the Image of Communism

In the United States, the secretary general of the Communist Party, Earl Browder, in order to make the party more acceptable to the American people, took the word *Party* out of the name of his organization and substituted in its place the much more acceptable word *League*. In Mexico the Communist Party became the Socialist Party, giving it a much less negative label and setting an example that was then followed by most of the communist parties of Central America. There was no need to do so in Honduras, where the Communist Party was not actually founded until 1954.

In Nicaragua, Mexico's top Communist, Vicente Lombardo Toledano, actually took a personal hand in local events. On May 1, 1944, May Day, Labor Day in most of the world, Lombardo Toledano publicly joined hands in Managua with the then dictator of Nicaragua, Anastacio "Tacho" Somoza Garcia, to found the Socialist Party of Nicaragua. This may have been one of the most ironic events in the history of our region, because this was the same Somoza who, ten years earlier, had assassinated Nicaragua's great revolutionary and patriot, General Augústo César Sandino. Shortly after Lombardo Toledano helped found the Nicaraguan Socialist Party, Somoza even declared in Nicaragua a socialist republic! It was precisely this sort of alliance that confused the public of country after country and legitimated the participation of communist parties in their normal political lives.

To facilitate the emergence of similar political alliances, in Guatemala the Communist Party changed its name to the Guatemalan Workers Party. But in that case a cosmetic effort was unsuccessful. Despite the name change, for many decades Guatemala was to be a nation in conflict where, both selectively and en masse, the extreme left did everything possible to destroy the extreme right and vice versa. Guatemalan Communist Party members and directors fell continuously as victims in one of the most violent campaigns of mutual extermination ever to take place in Latin America.

The only Central American country in which the Communist Party did not change its name during this period was El Salvador, where a revolutionary struggle had started in the 1920s. There Communist Party leader Faribundo Martí, a dedicated Marxist–Leninist forced out of the armed movement of Nicaragua's rebel General Sandino because of their incompatible ideologies, stood alone in his willingness openly to raise the flag of Bolshevism. But even there, after Martí was killed, the Communist Party began entering into alliances with other parties and continued to do so until much later, when it reverted to the path of armed revolution. It is one of the curiosities of history that despite the massive excesses visited on the country by all of the parties during its long and bloody internal conflicts, the Salvadoran people continued to demonstrate one of the region's strongest work ethics.

Honduras is a special case. In many ways Honduras has been one of the great tragedies of Central America. It had a war with El Salvador and has had to fend off numerous armed border incursions by both El Salvador and Nicaragua, it has been the scene of massive violations of human rights, and many of its military and political leaders have been caught engaging in both drug trafficking and money laundering. And yet without an armed revolution or the urging of a serious Communist Party, the people of Honduras were able collectively to reach the political conclusion that they must impose a regime of peaceful internal and external coexistence on their political system in order to promote the economic development of their country. This essentially revolution-free success has been made possible in large part by the emergence of an entirely new and much wiser variety of political leaders in Honduras in the wake of its neighbors' radical revolutions.

Costa Rica

Returning to the events of the World War II period, despite later armed conflicts, it is important not to forget that the wartime alliance between the superpowers and between democratic and socialist parties did yield some positive results. Perhaps the best example of this is Costa Rica, where an alliance of socialist and democratic parties made it possible to make the transition from a rural to a modern urbanized society without serious social conflicts or violent armed confrontations. It was there more than anywhere else in Central America where, in a relatively short time, the democratic tradition was successful when, beginning in the 1940s especially, important social advances were made that were later to have important influence on the emergence of democratic societies elsewhere in Latin America. At the beginning of the 1940s, during World War II, President Rafael Ángel Calderón Guardia staged a de facto social revolution without recourse to arms.[3] This revolution was founded on the establishment of a viable social compact among virtually all the people of Costa Rica and created for them one of the most advanced social security systems of the times. It was made possible by Calderón Guardia's success in enlisting in its support widely divergent popular sectors that, in other countries, found themselves violently opposed to one another. At the end of the 1940s, another president of Costa Rica, José "Pepe" Figueres Ferrer, came to power as a consequence of an armed confrontation with Calderón Guardia.[4] But, far from dismantling what his predecessor had wrought, as another might have done, once in power Figueres Ferrer not only respected but even improved upon the social contract negotiated by Calderón Guardia. He also abolished the very armed forces that put him into power, making Costa Rica the first country in the world to abolish its army.

In both instances, the creation and the preservation of Costa Rica's social contract under Calderón Guardia and its expansion under "Pepe" Figueres Ferrer, the Costa Rican Communist Party

(Vanguardia Popular), led by Manuel Mora Valverde, joined the alliance of political groups that created, protected, and preserved these social programs.[5] The Costa Rican case is so atypical that today, fifty years after these events, the leader of its Social Christian Party, Calderón Guardia, the leader of its Social Democratic Party, José "Pepe" Figueres Ferrer, and the leader of its Communist Party, Manuel Mora Valverde, all enjoy official recognition as Beneméritos de la Patria,[6] a distinction soon also to be bestowed on the nation's Roman Catholic leader of the period, Bishop Victor Manuel Sanábria, an act that will complete the process of recognizing the four key political leaders most responsible for the success of the country's social compact, for its social solidarity, and for the climate of peace that Costa Rica enjoys today.

Nicaragua

Let us now turn to the Nicaraguan problem. Throughout the centuries Nicaragua has traditionally been governed by rulers drawn from a very few families or their supporters and has been principally notable for the way in which old-line aristocrats succeeded one another in power as essentially the same families continued to govern. The result has been that the country has always suffered from exploitation at the hands of its governments regardless of the ideology they supposedly embraced. This has been true both in the past, when the country was in the hands of the extreme right, and more recently, when it was in the hands of people of the extreme left who claimed to be "the vanguard of the working class," and here I am speaking of the Sandinista Front. The pattern has never varied, nor has the nation's poverty diminished.

Nicaragua is one of the greatest storehouses of natural riches in Central America and potentially the richest country in the region. It has massive hydroelectric possibilities on both the Pacific and Atlantic that give it the potential of being the principal supplier of energy to all of Central America. It is also rich in many other things, in particular mining, fisheries, forestry products, and above all cattle and agricultural production potential. And yet this natural richness has been paralleled by an equally rich dedication to extravagant lifestyles by its ruling classes, which have demonstrated that far from being intellectually rich they suffer from a massive poverty of pragmatism. Massive poverty among the people amidst potential richness has been the result.

Nicaragua: The Roots of Revolution

Beginning in the middle of the last century, several world powers became interested in building an interocean canal through Nicaragua, which put that country into a special strategic situation, so much so that Nicaragua even came to have an American as its president, a medical and military adventurer named William Walker. He was soon removed and executed. But in the early 1900s the United States intervened directly, sending Marines to occupy the country. The struggle of the Nicaraguan people against this occupation became so well known throughout the world that when the 1928 Pan American Conference was held in Havana, Cuba, there were demonstrations in almost every country in favor of Nicaragua and against American intervention. These demonstrations took as their hero, a man known as "the hero of the Segovias," Augústo César Sandino. This worldwide public response to Sandino's fight against the United States even reached into the most isolated corners of China, where, during the Great March of Mao Tse Tung, one of the longest and bloodiest such marches in the history of the world, the name and banner of Sandino was raised and a unit was named in his honor.

Sandino was a revolutionary well versed in ordinary life, having worked for a foreign petroleum company in Mexico. While there he made contact with numerous politicians and businessmen and convinced them to help him in his fight in Nicaragua, which was eventually successful when the United States Marines, one of the world's great military elites, were expelled in 1933. But in 1934 Sandino was killed in an ambush laid by "Tacho" Somoza Garcia, which was followed by the massacre of most of his troops.

Only one leader of Sandino's movement, Pedro Altamirano, continued fighting, until he too fell in 1939, and only one of Sandino's generals, Ramón Raudales, survived Altamirano as an active opponent of Somoza.

Raudales slowly collected forces around him before again raising the flag of Sandino. This took him almost twenty years. Not until 1958, some twenty-four years after the death of Sandino, was this now aged but noble guerrilla prepared to return to combat. But when he did so he became an inspiration to new generations, not with words but with deeds. It was at this point that Raudáles became personally well known to many of the leaders who were to lead the struggle in the decades to come, among them Carlos Fonseca Amador, Alejandro Martínez, Edén Pastora, and other combat leaders who were to form part of what was later named the Sandinista National Liberation Front. Raúl Raudales, who was affectionately known as the "white-bearded patriarch," was to fall in combat soon thereafter. With his death the struggle inspired by a patriotism and nationalism alone ended, and a new form of revolution emerged, no longer purely nationalistic but also strongly influenced by political ideology.

The Cuban Revolution and the Cold War

The surge of guerrilla movements in Latin America during the cold war was primarily a consequence of the failure on the part of most countries either to resolve fundamental social problems or to at least reach accommodations with their socialist and communist parties as had been done in Costa Rica. But they occurred when they did because of, and were made especially vigorous by, the triumph of the Cuban Revolution under the direction of the 26th of July Movement, which was initially made up of revolutionaries of various ideological tendencies but which underwent a metamorphosis after Castro took power, principally as the result of the personality and political predilections of its leader, Fidel Castro.

This in turn had important consequences elsewhere in the region. Perhaps the two most important were the hardening of the attitudes of hard-line anti-Communist regimes throughout Latin America, particularly in Central America and the strengthening of revolutionary activities in a number of countries. From the triumph of the Cuban Revolution emerged a confrontation-filled environment that went far beyond mere attempts to obtain social justice and became quite clearly an ideological confrontation reflecting the positions of the West and the East. In other words, it was as a consequence of the Cuban Revolution that Latin America came to be part of the East–West confrontation known as the cold war. True, these confrontations themselves had been underway for a number of decades. But a number of countries had resolved them without violence, and in others they did not lead to armed confrontations but simply deepened discussions of economic and political processes.

The triumph of the Cuban Revolution greatly increased the intensity of confrontation between diverse forces in the region and caused a resurgence in national liberation movements throughout Latin America; many already existing guerrilla movements were greatly strengthened. This process was deliberately deepened by the creation of the Organization of Latin American Solidarity (OLAS), directed by Havana with a clearly Marxist–Leninist and pro-Soviet agenda. It was from within OLAS that a new concept, "revolution within the revolution," emerged that was to be so important in the thinking of Regis Debray, the famous French radical who later became an important advisor to the government of France. In those countries in which conditions favorable to guerrilla warfare did not yet exist because neither "objective" nor "subjective" conditions for revolution prevailed, Cuba was nonetheless able effectively to penetrate important sectors by targeting universities, labor unions, cultural societies, and other important segments of civil society. This Cuban penetration in return elicited a reaction from the right, known as the "doctrine of national security," which was strongly backed by the United States through its Department of State and its army operating primarily from Panama.

The Arrival of Peace

It was not until the end of the 1980s when, together with the fall of the Berlin Wall and the Communist regimes in Eastern Europe, along with their sponsors of the old Soviet Union, that this preference for the use of force fostered by the Cuban Revolution was to be largely abandoned. And it was only when the propensity to use arms to resolve conflicts was abandoned that the environment of violent confrontations in Latin America began to be transformed into a climate of peace, and democracy began to emerge throughout the region, with the sole exception of two countries, Haiti and Cuba. Today only Cuba remains as a dictatorship willing to use violence.

Repairing the Damage

Thus only after the Eastern bloc collapsed was there a significant reduction in the level of armed confrontations in Central America, where strongly political ideological roots were not just formed by the cold war but ran much deeper. Wars there had resulted in the displacement of millions of persons, in hundreds of thousands of deaths and injuries, in hundreds of homes destroyed, thousands of families divided, and national economies severely damaged. In the aftermath of the region's violent revolutions and wars, its severely damaged national economies will require near superhuman efforts to recover and rebuild so the region can effectively begin to participate in the world's new processes of globalization. Thankfully, repairing the damages caused by revolutions is not in the hands of communist or socialist movements or groups, nor of the military nor the hard right.

Rather, the massive changes that are taking place throughout the world are part of a silent revolution that began in Eastern Europe and the former Soviet Union when Gorbachev began to promote the concepts of glasnost and perestroika, and they are controlled by centrist parties, most important among them being moderate Social Christians and Social Democrats, parties without sharply defined ideological positions but rather that are based on the pragmatism that characterizes the modern world. It is into their hands that construction of the world's new democracies has been entrusted, democracies intended to be participatory and just and that avoid violent confrontations in favor of open public discourse and government by consensus.

Betrayal of the Revolution

But, returning to Central America, and more specifically to my personal experiences during the revolutionary process in Nicaragua, I would like to make a number of comments. The original Nicaraguan revolution, from 1958 to 1979, was a broad-based popular movement that mobilized almost all the political and social sectors of the country and generated hope among the people of Nicaragua and others by its example that it would be possible to overcome the problems created by grinding poverty. Initially it enjoyed wide popular support and levels of international support not even attained by the Cuban Revolution. This initial Nicaraguan revolution was the result of an extensive history of sacrifice, bloody battles, and personal heroism. This makes it all the more tragic that once a dictatorial clique from within the original FSLN took power in 1979, it was transformed into nothing more than a gigantic revolutionary fraud, for which those who ruled the country from 1979 to 1990 can never be forgiven.

Thankfully, Nicaragua's "Revolution of the Nine" lasted only eleven years, at which point a window was opened that allowed for democratic elections so that the people themselves could expel those who had betrayed them. And today, thanks to the people of Nicaragua, those who betrayed them will not return to power. These so-called revolutionary leaders, as a consequence of their inability to administer anything, even a daily newspaper, destroyed the real Nicaraguan revolution. Despite hundreds of millions of dollars in donations from throughout the world, the nine leaders of the 1979–1990 Sandinista revolution proved unable to develop a decent plan of government, although they did end up with some of the largest personal fortunes in Latin America, paid for by the pain, blood, and sweat of the Nicaraguan people. In short, what they did was shameful in the extreme. Luckily, the people opened their eyes and had an opportunity to eject them from power.

The leaders of the 1979–1990 Nicaraguan revolution are now in the process of being condemned by history, as analysts and historians begin to ask why they failed. The answer is really quite simple. Those who grasped power in 1979 had not paid their revolutionary dues. They did not live the clandestine lives of revolutionaries or risk their lives. Competent leaders cannot be formed in comfortable safe houses in Havana, Mexico City, or Costa Rica. To the eternal sorrow of the people of Nicaragua, those who really fought to overthrow the Somoza dictatorship fell in combat. The legitimate leadership of the revolution did not live to lead the subsequent process of social change. Among those killed were almost all the Sandinista movement's veteran political leaders and clandestine activists, including its most important leader, Carlos Fonseca Amador, along with Carlos Agüero, Oscar Túrcios, Ricardo Moráles, Juan José Quesada, Jonathan González, Eduardo Contreras, Pedro Aráuz Palacios, and many others.

Why the Nine Comandantes Failed

I have sometimes been asked by journalists if, had the natural leadership of the revolution not been killed but instead taken power, there would have been any guarantee that the revolution would have taken a route more favorable to Nicaragua. My response to that question has been simple and straightforward. Neither political maturity nor the ability to administer a program or manage people can be learned just by reading books or engaging in discussions with others. They must also be learned through experiencing actual situations. The natural leaders of the revolution, as contrasted to those who took power in 1979, were formed in the crucible of armed struggle over many years and were personally acquainted with how much it had cost in terms of personal sacrifice and pain. Persons with such backgrounds develop social consciences and learn to work in the interests of others, not just of themselves.

Among the things the natural leadership of the revolution would never have done was to try to reproduce a mechanical copy of Cuba in Nicaragua. The Nine followed the wrong blueprint. This is clearly demonstrated by their failure. It is important to remember that no process, revolutionary or democratic, can insulate itself from the changes taking place in the world around it. The collapse of the Sandinista regime was a consequence of the collapse of neither the socialist world nor the Berlin Wall. No such events were necessary in its case. Its collapse was a consequence of policies invented or adopted by the Sandinista Front itself that made the country ungovernable. When the fundamental dignity of the individual is undermined and constantly insulted by limitations on freedom of expression, by not allowing free travel in the country, or by establishing block committees to control every action, literacy programs are not enough, nor are health centers or sports activities. The results will always be negative. When the Nicaraguan people were repressed, they initially reacted not by engaging in violent opposition but by fleeing. Costa Rica alone received more than one-half million Nicaraguan refugees, most economic, not just political, refugees. In addition, another 200,000 went to Honduras, and tens of thousands more became refugees in the United States, Canada, and almost any other countries that would provide them refuge. But they, and others who stayed behind, also rebelled.

Some Reflections on Revolution

I would like to share a few personal reflections, both on the general subject of violent revolutions and on what happened in Nicaragua. I spent most of my life engaged in radical revolutionary activities, only in the end to reach the conclusion that humankind is designed to live in freedom and democracy, no matter how imperfect these may be, and that the key function of a government is to find the best balance between those with different ideas and ideologies and the various sectors of any social system, but always to do so without pointing rifles at the people. The natural intelligence of any people, their intellectual abilities, are so rich and powerful that they have an almost infinite ability to produce, to be free, and to make their nations richer in terms of production, freedoms, and culture. In the beginning these were, in fact, the primary objectives of the Bolshevik October Revolution in Russia, which had as its slogan "land and bread" and publicly dedicated itself to improving the standard of living for everyone.

To our eternal disgrace, power corrupts. And in revolutions directed by the few, the first to be corrupted are the leaders of the movement itself. And they become absolutely corrupted, because the greatest form of corruption of all is not putting a few million dollars in one's pockets or in personal bank accounts in well-known financial institutions in Switzerland; the most profound form of corruption of all is to enslave, exploit, and politically incarcerate an entire people.

Perhaps at the beginning of the century neither technology nor globalization were sufficiently advanced to provide the original Bolsheviks with an understanding of what really needed to be done, but that is not the case today. The world has continuously been improving the standards of living of its people, and armed revolutions are simply no longer appropriate instruments for seeking progress or change anywhere. In fact, war itself is no longer an appropriate approach to solving problems or differences. Even armies are no longer indispensable, and in most cases simple public safety systems are sufficient for maintaining internal order. Today the purpose of nations is to engage in dialogue, to promote international cooperation, and to facilitate internal cooperation and mutual support between all the actors in a society. Internationally, countries are still joining into geographic groups, no longer for the purpose of attacking or defending one another but for the purpose of helping one another develop economically and to confront the challenges of widespread misery and hunger.

On Central America Today

In Central America, now that its armed conflicts have been resolved, the region has begun making serious progress toward establishing political regimes based on participatory democracy, and these are becoming stronger almost on a daily basis. While little noted outside the region, this movement has advanced far enough to become an example to the rest of the developing world as it prepares to enter the next millennium. Perhaps it is because of the death and destruction, pain and misery, and hunger that the region suffered during struggles that touched so many lives that the region has been able to put violence behind and forge ahead toward a peaceful and cooperative twenty-first century.

Some Opinions on What Happened in Nicaragua

I would like to list a few opinions I developed during my lifetime of revolutionary activity about what happened that made the Nicaraguan revolution sour, many drawn from my personal experience as an anti-Somoza revolutionary:

1. In terms of Latin America and the world in general, most recent political changes and the revolutionary activities that followed were the consequences of alliances forged during World War II. Nicaragua was no exception.

2. In terms of the immediate antecedents of the Sandinista revolution, a number of major factors led to its final offensive and the fall of the Somoza dictatorship, the most important being internal political alliances that emerged just prior to the fall of the dictatorship. Of these, the two most important were the establishment of the Group of Twelve as a united opposition front and the struggle of Pedro Joaqúin Chamorro through his newspaper *La Prensa* and the reaction to his assassination.

3. Another major cause of the success of the revolution was the progressive international isolation of the government of Nicaragua and the worldwide condemnation of the dictatorship complete with the breaking of diplomatic relations with Nicaragua by country after country.

4 de enero.

Estimado Pepe:

Tuvimos el gusto de recibir tu carta de fecha 13 del pasado mes.

Esperamos que la presente te encuentre iniciando junto con los tuyos un año exitoso.

Por ahora tengo que referirme a que hemos hecho llegar una nota al diario "La Prensa" de Managua a nombre de Lucy con el objeto de que te lleguen a ésa los periódicos "La Prensa". Comprenderás el interés que tenemos de que una vez te lleguen esos periódicos a la vez nos los hagas llegar por la vía que tu sabes. Se trata de utilizar todos los medios de que disponemos para mantenernos al día sobre la marcha diaria de nuestro país. De manera que no se trata de simple curiosidad por conocer información sin interés sino cosas que sirven para tejer un cuadro más vivo de una serie de situaciones.

Con la nota que se les dirigió a los de "La Prensa" se les envió un giro por valor de 50 dólares, así no tendrás problemas económicos de ninguna clase.

Estamos entendidos de tu teléfono. Cualquier cosa nueva que tengas de las personas de que nos hables aparezca nos las hagas saber.

En nuestras cartas lo mismo que no puede faltar los saludos tampoco puede faltar la insistencia de la discreción de manera que se evite hablar lo que no es necesario y también se evite saber lo que igualmente no es necesario.

En la nota que referimos se puso a Lucy como profesora de periodismo para justificar la suscripción. Espero comprenda ella que no se trata de un abuso al utilizar su nombre, sino que es la confianza basada en nuestra seguridad de la identificación que existe entre ustedes dos. De antemano le agradecemos a ella esa tarea que estamos seguros tampoco trae complicaciones innecesarias.

Reciban ustedes nuestros saludos fraternales.

Humberto Ortega.

Letter from Humberto Ortega, then in Havana, to Pepe Puente concerning a news item to be planted in Managua's *La Prensa* newspaper, accompanied by a check for payment to the editors. Ortega apologizes for having signed the article with the name of Puente's first wife, Lucy, without her knowledge and warns him absolute discretion is required. The latter was accompanied by a check to pay *La Prensa*'s editors for running the story. The later assassination of *La Prensa*'s editor Pedro Joaquín Chamorro has been widely credited with triggering the final phase of the anti-Somoza Sandinista revolution. At the time then president Anastacio "Tacho" Somoza Debayle, the last Somoza dictator, was widely charged with the crime. Many in positions to know have since concluded the assassination was engineered by the Sandinistas both to act as a trigger for the expansion of their revolution and to remove from the scene their biggest rival for power.

4. Perhaps the most important precondition of all was the deliberate creation by the Sandinista Front of a false "social democratic" image that allowed it to gain the support of a number of important non-Marxist international leaders such as Carlos Andrés Pérez of Colombia, Omar Torrijos of Panama, Rodrigo Carrazo of Costa Rica, Olaf Palme of Sweden, López Portillo of Mexico, Felipe González of Spain, and above all, Jimmy Carter of the United States. It was their contributions that determined the outcome of the war and assured the victory of the Sandinistas, and all were soon disillusioned.

Revolution within the Revolution

At the very end of our struggle against Somoza, beginning on July 19, 1979, the day the Sandinista Front triumphed, an entirely different process began. The sudden flight of the third Somoza two days before created a serious dilemma for the radical leftists within the Front. Should they try to govern through existing institutions or simply take power in their own name? They decided to grab power, and it was that decision that ultimately defined the revolution's failure. The sharp differences between the Sandinista Front that had overthrown Somoza and those within its ranks who grabbed power did not become immediately obvious, but it was their decision that defines the moment when a fundamental transformation took place from a successful armed rebellion into a socialist revolution that failed.

A Vacuum of Leadership

For me the fundamental flaw in the entire process as pursued by the Nine was that, unlike elsewhere, with the natural leadership of the Sandinista movement dead, the Nine could not produce among them even one leader capable of pulling the Nicaraguan revolutionary efforts together. Every other revolution had one. The Bolshevik revolution had Lenin, the Cuban Fidel Castro, the Chinese Mao Tse Tung, the Korean Kim Il Sung, the Vietnamese Ho Chi Minh. All the Nicaraguan revolution had was nine nonentities. As a consequence the revolution in Nicaragua was the shortest in modern history. In fact, what transpired was not really a revolution at all. It was simply an armed uprising that ended badly.

Those Sandinista leaders who took power in 1979 did so with the idea that they would exercise power absolutely and that power could be based on three cornerstones: the party, the army, and the bureaucracy. It was their employment of these three instruments of power to the virtual exclusion of all else that resulted in a vertical hereditary state and a tightly controlled and carefully watched society. Perhaps the best proof of the inabilities of the self-appointed Nine was their defeat at the polls in 1990 by a simple housewife, Violeta Chamorro, who won thanks to three factors. The first was the eventual ability of the country's traditional and emerging political leaders to come together against the Sandinistas, in great part thanks to an educational process through which they learned democracy, including efforts by the Center for Democracy of the United States, supported by the National Endowment for Democracy from Washington, D.C. The second was the collaboration of almost all these sectors of society, except of course the revolutionaries, in efforts to end the Sandinista revolution, including businessmen, private educational institutions, labor unions, radio stations, and others in civil society. The third was the leadership of Cardinal Obando y Bravo of the Roman Catholic Church, fully supported by Pope John Paul II, who was able to synthesize a broad spectrum of ideologies and substitute Christian spiritual values for revolutionary concepts.

Corrosive Corruption

The example of the Sandinista revolution may be one of the best illustrations of the classic aphorism "absolute power corrupts absolutely." It was the corruption of the Sandinistas themselves as much as their revolutionary policies that destroyed the process. The Sandinista Nine, once in power, became a sort of committee of nine factotums who tried to watch everything and everyone every minute and to make all decisions, both large and small. But what they really did was contaminate everything by their own corruption. Their efforts to be omnipresent and omnipotent led to a growing paralysis of society and its energies. Put another way, what the Sandinistas established was a peculiar version of a late-in-the-day tropical Stalinism with overtones of folklore.

Armed Revolution Has Lost Its "Raison d'Être"

Today, with the world's attempts at radical revolution largely ended and with the world headed in new directions, armed revolutions are no longer acceptable. The struggle to better human existence today is best pursued by democratic processes, by nations and movements bent on constructing a new world order, not those bent on destruction. My message to all of the world's true revolutionaries today is that we now must join together to struggle for greater political opportunities within existing societies, to democratize political life, and to assure that all citizens participate in the building of democratic societies. The latter is especially important. To build democratic societies in Latin America it is necessary to do three things: (1) to promote democratic processes; (2) to reduce to the minimum the military role in society; and (3) to create solid systems in defense of basic human rights. The best antidote against both corruption and dictatorship is a constant struggle against impunity and in favor of the rule of law.

6

JOSÉ EDUARDO SANCHO CASTAÑEDA, *COMANDANTE FERMÁN CIENFUEGOS*

A BIOGRAPHICAL SKETCH[1]

Born in San José, Costa Rica, on March 6, 1947, of a Costa Rican father and Salvadoran mother, from 1966 on José Eduardo Sancho Castañeda was an active radical revolutionary, and for much of that period the military commander of the armed forces of the Faribundo Martí Liberation Front (FMLN). His Costa Rican father, Guillermo Sancho Colombari, a medical doctor specializing in hematology, initially went to El Salvador in 1942 to study medicine, but there met and married Liliam Castañeda Saldívar and settled in that country. Forced out of El Salvador during Eduardo's years as a guerrilla, as were Eduardo's two brothers, his father now lives in Costa Rica.

Eduardo traces his father's family on the Sancho side back to a Spanish Conquistador, Don Juan Sancho y Vélar, who arrived in Costa Rica in 1547 and settled in Cartago. On his mother's side, the Colombaris are descended from Pietro Colombari, who served with Giuseppe Garibaldi before immigrating to Costa Rica in 1884, where he made his fortune as an engineer during the building of a railroad. An important branch of the Colombari family, with whom Eduardo has visited several times, later immigrated to the United States and lives mostly in the San Francisco Bay area. Eduardo's maternal grandparents were often active in the military in El Salvador. One, Benjamin Castañeda, was killed in battle against Guatemala in 1904. Eduardo Sancho is thus from the upper middle class, and was educated first at the prestigious Externado San José by Jesuit priests and then at the National University, where he majored in sociology.

Eduardo's radicalization was progressive, growing both from a deep personal interest in history and the sciences, especially microbiology, and from three external influences. Eduardo Sancho is the first cousin of Plutarco Hernández and often visited his home in San José, Costa Rica. There Plutarco's father and Eduardo's paternal uncle by marriage, Abdenago Hernández, the son of Costa Rican President Rafael Ángel Calderón Guardia by a second woman, introduced him to numerous leftist politicians, including the leader of Costa Rica's Communist Party (Vanguardia Popular) Manuel Mora Valverde, who became a close friend. Plutarco also provided him with texts on Marxism, and Plutarco's mother, Graciela, also politically of the left, did her part as well. (All have been mentioned in previous chapters.) A second uncle who lived in exile in Mexico, Alfredo Hernández, also became an intellectual mentor, as did a Nicaraguan Jesuit priest, Father Chamorro, a member of the family of later Nicaraguan president Violeta Chamorro, who organized and directed a small political club of disaffected youths at the Externado. Eduardo's own comparisons between Costa Rica and El Salvador, and a short stint in Spain during the Franco dictatorship, did the rest.

Curiously, Eduardo Sancho began as a pacifist opponent of the war between El Salvador and Honduras in the 1960s. But soon thereafter he became an active revolutionary. In part as the result of contacts initiated by Guatemala's Fuerzas Armadas Revolucionarias (FAR), which had camps in Santa Ana, El Salvador, and along the border, in 1970 he and his companions turned to violence. They reached an agreement with Cuba, which trained small numbers of them in explosives, intelligence, and counterin-

San José 27 - II 73

Sr. José U Puente.

Recordado Pepe:

Al Hotel donde tenían que llegar nuestros amigos recibimos la súplica de avisarle a Ud que por favor
enviara lo ofrecido. Por motivos de la tragedia en ese
lugar ahora mas que nunca necesitan de ese origen
y están con la esperanza de que llegue pronto esta ayuda. De nuestra parte les aconsejo no esperarse a
semana santa que vienen Uds, sino hacernos el en-
vío antes, y si no han podido reunir todo lo ofrecido por lo menos una parte. Pues creo es de suma neces-
idad por los motivos expuestos por el desastre.
Realzan nuestro cariño para Lucy y niños.
Respecto a lo de Japi enviare recado donde ellos
al ver que resuelven y les avisare en el curso de la
semana que viene. De ella todo mi cariño y creo
que responderemos a ser, en carta anterior Armilca
me dijo la tragera a C Rica, pero luego me dijeron esperar noticias de estudiantes, y ya las
tengo Así le ruego esperar carta mía en México
Esperando lo deseado, lo abrazamos sus siempre
sinceros padres.

Chelita

Revolutionary period letter from Graciela "Chelita" Hernández to "Pepe" Puente requesting, in shaded language, assistance for her son Plutarco and other Sandinistas. In addition to raising their son Plutarco as a Marxist, Chelita and her husband, Abdenago, were instrumental in radicalizing their nephew Eduardo Sancho, who was to become Fermán Cienfuegos of El Salvador's FMLN. Private collection.

telligence. They were also helped by a retired Salvadoran army colonel who gave them weapons training. From that point until its conclusion in the mid-1990s, the FMLN and its various subgroups went through several permutations. The best known involved its decision to collect a large war chest by robbing banks and kidnapping prominent Salvadoran and foreign businessmen for ransom. This allowed them to build up a capital account of some $184 million, some of which they gave to the Nicaraguan FSLN through Eduardo's cousin Plutarco.[2] They also received arms from various sources, including, after July of 1979, the Sandinistas in Nicaragua. Many were carried to them in Panamanian air force aircraft provided by Panamanian president Omar Torrijos, one of which crashed near San Miguel, El Salvador.[3] According to Eduardo, who never met with Americans but did regularly meet with Torrijos, the United States government was kept fully informed of this through Ambassador Bowdler in Panama, who was regularly briefed on the details by Torrijos himself. Following the collapse of the Soviet Union and the Sandinista revolution, the FMLN abandoned its violent approach and reached a peace agreement with the government of El Salvador and has since become an important political party. Eduardo Sancho himself became, for a time, a national deputy.

□ □ □

THE BEST MILITARY STRATEGY OF ALL IS TO AVOID WAR

José Eduardo Sancho Castañeda

There are a number of lessons to be learned from the civil war in El Salvador. But perhaps the most valuable is that in the middle of such a war it is difficult, if not impossible, to listen to good advice and that once a civil war like ours starts it is all but impossible to stop before it reaches what seems to be an inevitably violent conclusion. The world may no longer have Hundred Years' Wars, but from even a twenty-year war like that of El Salvador the most important lesson to be learned is that the ideal military strategy is to avoid such conflicts altogether because, once they start, the only viable alternative that remains—and it is at best an extremely difficult one—is somehow to negotiate it to a peaceful end before it becomes not merely bloody but absurd.

Why We Fought

Perhaps a second set of important lessons can be derived from the reasons why the Salvadoran civil war was fought in the first place. This is especially important if we are successfully to make the transition to democracy. The first reason for the Salvadoran conflict was that those groups within the nation that had the most political, economic, and ideological power were not prepared to enter into a meaningful dialogue with one another. As a consequence, and especially in the absence of any governmental institutions capable of acting as intermediaries between these groups in the greater interest of society, this lack of dialogue led over the years to a gradual but very real increase in the levels of antagonism between these groups.

In the final analysis this suggests that El Salvador's armed conflict was caused more by the insensitivity of those who held power than by its capitalist political economic system. In other words, the Salvadoran civil war was caused not merely by the absence of democracy nor by a failure of its electoral system, nor even by military or civilian authoritarianism or the country's extreme poverty, but by a combination of all of these coupled to a political system that did not have adequate mechanisms through which competing powerful interests could intermediate their differences. To be precise, the political system of El Salvador lacked, and still lacks, the ability to engage in constructive dialogue between powerful economic interests and citizen groups. As a consequence, antagonisms between these groups festered and grew in an environment that lacked even the minimal necessary level of social cohesion between societal power groups to avoid conflict, and, as was also true elsewhere in Latin America, the government was incapable of playing the role of intermediator. The latter problem was the result of a system in which political parties in El Salvador, as elsewhere in the region, once in power, routinely exploit the institutions of government to give jobs to their supporters, family members, and constituents, and in the process assure that within the government bureaucracy personal relationships are more important than the governmental institutions themselves. The bureaucracy thus becomes the servant of the political party in power and not of the nation, which takes away from it the ability to act as an objective intermediary. This problem is so widespread that it can be considered Latin America's normal political tradition.

The Civil Conflict in El Salvador

Most external observers have tried to demonstrate that the civil war in El Salvador was caused by the two superpowers, but this is not true. It will be recalled that there were concurrent wars in other Central American countries as well, particularly in those controlled by military dictatorships or with only limited democratic systems, the sole exception being Costa Rica. But although the armed conflict in El Salvador began in 1971, the same year in which the war in Nicaragua to overthrow the Somoza dictatorship began in earnest, it was different from the others. Further, the Nicaraguan war was concluded successfully in 1979, but the one in El Salvador never was. In the case of El Salvador, unlike in Nicaragua, the two superpowers had no direct influence on the beginning of our revolution in the decades of the 1970s, nor did they play important roles even after it became a larger civil war in 1981. True, the two superpowers, locked as they were in a Cold War, later played roles on both sides of our conflict, but they did not at the start of it. In fact, it started and continued for many years without their involvement and without any important extra-regional involvement until 1983, the year when the first serious efforts were also made to design a strategy for restoring peace.

Elite-Led Warfare

In the introduction to a book published by the National Defense University in Washington, D.C., entitled *El Salvador and the War,* by Air Force Lt. Gen. Bradley C. Hosmer, the claim is made that our war was not a cohesive mass movement but rather a coalition of several small groups of insurgents, organized in accord with a strategy designed and led by a tiny disciplined and educated elite. And yet from its very beginnings in 1971, even before the war began, through 1991 we were both organized and constantly making efforts to enter into political negotiations, because the tiny elite to which the general referred, of which I was a member, understood very well that war is destructive and not part of any constructive political process—especially not, despite the theses of strategists like Von Clausewitz and Machiavelli, in countries as poor as ours. As it turned out, the Salvadoran radical revolution became a sort of "armed debate" between the armed left and the superpowers that paradoxically served principally to open doors to a national dialogue, to force the government to create new institutions, and to increase the participation of the people in the process.

Peace, Not War, Is the Hard Part

Regrettably, today [1998], although much has been achieved, we find that the most difficult part of this process has proven to be the effort to establish a lasting peace because, although the war has now ended, it ended without our having first developed a plan for reconstructing the nation, for integrating it into the rest of Central America, or for establishing a durable and lasting social dialogue. As a consequence, peace is fragile because El Salvador's fundamental social problems have not yet been resolved. Nonetheless, peace is better than war, and I am pleased that I participated in the transitional process from 1992 to 1997 that culminated in the signing of a formal peace agreement that moved El Salvador toward the establishment of a true republican democracy, complete with three separate branches of government. I do regret, however, that the resulting peace has remained fragile due to insufficient economic development to satisfy the needs of the populace, a failure that in turn can create the conditions for a possible return to conflict. Until El Salvador's fundamental economic problems are resolved, it will always be possible for others to stage armed insurrections for the purpose of coercing the nation into following a particular political line. Thus even today there remains real danger that there might be another armed conflict, doubly so because of both growing public disorder and the actions of populist parties that continue to agitate and thus to generate the potential for another social war.

Based on this experience in El Salvador, it is therefore important to learn that the transition from war to peace must be followed by a second transition. Peace is a beginning. But it is not enough unless followed by a process of national reconciliation, a second process that tragically has not fully taken place in my country. Until it does, Salvadoran society will remain highly polarized, and such excessive polarization can be the precursor to more war.

The Three Stages of the Civil Conflict in El Salvador

It might be useful at this point to review the history of the civil conflict in El Salvador, which I see as having taken place in three stages. The first stage, from 1971 to 1980, was an urban and suburban guerrilla war. During this stage we on the armed left adopted a deliberate strategy of avoiding, insofar as possible, armed confrontations with the army. The second stage involved a strategy of attempting to avoid an all-out war by establishing an alliance between our guerrilla forces and a faction within the army. This second stage reached its denouement on October 15, 1979, when two midlevel army officers, backed by us, staged a coup and took over the government.[4] But it failed very shortly thereafter, on December 23rd of that same year to be precise, when they lost power. The third stage of El Salvador's civil conflict, which was made necessary by that failure, was a more general war beginning in 1981 during which we sought to control selected strategic positions and geographic zones and which became a war of maneuver for the military forces of both sides in conflict.

Lessons to Be Learned

There are perhaps two important lessons to be learned from this progression from urban and suburban guerrilla activities to general war. First, one should never underestimate the importance of even the smallest of guerrilla *focos.* Just as soon as one develops, the best thing to do is to seek a political solution. The second lesson may be that one should not create a mythology concerning the importance of external logistical support reaching a guerrilla force. In the case of El Salvador, the myth that was created by our opponents seemed rather like comparing a Coca-Cola-sized drinking straw to a giant pipeline like the one linking the United States and the Salvadoran government and army. In our case, logistics was not our problem. Politics was. It would have been better by far for our opponents to have acted as though there is no such thing as a small or limited war. Rather than attempting to decide whether the war in El Salvador was a low- or high-intensity conflict, it would have been far better for them to have accepted that it, like any war and regardless of its size, needed to be negotiated to an end as quickly as possible.

Our Strategy of Permanent Dialogue: The Process

The process of negotiation, mediation, and dialogue between parties in conflict invariably seems to take a long time to come to fruition. Perhaps the nearest analogy is the process of negotiating a collective contract for union workers. In the worst of cases, union negotiating processes grow from being simply labor disputes into attacks against the political system in the form of confrontations between workers and duly constituted legal authorities that end either with the workers finally sitting down with their adversaries at the negotiating table or in violent confrontations that result in their leaders being jailed or killed. When confrontations become even more complex, such as is the case with the seizure by workers or peasants of buildings or land, such conflicts may even result in organizations such as the Red Cross or foreign embassies becoming involved as mediators. This is most likely to take place in countries that lack government institutions that can act as honest interlocutors, either because of the power of opposing pressure groups or due to the authoritarian attitudes of a dictatorship. In such cases there exists a vacuum that can only be filled by extraparliamentary institutions.

In the case of the civil conflict in El Salvador, from 1972 to 1984 the state pursued a policy of attempting to exterminate the armed opposition on the left. This left the armed opposition no other alternative than to seek out international and national intermediaries, especially between 1977 and 1980, because there were no institutions at any level of the Salvadoran state prepared to engage in a dialogue with us, to act as honest brokers, or otherwise to bridge the gap between us and the rest of the government. Because of this we were left with no alternative other than to seek out others who could substitute for the state, since the state itself was not prepared to enter into even a simple direct dialogue.

For those looking for lessons in how to promote a transition from war to peace, there is an important lesson to be learned from this. When the political and daily life of a society becomes so polarized that it does not, even in the best of cases, recognize the importance of dialogue, one must either look for institutions to substitute for the state or accept that violence will occur, because it is in precisely such situations that civil wars begin and armed uprisings are most likely.

In the case of El Salvador, international public opinion became aware of the government's determination to pursue a war of extermination against us almost from the moment the conflict began in 1971. But it was not until 1979, when the International Committee of the Red Cross from Geneva first visited El Salvador to observe the treatment of prisoners of war by both sides in the conflict, that international public opinion became seized with this issue, and the government found it necessary to change its strategy. Up until then, the government had insisted that there was no state of war in El Salvador. But with international witnesses like the Red Cross giving credibility to the alternate view that in fact a state of war existed, the government began to lose credibility in the eyes of much of the world and was forced to change its approach. It was at this point, with two armies engaged in what was finally recognized as a civil war, that many concluded that to avoid even more destruction it was important to bring the two parties in conflict together and to try to start a dialogue, mediation, and negotiation process between them. This was especially true because neither side seemed able to gain a military victory over the other.

In El Salvador at the time both the government and the guerrillas were seeking a purely military solution to the conflict, objectives that required both of them to insist on defining precisely who were their friends and who were their enemies. In such situations there are no brothers, only enemies, and a sort of armed polarization that inevitably prolongs the conflict. In such a situation, the absence of institutions at the national level that can facilitate a dialogue deepens the conflict even further. It was in such circumstances, coupled both to our earlier failure to avoid civil war and the 1981 failure of what we had hoped would be our final military offensive, that we found it necessary to seek international mediation.

The Diplomatic Track

The guerrilla movement in El Salvador may be unique among such movements during this century because it consciously put diplomacy first and used military actions primarily to bring pressure to find a political solution to the conflict. Our military campaigns of both 1981 and 1983 were specifically designed to advance this political objective. We chose to use military force in this way because in our particular political society those who wish to be heard must use pressure, and in our case the country only seemed to understand the language of our arms. In the end, we were able to turn what appeared on the surface to be a military defeat in 1981 into a diplomatic victory because there was a strong international reaction in favor of third-country mediation as the sole alternative to what was otherwise feared would be an inevitable bloodbath. In concrete terms, it was the subsequent official Declaration of a State of Belligerency between us and the government by Mexico and France in August of 1982 that created the opening that made possible the establishment of a real dialogue. For El Salvador, international participation was to prove positive.

Approaches to the United States

In addition, and because one of our fundamental strategies was to avoid insofar as possible all direct confrontations with the United States, we also made two attempts to open dialogues directly with United States. The first was an attempt to avoid the civil war itself, which we made with the help of the Salvadoran Catholic Church. In this instance Bishop Monsignor Rivera y Damas, on December 17, 1980, delivered a letter from us to the ambassador of the United States in San Salvador asking that the United States enter into a dialogue with us. Although I can perhaps understand why the United States, the most powerful country in the world, would wonder why it should dialogue with a flea, this opportunity to avoid war was lost because the United

States did not respond. We made our second attempt in January 1981, when we asked Mexican Foreign Minister Jorge Castañeda, Sr. [no relation], to bring to the attention of both William Casey, then the director of the Central Intelligence Agency, and Richard Allen, the director of the National Security Council, our interest in a dialogue with the United States. Neither attempt elicited a positive response, perhaps because at that point President Reagan was not interested in dialogue.

Dividing U.S. Opinion and Its Government

The failure of these two attempts to open a direct dialogue with the government of the United States led us to take the peculiar step of opening an office in Washington, D.C., which, from 1981 on, actively lobbied the Congress of United States. It was during our earliest lobbying efforts that we first made contact with Bernie Aronson, then working in Congress, who became both a friend and ally and who, after he became Assistant Secretary of State for Latin America in 1990, played a decisive role in switching the course of events in El Salvador from the pathway of war to the pathway of negotiations.

Up to 1990, however, the Pentagon and the Department of State were our openly declared enemies, whereas we saw Congress as our ally. I must admit that it was quite difficult for those of us on the radical left in Latin America to comprehend this sort of political surrealism, the kind of two-track approach to a problem that only a major power can afford. But, in the end, this division within the United States government was to be the key to resolution of the conflict.

On the official diplomatic side, the United States tried hard to neutralize European and Mexican efforts to negotiate our conflict. One such effort was the Stone Commission of the State Department, which, in its final report, quite simply asked us to surrender. In the end this proved to be one of very few strategic mistakes made by then American assistant secretary of state for Latin America Tom Enders, an exceptionally intelligent and experienced diplomat who, together with Ambassador Thomas Pickering, was to coin the famous phrase "the guerrillas in El Salvador are trying to win at the negotiating table what they cannot win at war." Perhaps because for 100 years American diplomacy simply had no experience with negotiated solutions to Central American conflicts, it did not know how to do so, the only exception being perhaps Nicaragua in 1979, when United States ambassador William Bowdler tried to negotiate a solution to the conflict there that would have allowed for the peaceful departure of the dictator Somoza. But that effort was unsuccessful.

By way of contrast, Europe, after the joint Mexico–France declaration of 1982, continued committed to a policy of mediation and the search for a political solution to the conflict. This was also true of Panama, which, under the direction of General Omar Torrijos, tried from 1979 through 1982 to mediate between us and the army of El Salvador. The Central American countries themselves came late to the process, beginning their own participation in the dialogue only after finally reaching an agreement in 1987, known as Esquípulas II. One of the main reasons it took them so long was that they themselves were severely limited by having several of their own armies engaged in similar conflicts, especially in Guatemala, and because Honduras was closely allied with the United States. It is always difficult for countries that are themselves participants in conflicts to act as honest brokers between other parties that are at war. Nonetheless, and despite all these difficulties, this process of external intermediation did create the political conditions that allowed us to engage at least in a limited dialogue from 1980 through 1989. However, despite positive developments, the war continued to worsen and finally reached its most violent extremes in 1987 and 1989. In 1987, supported by the American Pentagon and with help along the border of Honduras from the Honduran army, the army of El Salvador attempted to resolve the war militarily but failed. In 1989 we tried to do the same thing but also failed. I now realize that had either side won, it would have been disastrous, because the causes of the conflict itself would have remained unresolved. But in the end neither side won the war militarily.

The End to the Conflict

At this point peace came to be the most important objective, and this seemed best accomplished via what had to be a negotiating process of almost jewel-making precision that could withstand gilding the reality of war in a brilliant, almost golden bath of peace. The first step was to identify an acceptable intermediary capable of bringing together at the negotiating table the participants in such a violent war. Our first thoughts were that the Organization of American States (OAS) might play that role, but in those days the OAS was not what it is today. True, the Esquipulas II plan had opened up some limited spaces for negotiations. But it did not guarantee sufficient autonomy to assure that a negotiated solution to the conflict could be reached. Further, the OAS was for us not diplomatically acceptable because, during an earlier attempt at dialogue in 1984 in the city of Palma, it had asked us to disarm merely in exchange for our inclusion in the negotiating process, a condition included in the Esquípulas II plan but not acceptable to us.

Therefore we concluded that it would be much better to engage the United Nations (U.N.), together with a group of Spanish and Latin American "friends" of the U.N. Secretary General, which included Mexico, Colombia, Venezuela, and Spain, with the full support of the European community as guarantor of outside impartiality. These countries came to be known as the Group of Four, later expanded to become the Group of Four plus One when the United States became a participant. It was at this point that our ally Bernie Aronson and his team from the Department of State came to play a decisive role in support of the negotiations process and of international mediation. Regrettably, it later became apparent that several critical problems were not addressed during this 1989–1990 negotiating process. The most important was economic development and how Central America would integrate in the postwar period. This failure to complete the negotiations adequately was apparently a consequence either of inattention, forgetfulness, or simply an inability to identify and set priorities.

Postwar Institutional Transition

Even though a peace agreement was signed on January 16, 1992, El Salvador found itself still walking a high wire strung between hopes for a durable peace and the reality of a fragile one. This difficult situation developed because the Salvadoran state was not, in and of itself, able to assure compliance with the agreements that had been reached. In its place an observer mission of the United Nations [ONUCA] was charged with this responsibility, a level of involvement not considered intervention only because it was part of an accord signed by the government of El Salvador, known as the Agreement of Chapultepec. Had it not been for this U.N. presence, even a fragile peace would probably not have endured, because so many important interest groups felt they had lost too much as a consequence of the peace accords. Walking the high wire created by the peace agreements at all without a U.N. presence would have been extremely difficult, because the accords would have been in constant danger of being abandoned under pressure from those who dominated the apparatus of the state and would have caused constant problems in efforts to gain advantages or delay implementation.

As it was, numerous delays were caused by interest groups, forcing the U.N. to grant a number of extensions to the original calendar of verification and compliance with the peace agreements. This was a problem caused both by ill will toward the agreements themselves and resistance to compliance with them by those who felt they had lost advantages. This is why so much constant international pressure was necessary. Powerful political and economic interest groups entrenched within the apparatus of the state were simply not up to the challenge of the moment and cooperated, if at all, only with a great deal of reluctance. What developed was a set of entrenched interest groups that were opposed to the positive changes caused by the revolution, resistant to the process of transition to peace, and unwilling to be creative or to accept any new initiatives. These groups were convinced that sufficient concessions had already been made to the guerrillas in the peace accords, were willing to act on this belief, and were unwilling to accept that the revolution had any positive results beneficial to the country.

What then took place as a result was nothing less than a campaign of resistance by certain groups to the program of reinsertion of the guerrillas into civil society. The preference of some of the most conservative groups was simply to abandon the guerrillas in the streets, in fact simply to forget the soldiers of both sides. It was as part of this campaign that several of the economically and politically most powerful groups joined with a tiny faction within the army in an attempt to stage an old-fashioned putschist-style coup d'état, which the government of President Cristiani and the army general staff were able to defeat. Had the coup succeeded it might well have taken the nation to the brink of another civil war.

There were other groups that, with their minds closed to new ideas, believed that the negotiations that had taken place were simply a ruse designed to create some new political space for the revolutionaries and that once the guerrillas were disarmed commitments to them could be ignored. The shortsighted and nationalistic reactions of so many against the U.N.'s presence were a clear reflection of this sort of thinking among sectors that preferred a fragile to a durable peace and were opposed both to any real institutional changes and to the presence of international observers. They were convinced that there were no real reasons to make serious changes in the nation's political economic power structure and that it was only necessary to accept participation by the guerrillas in the process in order to coexist with them. Even this was, of course, a great advance over the past. But in reality the peace agreements had ushered in a much more positive revolution than that. There were yet others who believed that the process did require structural changes to the political system but that there was no need to touch the economic system. They were convinced by the political opening up of the world since 1985 and the fall of the Berlin Wall that all that was really necessary was some minor economic reengineering. This led them to visualize a process in which mere improvement in the social sensitivity of powerful economic groups would be sufficient. But in reality the actual result of the process was a sort of beneficial revolution similar to those that had opened up political spaces elsewhere in Central America, particularly in Honduras and Guatemala, as well as in Panama and even Haiti. In short, democratization was under way.

Lessons Learned by the U.N.

For the U.N., El Salvador has been a "school" in which it learned quite a bit about how to resolve armed conflicts and civil wars, lessons that it is applying today in a number of countries of the Americas, Europe, Africa, and Asia. Perhaps the most important lesson it learned in Central America was that to resolve internal armed conflicts it is necessary to engage in a process of negotiation about what caused the conflict in the first place, a useful lesson that is also applicable to regionwide stabilization efforts. In our region this approach included addressing what is perhaps the most difficult problem of all, that of the region's armies. In our case, UNESCO proposed the creation of peace commissions to help move the region's armies toward the pursuit of new missions related to development and democratization. Today the traditional idea that national security is solely the domain of Latin America's armies has been replaced by a belief that this concept has no place in the new globalizing world.

We need now to address two other regional problems. The ending of the wars in Central America has made it possible to reinitiate discussion of real Central America integration, which has been stalled since 1960. It has also become possible to resolve border demarcation problems through peaceful dialogue, thus increasing stability in the region. Both are opportunities made possible by the democratic openings that have taken place in the region.

In El Salvador the main lesson learned as a consequence of engaging in the postwar process is that the Salvadoran state continues to be weak. That is why it was necessary provisionally to enlist outside organizations to reinforce the powers of the state in order to assure the transition agreed to as part of the Agreement of Chapultepec. It was the only way compliance with the terms of the agreement could be enforced. The case of El Salvador has also demonstrated that the Latin American state by itself has not found it possible on its own to make important constitutional reforms to old systems and therefore has required external help to accomplish this task. The U.N., external diplomatic pressure, and internal actions were required to assure that the first phase of the transition as envisioned by the peace agreement was implemented. Measures that were successfully promoted by these external actors included a 1990 transitional measure to insure the participation of all the legal parties in the country in the political process and the formation in 1992 of the Commission of Peace, or COPAZ, made up of representatives of those same parties. Their involvement also helped make possible the creation of national institutions responsible for the distribution of land and guaranteed timely compliance with the peace agreements and their verification.

But the long-term keys to the situation are constitutional reforms. In El Salvador the first major change in the constitution was made in April 1991, when the National Assembly approved a constitutional amendment designed to remove the armed forces from the political arena and transform what had once been the national army into simply another democratic institution dedicated to political stability, a role they have in fact played since then. But too many delays have occurred, and it was not until April of 1994 that the National Assembly was able to approve portions of some of the other reforms required by the peace agreements. In particular, reform of the judicial system has been going forward, at most, at the pace of a very slow turtle. What is needed is reform of the system itself and a shakeup of both its corps of judges and its corps of lawyers. But excessive delays in the legislature's review have been so slow they have actually become detrimental to individual legal rights. Just now is the assembly beginning to take the necessary steps to unfreeze the system of judicial appointments.

Nonetheless, there have also been positive developments. For the first time in 150 years, as a result of governmental reform efforts the three branches of the government are independent of one another, and this has begun quickly to generate an acceptable balance of power between them. In 1992 the National Guard was also symbolically dissolved because of its reputation for brutality. Regrettably, this reform did not extend immediately to the secret police apparatus within the National Police, and they managed to organize extralegal bands of veteran National Policemen that then engaged in political persecution in favor of a new national political organization. It would have been better to dissolve the old police, together with their intelligence system, at the same time that action was taken to reform the army so they could not have been used to create a new extralegal system of repression during 1992–1994. On the other hand, one success story has been the establishment of a new institution, the Office of the Public Defender of Human Rights, which has played an important role in controlling abuses of authority and in protecting individual rights. Perhaps its greatest success has been in fostering a climate that supports the exercise of freedom of opinion, something we previously did not enjoy.

It may be useful to try to extract a few lessons from these experiences. First, when dealing with a nation that has not enjoyed extensive individual freedoms for more than one hundred years, the establishment of a new system that allows for such freedoms to be exercised also requires that the populace be educated on how to responsibly exercise them and that the government learn how to properly administer a regime based on personal freedoms. People must especially be educated in how to exercise the freedom of information. In the absence of such an educational effort, what we have seen in El Salvador is an explosion of defamatory discourse and the emergence of styles of public debate that are, to say the least, inappropriate. El Salvador's political parties have played an especially unfortunate role by setting bad examples for the general populace that have not improved the nation's governability.

When dealing with a country whose traditional political culture has been basically antidemocratic and anti-institutional, there are too many people who neither respect nor are prepared to work through new or reformed institutions, often claiming ignorance of law, a partly valid argument when national authorities have not kept the people sufficiently informed about new laws and changes in systems. As a consequence, Salvadoran political culture is still basically anti-institutional because the people lack confidence in their institutions and prefer to act extralegally. The result has been to leave a giant gap between the people and their new laws and institutions and failures to comply with the new norms that have been exacerbated by a crisis of the political parties, with the parties becoming mere parasitic growths attached to the new democratic system, a development that, in turn, has alienated the electorate and others who wish to take part in the country's new political life. This in turn has created a crisis for the new state. In El Salvador, in fact throughout Latin America, there is another new phenomenon. Recent changes in political processes require that bureaucrats working for the state become more open to dialogue with the public. But the region's public functionaries remained insensitive to this new demand because they are still wed to the old system in which they receive their orders from the party that put them into their positions and made them obedient to the party, not the government.

Nonetheless, the region's new electoral systems have also, despite their many imperfections, allowed for greater exercise of political freedoms, resulted in the redistribution of power, increased popular access to the legislative system, and increased the importance of municipal and local government and of those legally constituted parties that support diverse ideologies. This has resulted in a real redistribution of political power. It can also be said that the new electoral systems have reduced opportunities for fraud, which in reality was usually organized by the very same political parties that were competing for power. What has not yet been learned is how to live together in peace, how to share fairly between minorities and majorities, or how to insure that the presidency alternates after the first postwar election in 1999.

With the arrival of peace, the National Assembly has also been required to perform new missions. Specifically, from 1994 to 1997 the National Assembly, in which I was a deputy, was required to complete the legal reforms that formed part of the peace agreements, to initiate the modernization of the government's structure, and to establish policies for incorporating the nation economically within the globalization process. The 1997–2000 assembly is required to deal with the problem of decentralizing the government, making the financial system transparent, and privatization.

El Salvador Is Still Not Reconciled

The political transition from war to peace required by the Peace Agreement of Chapultepec has been technically completed, and the requirements of that agreement have been largely complied with. We can therefore conclude that we have now begun the second required process, to transform the nation completely. Unfortunately, many political groups have forgotten that there was a war and act as though it did not even take place. Even worse, many act as though we have a hundred years' experience with democracy and live in a free society accustomed to political dialogue. But this is not true. It is as if the participants in the United States Civil War of the 1860s or in Mexico's revolution had instantly forgotten those wars even took place.

In fact, inside the process of transformation there remains a large and dangerous vacuum related to the reform of the system of government itself. This is clearest in the economic sector. All attempts to develop a national plan for economic development in agreement with all the major sectors of the nation's public life and with its local governments have thus far failed. In large part this has been caused by the failure of the central government to develop a nationwide plan. Instead it has dedicated itself primarily to short-term planning, a process that has weakened the government's ability to act. The only exception to this has been a 1995 long-term educational reform initiative produced by a national reform commission. The main task has been passed along by agreement among the parties to the three branches of the central government, which have been asked to design new policies in the absence of participation of the political parties, which have refused to become involved. Several have even claimed that the process itself is contrary to their electoral interests. This is not the proper way to proceed. Transition to peace requires agreement between all the political, economic, and social groups of the nation and the government. All of them should participate in the process and then commit themselves to supporting change. In the absence of a national plan of integration, what has moved into the vacuum is a form of favoritism toward the party temporarily in power and its supporters that has in turn generated distrust and uncertainty among the populace in general.

The Saddest Lesson

This has taught us a sad lesson. When political parties themselves do not cooperate in a peace process, the resulting peace is fragile, not durable, because the nation continues to be polarized. This leaves the nation as a whole trying to walk a very narrow tightrope. Civil wars such as our revolution polarize a nation and leave it with a heritage of serious problems. They leave behind sores and resentments that, if not properly tended, cause serious problems. In particular they inoculate into society the viruses of extremism and distrust. This is especially true when in their aftermath the leaders of political parties refuse to change their leadership styles or to work with other parties. If the parties continue as they are it will not be possible to resolve the nation's problems.

Instead the parties themselves will simply become parasites on the body politic, unable to assist in the development of the country, which will be a tragedy for the nation's poor and for those attempting to make the postwar transition. Regrettably, as of today [1998], El Salvador's existing system is not inclusive, there is no national consensus on how the state should proceed, there are no agreements on how to unify the nation, and the political parties remain primarily interested in collecting up booty after each election. This must change.

Recommendation

What is recommended here is that the government join with all the recognized political parties, the business community, and the workers to develop a plan of government that could serve as an instrument of national reconciliation and economic development. Unfortunately, not even all those who signed the peace agreements have been prepared to work toward reconciliation during this period of transition. Our war generated extreme social polarization. To erase this polarization completely many generations must pass, and even then it will be necessary to teach people how to forget and forgive rather than how to hate, how to trust rather than distrust, and how to accept what has happened. Not enough attention has been given to this problem. Instead, some political leaders have tried to forget that the war even took place and act as though we have a hundred years of experience with institutionalized democracy. In addition, some economically powerful groups continue to be insensitive to the social and economic changes being caused by modernization and seem merely to believe that peace is good for business, which, even if true, is not sufficient to ensure future prosperity.

Despite these problems there is still time to promote a culture of peace in El Salvador based on the sort of goodwill that was promoted by the U.N. during its presence as an observer of the postwar transformation process. This is the only way that will allow for new generations of businessmen, politicians, and workers to be to be sensitized to the reality of what happened and learn how to pardon what was done without forgetting the lessons that the war taught us. National reconciliation is thus the principal challenge during this second transitional process, which should lead to both economic and social growth in accord with a set of national objectives to include Central American regional integration, another major vacuum created by the failure as a region to act in unison to promote economic development, which in turn has been a consequence of the lack of integration between the states of the region and a lack of cooperation on the part of its political parties and businessmen. Unfortunately, there is no agreement to support this nor is there a consensus on negotiating a national plan.

PART II
GUERRILLAS

7

ENCARNACIÓN BALDIVIA CHAVARRIA, *COMANDANTE TIGRILLO*

A BIOGRAPHICAL SKETCH

Encarnación Baldivia Chavarria, *Comandante Tigrillo* (Wildcat), is a living legend in Nicaragua among the mountain peasants.[1] A peasant farmer with little formal education who speaks Spanish with a heavy campesino accent, and who still makes his living raising beans, corn, and a few cattle on a small milpa reachable only by four-wheel drive, he may well be the best natural guerrilla leader produced this century in Latin America, a claim not lightly made. Slight of build and at first appearance unusually modest and withdrawn, he has a native charisma that very quickly draws others to him. He was just twenty-three years old when he first went to war, joining in 1977 the Sandinista guerrillas in his home region near La Concordia in the rebellion against the third Somoza dictator. Although lacking any formal education, *Tigrillo* proved to be a natural soldier and leader and rose through the ranks to become the Sandinista equivalent of a company commander at the war's end. After Somoza fell, *Tigrillo* at first remained with the Sandinista military and was commissioned a first lieutenant. But he soon became disaffected with the radical course of the Sandinista revolution, which he considered especially injurious of independent peasants, and took up arms against it in 1980 by organizing one of the first guerrilla MILPAS groups. For two years he led one of the three major MILPAS guerrilla groups, the real predecessors of the Nicaraguan Resistance Contra army. In 1981 *Tigrillo* was also one of the first to make contact with former Guardia in Honduras and enter into an alliance with them in order to receive American paramilitary assistance. From then until 1989 he was a key Contra field commander and built and commanded a major guerrilla unit, the Regional Command Rafaela Herrera,[2] for several years the largest unit in the Contra army.[3] Those who have campaigned with him, from Sandinistas who served with him during the war against Somoza to comando comrades of the Resistance, say he has an almost preternatural ability to smell out ambushes, to place his men to assure minimal casualties for maximum results, and to gain the confidence of those around him. In short, he is a natural combat leader.

During the 1990–1996 silent war of the Chamorro era, or re-armed former Contra period, he demonstrated time and again the ability to resolve dangerous situations in the countryside, to win the confidence of that least trusting of all Nicaragua's population groups, the Segovian peasant campesinos, and to be an effective political leader at the grassroots level. In recognition of his abilities and influence, after his election in 1996, Liberal President Arnoldo Alemán convinced Baldivia to become a regional delegate of the Liberal Party and a political leader of its rural peasant wing throughout the highlands. As a consequence, *Tigrillo* has grassroots-level political influence over a surprisingly large area and can even influence some policies at the national level. For an unlettered small farmer peasant, his is a fascinating personal record.

□ □ □

A GUERRILLA'S GUERRILLA

Encarnación Baldivia Chavarria
(as told to the editor)[4]

I've been asked to describe a little how I went from being just a poor peasant to being a political leader trying to help my country, Nicaragua, become a democracy. I hope it's an interesting story.

My Years as a Sandinista Revolutionary

Before I got into my first war, I was just a peasant farmer raising beans and rice on my milpa near the town of La Concordia up in the mountains of Jinotega. This was when the Sandinistas were trying to overthrow the Somoza government. One day a small Sandinista patrol that was operating clandestinely near my farm showed up at my place. After we talked for a while, they asked me to go with them. I wasn't sure I wanted to do that at first. I knew I didn't like the (Somoza) Guardia because they acted like savages, and I had not forgotten one time when a Guardia soldier beat me up. I was only fifteen years old when he did that. So I really didn't like them. Even though I was young, I could also remember when Nicaragua had been a peaceful place. So at first I told them I didn't want to go with them. But I thought about it, and when they came back about eight days later I had changed my mind. When they invited me one more time to join them, I was ready, and went with them.

After I got to their camp, which was up in the mountains at La Esperanza, in the mornings they would give me military training and in the afternoon they would give me political training. That was where I first met the founder of what was to be the Contras, *Comandante Dimas*, Pedro Joaquín González. Their message was against Somoza and against the Guardia. I agreed with that message even before I had joined them. After a few months of training I went to another place called Zapote Kum, which was where I first got involved in fighting.

All together I was with the Sandinistas as a guerrilla during the war against Somoza for about two years. I went into combat with them a number of times. A first I went on some smaller missions, mostly not too important. But after a while I moved up in rank and started becoming involved in more important battles over a larger area. As I moved up, I also got to know some other groups that were fighting. For example, I got to know the group of Germán Pomáres, *El Danto*. I found that the one thing we all had in common was that we wanted to fight against the Guardia. They were very tough, and everybody was afraid of them. I was afraid of the Guardia myself because I was a simple peasant and the Guardia could be pretty bad, so I thought that when I got to the battlefield I was going to be very scared. But it didn't turn out to be that way. From the very first time I went into combat against them I lost all my fear. Instead, I found myself fighting hard.

At first, as I said, most of our confrontations with Guardia were pretty small. But after about two years we got into our first real battle, which took place at Estelí. That was a really tough battle. We fought for almost twenty-two days straight but never took the town. Then we went on to Ocotal and attacked there. From there we went to capture the small Guardia based at Yalí, which wasn't too hard because there were not many Guardia there. After that we attacked San Rafael, which also didn't have much of a Guardia presence, and, besides, most of them were fairly old and really didn't have the energy to fight. All we really did there was just capture them and their weapons and then let them go because they weren't even worth killing. From there we went back to a place called Las Mulas, which was one of our secure base areas. While were at Las Mulas, we spent a lot of time planning another attack against Estelí. We were successful in our second attack and liberated it from the Guardia. From there we continued to fight until we eventually captured first Matagalpa and then Managua. In short, we liberated Nicaragua from the Somoza regime. That had been our only goal when I was fighting, and so it made me very happy because that was the reason why I had gotten into the war in the first place.

The Sandinistas Change Their Goals

Then the Sandinistas asked me to stay on as an officer, and I agreed. But then some of the higher officers above me began saying that although we had liberated Nicaragua from the Somozas that wasn't enough, and there were other battles to come. They said that now we had to liberate El Salvador and Honduras and Guatemala and eventually Costa Rica, because those other countries were still dominated by the Yankee imperialists, who were our real enemy. That was when I realized things were not going the way I thought they were supposed to go and that Nicaragua in fact was not going to be turned into the democratic country they had talked about before. Instead, they were now talking about other things.

A lot of what they talked about had to do with praise for Cuba, and I remember that they were especially admiring of "Che" Guevara. I said to them that I thought we had been fighting so that Nicaragua would be free and that I wasn't interested in those other countries. Besides, they were all at peace, their people were all working, and they didn't have any problems. In fact, everything seemed to be okay in those other countries, so I couldn't understand why we should be worrying about them. The Sandinistas then sent me off to take another course, which turned out to be political. At the end of the course the Sandinistas asked me if I wanted to go to Cuba for some advanced training, but I didn't.[5] I told them that we had already beaten the Guardia and there wasn't really anybody else to fight, so I couldn't see why we were preparing for more war. Then I said there also wasn't anybody to fight in Cuba, so why would I go there? They answered that we were getting ready for a gringo invasion and that's why we had to get ready to fight another war. We were preparing for an American invasion. So as the months passed, even though I didn't go to Cuba, we spent most of our time sitting around waiting for an invasion by the Americans that never came.

Making War on Our Own People

What we did begin to do was go on military missions against our own people, and what I then saw was savagery being committed by us against Nicaraguans, not foreigners, and especially against our own peasants. As I watched with my own eyes I saw the security police and sometimes even army soldiers beat up peasants or arrest them without any good reasons, and that began making me very unhappy. I also remember that some of the comrades I had fought alongside in the mountains went to Cuba. When they came back, they began asking me whether or not I believed in God. What I said yes, they told me I was a *baboso* [slug; literally stupid], that there really was no God, and that what I believed was just *pura mierda* [pure crap]. What I believed was just a lot of lies told to me by people who really just wanted to oppress the people. They also said that we should forget all of that old-fashioned stuff because the only God that existed was us.

I didn't agree with them and realized we would never get along anymore and decided the best thing I could do was just leave and go back to my farm, which I did. I made that decision during a mission when they sent me out to fight against somebody I had known very well during the war against Somoza, Pedro Joaquín González, *Dimas*. He had about twenty-two guerrillas with him and was once again fighting, this time against the Sandinista revolution. I went on the mission against him even though I knew he was very much an anti-Somoza soldier and had been a very good commander of the Sandinista guerrillas in the mountains during the war against the dictatorship. After all, I had been one of his comrades in arms. Anyhow, we went looking for him but couldn't find him in the mountains. We didn't catch him, of course, so after a week we came back. After we got back I asked for permission to go home for a while. When the Sandinistas said I could go, I packed my suitcase and left. I never went back. After about four days some of my comrades from my battalion came to my farm to warn me that I should hide because the Sandinistas were looking for me and intended to arrest and maybe kill me. An order had been issued that I was to be captured dead or alive.

My Years as a MILPAS Guerrilla

Because of the warning I got, I went into hiding. At first I just went into the mountains without any plan. At that time I didn't intend to fight against the Sandinistas. But I remembered that the Sandinistas had ordered me captured dead or alive. For the first six months I was hiding out in the mountains with some family of mine and did not get into the war against them at all. But after a while I realized I had to do something, not just hide. Besides, some of my Sandinista comrades came to talk to me and said they wanted to fight against the Sandinistas. After while it became obvious to me that I was going to have to fight again, and so I began organizing a small group of guerrillas of my own. At first we had almost no weapons, although little by little we did manage to collect up a few pistols and shotguns.

My first group was made up of twelve comrades who had served with me in the war against Somoza. Our first action was to attack a Sandinista post in a place called Plan de Grama. There were only three Sandinistas there, and they ran off pretty quickly. They had been protecting a warehouse full of food, which we took and shared with the peasants. It was there for the first time that I identified myself to them [the peasants] by the name of *Tigrillo*. One of our other men identified himself to them as *Tiro al Blanco*, and my brother, who was with me, called himself *Dimas de Tigrillo*, because he wanted to be identified both with Pedro Joaquín González and me. That was important because for reasons of our own safety we had to have names that were different from our real names. I always liked the wildcat as an animal, so that's why I called myself *Tigrillo*.[6]

After the fight at Plan de Grama we attacked another place called Santa Teresa. It was close to the house of Oscar Sobalvarro,[7] and we had a shootout near there with a small group of Sandinistas. They had machine guns and lots of different weapons and all we had were pistols, but by then there were twenty-four of us and they were badly outnumbered, so they quickly broke and ran. As our next operation we planned an attack against a larger Sandinista unit in a place called El Cuá. That attack was also successful, and we captured seven rifles, six submachine guns, and a machine gun. Once we had these weapons I felt much stronger and was more ready to take even bigger actions against the Sandinistas.

By then we were also being chased by the army. One Sandinista *comandante* who was after us had been my commanding officer for quite a while when I had been serving in the Sandinista army up around the Honduras–Nicaragua border, and I heard that actually he was much more interested in talking with me than capturing me. Of course, it was pretty hard for us to get together to talk because by then I had made my first few attacks and had killed quite a few Sandinista soldiers, as I remember about eleven. So I couldn't talk directly with the *comandante* chasing us. But I did sneak into his base, where I talked with one of his men who had been with me in the war against Somoza, a man by the name of Regadillo, and tried to convince him to join us. I was successful, and he deserted to join us and brought with him eleven more weapons. That let me arm another group of men.

By then the Sandinistas were sending battalions after me into the mountains. Finally the pressure from the Sandinistas became so heavy that I took twelve men and went to Honduras to look for help. In Honduras I made contact with Colonel Villegas, who was an Argentine army officer who was offering to help people fighting against the Sandinistas, and also with *Comandante 3-80*, Enríque Bermúdez. Some of the guerrillas who had been fighting with Pedro Joaquín González's group were in Honduras when I arrived.[8] They were calling themselves MILPAS, or the *Militias Populares Anti-Sandinista* (People's Anti-Sandinista Militia). I liked the name, and we also began using it for ourselves, and calling our guerrillas Milpistas.

My Years as a Resistance Guerrilla (Contra)

I stayed in Honduras for a few weeks until I was able to get a few more weapons, which were given to me by some of the other MILPAS who were there. With these I went in back inside with my twelve men, made contact with those I had left inside Nicaragua, and once more attacked Plan de Grama. By that time it had grown and become a bigger Sandinista camp and had quite a few new militiamen defending it. They had about fifty men, fairly well armed. But I had 120 with me and, even though only 40 of my guerrillas had arms, we were entirely successful. From Plan de Grama, I went back to Zapote Kum and then on to Waslála. For quite a while we operated all over that part of northern Nicaragua, until we went back once again to Honduras. This time when I got to Honduras, I had 270 guerrilla fighters with me.

When I got to Honduras I made contact once more with *Comandante 3-80,* and he told me that the arms they had been waiting for had arrived. He said that we had to fight for Nicaragua, which I was more than ready to do, and in fact was already doing. But first he said I had to go through a military training course with at least sixty of my men, which I agreed to do. Actually, it seemed a little strange because the people who were trying to teach us didn't know anywhere near as much about guerrilla warfare as we did, since so many of us had already been fighting for over four years in the mountains, first against Somoza and then against the Sandinistas. Still, since that was what we had to do to get arms and ammunition and other support, we did it. When we finished the course, they gave us some better weapons and other military equipment, and I took my unit back into Nicaragua and back to war.

Back to War

This time it wasn't as easy. On my way back into Nicaragua, a Sandinista army battalion chased me for sixteen days. Finally I set an ambush for them. Actually the unit that I managed to am-

FDN basic training formation, August 1982, at Guacamaya, Paraiso, Honduras, near the Rio Grande. Unidentified instructor in foreground may be an Argentine advisor. Courtesy ACRN.

bush had only twenty-five men, since most of the battalion had stayed behind in some houses resting. Of the twenty-five, we killed twenty-one. We also captured a radio, a lot of ammunition, some pistols, and a lot of other military equipment. We had a radio with us as well, and I called back to the headquarters in Honduras to let them know what we had done. I explained to them the action and remember having talked personally by radio with the Argentine Colonel Villegas, who was very happy.

After a few months, I took some more Milpistas back into Honduras for training, and left my brother *Dimas de Tigrillo* in charge of the troops inside Nicaragua. When we returned to Nicaragua, the Sandinistas had a really big force of soldiers operating in the area around Wina. They had also cleared everybody out of the area through which we had to infiltrate. They had even taken the pigs, dogs, chickens, and everything. At first we thought there simply wasn't anything or anyone there anymore. But when we started looking around we began to find people who were hiding in the mountains, so I started gathering them up. Altogether we found several thousand people, including 1,200 young people who wanted to join our forces. So I put them all together and took them back to Honduras so that those who wanted to fight could be trained in the camps in Honduras and then armed and sent back to join us inside Nicaragua. There were so many of them that after they were trained they were put together in five different task forces, which is what by then we were calling our big units. That was when we established several of our new units, including the Jorge Salazárs, the Arieles, and my own unit the Rafaela Herreras. We also established a unit called the Pino-1s, and some others.

I wanted to spend as much time as I could inside Nicaragua, so I also established a training camp inside. The idea was that instead of taking people out to Honduras, they would send arms inside and I would train the people there. As part of the plan, I collected up another 1,200 civilians to train. But the arms never arrived. The first pilot who was supposed to drop their rifles to us overflew my position but never did drop off weapons. They radioed me to ask whether or not I had seen the airplane. I told them: "Yes. I saw the airplane, but it didn't drop the arms." They called back later to tell me that the airplane that was supposed to drop weapons had been shot down at Mulukukú. So instead I took the people out to a place on the Honduras border known as Banco Grande, where I did get the weapons I needed.

Antiaircraft rocket gunners pose in front of signpost for FDN's Centro de Instrucción Militar (CIM), New Year's Day, 1986. Weapons are surface-to-air Red-Eye missiles supplied by the United States. Officer in right background is José Benito Bravo, *Mack*; at left is unknown. In 1998 *Mack*, after a postwar stint as a Sandinista police officer, was farming just opposite the La Concordia *milpa* of Encarnación Baldivia, *Tigrillo*. Courtesy ACRN.

But when I got to Banco Grande that time I also was told that we were no longer going to have any help from outside and that we would have to find some other way to take care of ourselves because the assistance was running out. Even so I had my people, so we went back inside as part of a mission to block the main highway near Plan de Grama. There were about 1,800 comandos in the operation altogether. I managed to accomplish my part of the mission and attacked, but some of the others didn't, while others attacked but were pushed back. Some of them never attacked at all. The Sandinistas poured into the area around Kilambé, the mountain I'm talking about, and they managed to surround us. But a force led by *Tiro al Blanco* came to my rescue and helped us get out. I sent part of my force back out to Honduras again, but I stayed inside Nicaragua myself. I broke my own forces up into small groups and had them scatter into the mountains. I also established a new safe area where we stayed for about six months. By then we had altogether almost 6,000 troops in the region, but the Sandinistas attacked us constantly, using rockets and helicopter gunships against us. Between the helicopters and their rockets, it made it difficult for us to keep away from them. It got so bad that finally I pulled most of my troops back into Honduras to rest.

A Visit Home

As soon as they were in Honduras I myself went back in with a small group of only twenty guerrillas, all the way to my home in La Concordia. I hadn't been home for over five years and was interested in seeing how things were with my family and friends in the area where I used to farm. But while I was there all sorts of

Comandante Chinandega, Task Force San Jacinto, FDN, during combat operations at El Cuartelón, Nicaragua, May 8, 1987. He was killed in action three days later, on May 11. Courtesy ACRN.

people came looking for me, and I ended up gathering another 1,300 people and taking them back to Honduras with me. It took fourteen days to get them back to Honduras, and we had to cross lots of highways, fighting to cross every one of them. During one of the fights to cross a highway we captured five Sandinistas, three women and two men, all from a big Sandinista base in Pantásma. They had propaganda books, I remember. We also had some wounded with us and things were pretty bad. I remember that three of my men tried to desert and I had to shoot all three. I also had the three women prisoners with my force and remember that one of them was wounded badly and we didn't know if she would live or not. But we managed to make it back to Honduras with all of them still alive and when we got there we just let the women go.

A few months later, after I had been back inside for a while once again, I was wounded in a fight in a place called Volcán, not too far from Yalí. It took four days to get out of where I was, and I only made it because they sent a doctor in to help me get out because I was so badly wounded.[9] The doctor got me out to Banco Grande on the Rio Coco. From there he took me to our hospital at Aguacate. But I was so bad that from Aguacate I was taken first to Tegucigalpa, and then to New Orleans. After I was better, the CIA took me from New Orleans to Washington to meet with *Comandantes 3-80, Aureliano,* and *Rigoberto.*[10] We went there to discuss our needs for military assistance, which led to our getting a $100 million package. That's what we got in 1987. But at the same time we also began considering negotiations with the Sandinista Front.

The Americans Manipulate the Peace Process and Us

There was a lot of pressure on us to negotiate with the Sandinistas, especially from the Americans. But this also caused a lot of unhappiness in our ranks. I remember that some of us asked *Comandante 3-80* to resign, or at least step aside, because we were so worried. But he did not want to resign and was quite unhappy with us. Our situation became particularly difficult toward the end of 1987 when our lethal aid was cut off and we were pushed into the hands of AID (the Agency for International Development).[11] We were very unhappy and said so to the CIA's station chief, who had us detained and shipped five of us off to Miami. We stayed in Miami because we had no choice, but we never lost the hope that someday we would be able to go back, maybe even to a free Nicaragua, even though the Americans who talked with us in Miami told us that our struggle was over and the war would not continue, and kept us informed about the negotiations with the Sandinistas. We all hoped they would do well enough for us to go home safely.

Later we found out what many others found out first, that the peace was very badly negotiated. For example, we were all certain it would take quite a while for us to disarm safely, perhaps as much as a year, but in fact we were forced to disarm almost from one day to the next, much too fast to be done safely or well. Much too fast. Even so, little by little we did manage to accommodate ourselves to the arrangement. I remember how it went in a place in Honduras called El Alméndro. I had come back from Miami and was there to watch what was happening. It was February 25th, 1990, and the Americans had only told me I was going back the day before. It was so bad that, instead of officially disarming, I went back to Miami and stayed there about twenty days before going directly to Managua. I was very concerned by the process because it was so difficult to watch as the Sandinistas got to keep their guns even as we had to give ours to the United Nations. When I arrived in Managua I went to the hotel Las Mercedes, where our top *comandantes* at the time, *Franklyn* and *Rubén*, were.[12] They told me there was nothing else we could do because there was too much pressure from the Americans and everyone else, but that things were going to go badly. They turned out to be right.

I went to a disarmament point, where they told me I had to give up my weapon. But I didn't have one, so I told someone "give me some pieces of something and I will turn them in so I can go home and see my family," which is what happened. Some of the comandos who were giving up their guns had lost almost all of their families and had neither mothers nor fathers to go back to. Some had both their mothers and fathers in jail. While I was in Miami, the CIA had been giving me barely enough money to survive on, but still I had saved some and gave some to a few of those who were in the worst condition. After I laid down my own gun, I went to see some of the others who were disarming in a place called San Pedro, just to see how it was going for them. A couple of them asked me whether or not I had hidden any weapons, and I asked them why. Some of them did hide arms up in the mountains, and in other places, but most just wandered around the streets lost.

My Time as a Peacemaker

After three days of looking around, I packed up my bags and went up to Jinotega. The place I went to was way up in the mountains. About the only thing up there were wild animals. I didn't want to do anything except stay in the shadow of the mountains. It hurt to see what was happening to people. All I did was just stay by myself. But the Sandinistas began claiming that I was up in the mountains killing babies, robbing people, and doing other terrible things. It was all untrue, but I had to come down out of the mountains because of the lies they were telling about me.

I will never forget that it was the director of CIAV (*Comisión Internacionál de Apoyo y Verificacíon* of the OAS), Santiago Murray,[13] who came with some of his people to bring me down safely. Otherwise the Sandinistas would have tried to kill me. I am still grateful to him for the help he gave me. He told me that I had the right to go home in peace and to have my own home and milpa. There were a lot of people in those days [1990–1996] saying that in Nicaragua there was freedom and liberty, but that was not true. For thousands of comandos and their families the war had not ended. It's just that we were unarmed while the Sandinistas who kept on killing us still had their guns. In any case, I came safely back out of the mountains with him, and thanks to him I also got a little money to help to start my life again, about $400.

The Minister of the Interior, Carlos Hurtado (who had been part of the Resistance's Southern Front), also asked me to help him with the problem of comandos who were rearming themselves [known as Re-Contras]. I agreed, so he gave me a pickup truck so I could move around and help with the problem of Resistance soldiers who had not yet laid down their arms or who had taken them up again and gone back to war. Actually I was still not in very good physical condition and still limped badly from the wounds I received during the war against the Sandinista revolution. But with the help they gave me I was able to go back and plant beans and get around my farm to do what had to be done.[14]

Every once in a while CIAV or the government would call on me to do things for them. For example, Minister Hurtado once called and asked me to go talk to several rearmed groups of former comandos who were fighting once again. One of the groups was led by my brother Francisco, *Dimas de Tigrillo*. Another was led by *Indomable*, another by *Campeón*, others by *Bigote de Oro*, *Bolillo*, and *Rojíto*. They brought them down to a place called San Marcos, where I would talk to them. I told them that the wars were over everywhere, not just in Nicaragua. They were also over in El Salvador, in Guatemala, and other countries, and I also told them that going back to war simply made no sense anymore, but many of them did not want to believe me. I also told them there was no reason for them to continue operating clandestinely. Instead, they should negotiate decent arrangements with the government and go back to work. But many stayed in the mountains, and soon there were also rearmed Sandinistas called Re-Compas.[15]

Working on a New Peace

As a consequence of this problem of rearmed soldiers, the government created a combined brigade of Contras and Sandinistas to work on bringing peace to the [central mountain] region. I was put in charge of the former Resistance side of the effort. The representative on the Sandinista side of the brigade was an army colonel named Sosa. I would not say we ever became friends. About eight days after we began trying, a group of former Resistance fighters ambushed a Sandinista army group and killed some officers during the ambush. Because of what they did, I had to go find those who had ambushed the Sandinistas and bring them back under control. But when I went up into the mountains to do so, the Sandinistas in turn tried to kill me. They laid a well-designed ambush they thought I couldn't escape. But obviously, more thanks to luck than anything, I wasn't killed. But I was seriously wounded, and the OAS had to come into the mountains once again to find me and then to take me first to the hospital at Trinidad, then to a hospital in Managua, and then to a hospital in Costa Rica.

By the time I got back to Nicaragua the group that was with my brother *Dimas de Tigrillo* had negotiated an arrangement to lay down their arms that had worked, and they were back working at civilian jobs. I came back from Costa Rica supposedly cured and in good condition but actually wasn't. While I was gone my pickup had been given to someone else, so the government gave me another one so I could keep on helping them. After a while, my work was over, but they told me to keep the truck, so I exchanged it for a small piece of land. Since then I've been working my little piece of farmland.

My Time as a Politician

I have since become a little involved in politics, mostly because a lot of people who are in that business have always taken me into account a little bit. When Dr. Alemán, who is now [1998] president of Nicaragua, started his campaign for president I was invited to go to Miami to talk with possible supporters and so that I could explain to the Cuban-American community in Miami that a man there who was pretending to be the leader of the Resistance Party, a Sr. Quiñones, had not actually ever been one of us. In fact, he had been a Sandinista. In fact, the man they were trying to help make the president of the Resistance Party was actually an enemy. But he had a lot of money and had been able to buy the support of some former comandos who were very poor and willing to pretend he had been a *comandante* of the Resistance. In Nicaragua everybody knew better. In fact he had been the commander of a Sandinista battalion known as the *Pablo Úbeda,*[16] one of the Sandinistas elite hunter–killer units. He was telling everybody he had been one of our commanders and had fought on the side of the Resistance, but that was just a big lie. But a lot of our Cuban friends had believed him. There was a public debate, and when Quiñones was asked how many men had been with his unit, he gave the wrong answer.

He was just one example. It was a real mess, because there were also other people who were trying to pretend to be Resistance political leaders when in fact they had been Sandinistas and were just trying to take advantage of our popularity with the Cubans and Miami. In fact, many of those in Miami trying to take over the Resistance political party had actually been Sandinistas, and they had everybody all confused. Finally, because Quiñones kept pushing so hard, some people of the real Resistance Party had to grab him virtually by force, put him on an airplane, and send him back to Nicaragua. That was one of a number of things I did in support of Alemán. For me, those who were in favor of democracy all went with the Liberal candidate, who was Alemán. All those in favor of communism went with the left, which was the Sandinistas. And of course, since all of us who had been with the Resistance were in favor of democracy, we went with Alemán. Since then the Liberals have called me quite a few times to go to political meetings and reunions around here and in Managua.

I don't really want to get involved in politics. But at the same time I feel like I have to do something so that the situation in Nicaragua doesn't go bad again. I also believe that the people have to participate because if not they will live in ignorance of what's really going on and, while it's true that there is not a shooting war going on, there is still very much a political war going on between the Liberals and the Sandinistas. For me, blessed are they who continue to try to bring freedom to Nicaragua, even though it's going to be a long, hard struggle.

At least now, after all of my years and after having been fooled so many times by people like the Sandinistas, I understand a little bit about politics and what can really be going on behind the scenes. I don't actually like to talk when I go to meetings. But I do very much like to listen closely. For example, on July 9, 1998, there was a meeting between the traditional Liberal Party and the Party of Resistance. At that meeting we decided to rename our particular party the Liberal Resistance Party. Two days later, on July 11, there was a convention in Managua. I was in that convention because I very much wanted to see how the political scene was developing. That's what I consider to be my important role now, to participate in the political process and try to make sure that Nicaragua continues to become a free country and a democracy.

8

OSCAR SOBALVARRO GARCIA, *COMANDANTE CULEBRA/ RUBÉN*

A BIOGRAPHICAL SKETCH AND SKETCH OF HIS MOVEMENT

Oscar Sobalvarro Garcia was known during his guerrilla life first as *Culebra* ("Snake," 1980–1983) and then as *Rubén*, after Nicaragua's premier poet Rubén Dario (1983–1990). Although little known outside Nicaragua, he was a founding leader and then a top field commander of Nicaragua's armed Resistance for more than a decade. As of this writing he was president of their main veterans organization, the Asociación Cívica Resistencia Nicaragüense (ACRN). The label "Contras" was given to them by their enemies. From the perspective of the Sandinistas it was a not unreasonable label, standing as it did for counterrevolutionaries. But the Contras considered themselves the legitimate defenders of Nicaraguan nationalist traditions against Sandinista internationalism and the legitimate heirs to Sandino. Like Sandino they were almost to a man staunch Liberals and convinced nationalists and, like virtually all of Sandino's army, from Nicaragua's Segovian highlands peasantry. Although Sandino's name had been appropriated by the radical branch of the Sandinista Front, in the

Contras' view this merely meant his image had been usurped by outsiders.

The Resistance movement consisted of a relatively small army supported by a mass peasant base of highlanders. It first emerged in early May 1979 before the fall of Somoza, from within the ranks of an anti-Somoza Sandinista peasant guerrilla force known as the People's Anti-Somoza Militia, or MILPA, the name being both a play on the words and a claim to indigenous identity, since a milpa is an Indian peasant's cornfield.

The Godfather of the Contras was Sandinista war hero Germán Pomáres, *El Danto*, who has been mentioned by several of the previous authors. An anti-Somoza guerrilla since 1958, *El Danto* was a product of the Conservative youth movement. In early May 1979 when plans to stage a post-Somoza socialist revolution were disclosed, *El Danto* objected loudly and strenuously, arguing that that was not what he or his men had fought for. On May 24 he was killed in battle by what the Sandinistas said was *una bala descarriada*, a stray bullet from within his own ranks.[1] His second in command, Pedro Joaqúin González, *Dimas*, immediately began to organize an anti-Sandinista guerrilla group from within the ranks of *El Danto*'s MILPA. This group, with roots deep inside the anti-Somoza Sandinista camp, became the first armed anti-Sandinista force.

Dimas named the new movement the People's Anti-Sandinista Militias (MILPAS) deliberately to identify them with *El Danto*'s force. Its combatants continued to call themselves Milpistas. *Dimas* was killed in 1982 by a close friend or cousin, Mamerto Herrera, but the movement continued to grow, and many of *Dimas*'s Milpistas went on to become top combat commanders of the Resistance movement's army.

From 1979 through 1981 the MILPAS were the only armed Resistance force fighting inside Nicaragua, and by late 1981 they were under serious military pressure. Lured by promises of arms made by Argentine military intelligence agents acting for the CIA, the Milpistas entered into an uneasy alliance with former Somoza Guardia Nacional soldiers organized as the Legión 15 de Septiembre. In recognition of this new alliance, the Legión's leaders changed their name to Fuerza Democrática Nicaragüense (FDN). The result was a largely peasant army led at the very top by a few former Guardia. The number of Guardia peaked in mid-1982 at 237 out of about 9,000, and then gradually dropped due to attrition—deaths, desertions, voluntary departures. By 1987 at least 97 percent of the FDN consisted of highlands peasants. Outsiders usually confused this army with a very different, smaller and unarmed, but much more visible political movement centered in Miami, also called the Nicaraguan Resistance. But in reality there was never a real organic link between the two, and at no time during the war did the leadership of this external movement have a voice in military operations.

Oscar Sobalvarro and his extended family are a prime examples of the key role played within the Resistance movement by highlands peasant clans.[2] His father, five brothers, several uncles, and dozens of relatives were from one of some twenty-two clans that provided about 40 percent of the FDN's comando force, which by 1988 numbered about 18,500. The farms of these highlander clans are all within a relatively small region in the provinces of Nueva Segovia, Jinotega, and Matagalpa, deep in that country's central Segovian mountains. The Sobalvarros are typical peasants of the region, which provided soldiers to both General Sandino during his Constitutional War and his 1927–1933 guerrilla campaign against the American Marines and to Ramón Raudales, who was discussed earlier by "Pepe" Puente, Alejandro Martínez, and Plutarco Hernández. They were also largely supportive of Sandinista efforts to overthrow Somoza. But because they were independent peasants, their ideas lay much closer to the nationalist, populist, and liberal ideology of the original General Sandino than to the radicalism of the 1979–1990 Sandinista social revolution.

Four Sobalvarros rose to key command positions in the FDN, Oscar, Luís, Julio César, and Manuel de Jesús. Oscar's own passage took him from simple peasant farmer to chief of staff of the FDN in 1989, when, after the United States pulled the supply plug for the last time, almost all the former Guardia left, and the original peasant leadership of the MILPAS reemerged and were found to have been the movement's real leaders all along. It was they who in 1990 negotiated an end to their war, the disarmament of their men, and the reinsertion of their forces and followers back into Nicaraguan society.

At first the newly elected Conservative government of Violeta Chamorro appeared to recognize Sobalvarro's importance to the movement by naming him Vice Minister for Repatriation. But once that effort was completed, he was dismissed. In 1999 he was still the president of the ACRN. He had also established a lumber exporting business and was president of a private lumber exporting company, Nicamadera. Still widely respected by his former comrades in arms, he had largely withdrawn from the active political arena.

□ □ □

THE CONTRAS AS THE SONS
OF SANDINO

Oscar Sobalvarro Garcia

I would like to thank the Hoover Institution and Timothy Brown for giving me this opportunity to reflect on my personal experiences during the recent civil conflict in Nicaragua.[3] This is the first time I have been able to do so, and I would like to explain why I fought, how we won our war but at first lost the peace, and what I have tried to do since our war ended to help establish democracy in my country.

My family is of peasant origins. My mother Julia María Garcia and my father Justo Pastor Sobalvarro are both natives of the province of Jinotega in Nicaragua's central mountain region, where they had farms near a place called Planes de Vilán on which they grew mostly coffee. While I regularly worked in the fields, my family was able to send me to school in Jinotega, so I managed to finish the third year of high school. I remember being raised on the stories of the highlands, including some about the war of General Sandino against the American Marines. But my father was a minor local magistrate during the Somoza period, so even before the fall of Somoza and despite the presence of many of my family in the ranks of those fighting against the government, my father and I came under pressure from the Sandinistas.

I remember one incident especially well. At the time I was just nineteen years old. While going to our farm, my father and I were detained by a Sandinista guerrilla unit. At first, because my father was a magistrate, they told me we were to be tried before a People's Tribunal and then executed. But when we arrived at their camp, we found that most of those on the tribunal were friends of ours, and several declared that my father was a good magistrate and neighbor who had never exploited his position and that we should be released. The Sandinistas not only released us but asked me to join their forces. I begged off, claiming my father needed my help on his farms. But being sentenced to death bothered me a lot.

After the Sandinistas took power they continued to treat us badly, arguing that my father was a Somocista because he had been a magistrate and that we were rich because we owned our own farm. We saw ourselves simply as more fortunate hardworking peasants. But in the revolutionary world of the Sandinistas, even though many of my family had supported the overthrow of Somoza, owning land and having had a position, no matter how minor, made us enemies, and that is the way we were treated. We were not alone in this, of course.

Unlike the peasants in western Nicaragua around the big cities who rarely own land and usually work on big plantations as laborers, almost all the peasants in the mountains own their own land. They are also by tradition Liberals, so they were from the very beginning treated like enemies of the revolution and reacted just as you would expect to this treatment. Within just a few weeks of Somoza's fall, Sandinista cadre from Nicaragua's cities began pouring into the mountains for the purpose of revolutionizing the peasants. They criticized the peasants' families as antiquated, attacked their Catholic beliefs, and pressured them to join new mass organizations of women, peasants, youth, Committees for the Defense of the Revolution (CDS), and a new militia.

I remember that the young city *brigadistas* of the Sandinista's literacy brigades were the worst. In theory they should have been warmly welcome, since their mission was supposedly just to teach the peasants how to read and write, and this was something the peasants very much wanted to learn. But the messages they taught along with reading were almost entirely political and deeply shocked the peasants. Not only did the *brigadistas* preach to the peasants that the idea of family was outdated and religion was bad, they also tried to reteach parts of Nicaraguan history that the peasants knew better than they did. Their lessons were full of praise for Fidel Castro and Cuba and for the communist world. The only Nicaraguan they sometimes mentioned was Carlos Fonseca, the founder of the Sandinista Front, who had been killed during the war against Somoza, but they clearly depicted him as just a minor figure, and except for him almost all the heros they talked about were foreigners and communists. The peasants were especially incensed by the *brigadistas'* complete failure to talk about General Sandino, who had after all survived in their mountains during his fight against the American Marines only thanks to their support and was to many of the mountain peasants Nicaragua's biggest hero. This omission of Sandino by the very people who claimed to be his legitimate heirs, even more than what they did teach, was what most convinced the peasants that the Sandinistas were actually internationalists preaching a foreign message, not Nicaraguan nationalists, and this was something they strongly disliked.

I remember clearly the day when I made my own decision to enter into the struggle to save democracy in Nicaragua. It was March 20, 1980. At first I had tried not to get involved. But the more I saw the more I came to realize that my country had been captured by a Marxist internationalist regime disguised as nationalists and headed by just one man, Daniel Ortega, his family, and his closest allies. It was a pattern they called Sandinista instead of Liberal, but it was really just a repetition of the family-style dictatorship of the Somozas.

When I was a child I had never dreamed the time would come when I would take up arms against my brother Nicaraguans. But the situation had changed so drastically that it became necessary. The dreams of tens of thousands of Nicaraguans, including my own, had been transformed from the euphoria of hope after the fall of Somoza into growing despair. I did not take my decision alone but rather did so with my father and five brothers. It was a difficult one to make, but we all agreed it had become necessary to take up arms against the international communism being preached and in fact implanted in Nicaragua by the Sandinistas before it could consolidate in our part of the country or even become a threat to neighbor countries. The Sandinista revolution was in the process of trying to destroy all our basic rights, our freedoms, our traditions, and our religion, and had even begun to put in danger the most important of all rights, that to life. From the very beginning of their taking power, the Ortega brothers made it impossible for Nicaraguans to live in peace unless they were prepared to submit themselves completely to the Sandinista government's political model, which involved the expropriation of properties, jailing people without trial, psychological manipulation, and physical torture. Opposing what they were doing could easily lead to being killed. In short, Nicaraguans had only two alternatives: submit completely to the will of the Sandinista revolutionary regime or join in an armed struggle against the Sandinistas. Given these two alternatives, we didn't even consider going into exile; we decided we had to fight. We also concluded that our struggle would be both legitimate and necessary.

That decision made, my family at first stayed home while I began organizing a small opposition group in the mountains near Planes de Vilán. In the beginning there were fifteen in our group, all young men. We began by getting together mostly on weekends and pretending to be two baseball teams. It was probably the safest disguise we could have invented, although it didn't last too long. We made contact with other peasant families nearby and they gave us a few hunting weapons. The Sandinistas had swept through the region almost immediately after Somoza fled in an effort to collect up all the peasants' weapons, but the people had hidden most of them, and most families still had two or three. Everyone we contacted gave us one or two of these, shotguns, .22 caliber rifles, small pistols, which became our first arms. Our leader was Antonio Jarquín, who took the pseudonym *Chilindrín* ("Rattle"). I was his deputy. We began to organize a system of supporters, *correos* to carry messages and keep us in touch with the other peasants. We also organized the peasants who were helping us into committees that became our *base social,* or social support base.

We didn't do too much patrolling at first, although we did stage some raids to capture weapons from the new Sandinista militia. This was actually fairly easy, since most of them were already sympathetic to us. We would prearrange a time with friends who were members, usually involuntarily, of a militia group, "attack" their post firing into the air, they would "retreat under attack," leaving their weapons, and we would pick them up and take them with us. That way they could claim to have lost them in battle, so they wouldn't get in trouble, and we got weapons without hurting anyone.

Of course it didn't take the Sandinistas very long to realize who we were or what we were up to. One night a few weeks after we began, a Sandinista helicopter flew over my family's house and dropped some small bombs. Although the house was badly damaged, no one was hurt. But my father, five brothers, and some other relatives fled to join us in the mountains. The Sandinistas alleged in their propaganda that we were just a gang of former Guardia and began painting what we later came to call the Black Legend of the Contras (*La Leyenda Negra de Las Contras*) that claimed we were all former Somoza soldiers. The peasants knew better, of course, but most other people didn't, so while it was a lie, it was a lie that stuck to us throughout the war. In our case, we did have one former Guardia, Jarquín, but he was just a peasant private who had been drafted near the end of the war, not a professional soldier.

At first we thought we were the only ones fighting, but we soon heard about some other groups, although we had no contact with them until much later. One we heard about was led by Pedro Joaquín González, *Dimas,* who had been a top Sandinista commander during the anti-Somoza war. He called his group the People's Anti-Sandinista Militia, or MILPAS. He chose that name because he considered his guerrillas legitimate descendants of his earlier anti-Somoza Sandinista revolutionary force, which had been known as the People's Anti-Somoza Militia, or MILPA. We thought that was a good name, and soon we also began to call ourselves MILPAS.

Dimas's guerrillas were all former anti-Somoza revolutionaries who had fought alongside the Sandinistas only to see their leader, Germán Pomáres, *El Danto,* killed and find that their struggle for a Costa Rican–style democracy had been stolen in the last weeks of their war. Talking to them later, we found that they were certain Pomáres had been assassinated on orders from the Marxist leaders of the Sandinista Front. In our case it was different. We had mostly not fought against Somoza but did think that the fight against the Somoza regime had been, in many senses, just an extension of the efforts of Sandino and his successors to establish a democracy in our country. What we were fighting against was very different, a revolution run by a small clique of Marxists who were pursuing a communist plan that was unlike anything Sandino would have supported. So we had no problem at all accepting *Dimas* or his MILPAS. It was a little different later when we joined with some former Guardia.

Our own group and the MILPAS movement in general was born in the mountains and grew rapidly because it had massive support from the peasants of the region. From the very beginning, in March 1980, ours was a peasant struggle made up almost entirely of peasants, many of whom had been participants in the armed struggle against the Somoza dictatorship. The Somozas had maintained power in Nicaragua for more than forty years prior to the arrival of the Sandinistas and treated the country virtually as their private property. More than one-third of my country's territory and much of the nation's capital, Managua, had belonged to the Somoza family and their supporters. But the peasants who had flocked to the flag of those fighting to rid Nicaragua of the Somozas quickly found that their rebellion was being betrayed by the Sandinistas, who, rather than sharing with people, simply grabbed the property of the Somozas for themselves and became even more economically all-powerful in the country than their predecessor dictators had been.

As I mentioned earlier, we began our struggle against the Sandinista revolution armed only with hunting weapons, shotguns, .22 caliber rifles, and small pistols. Those we were fighting against were receiving massive amounts of military support from the socialist camp, principally from Russia via Cuba, and had the full support of the Russian's favorite Latin American comrade, Fidel

Castro. Even so, by the end of 1980, well before the decision of United States President Ronald Reagan to provide us with military support, our organization had an armed military force of more than 2,000 combatants and a social support base numbering twenty or twenty-five times that many persons, mostly peasants, although some lived in mountain towns. Most of our arms were captured from the Sandinistas. But they were receiving massive quantities of military help from abroad, while we were able to capture only relatively smaller amounts. As a result of the growing imbalance between their supply of arms and ours, if we were to continue our struggle we had to look for a better way to get weapons, ammunition, and other military necessities for our combatants.

In early 1981 we heard through the peasant grapevine that there might be arms available in Honduras. This caused us to send teams out of Nicaragua into Honduras to search for help. I went in one of them. At the time what we had was a small stock of military weapons we had captured from our Sandinista enemies, mostly of Soviet manufacture. The best was the famous BZ, so we took a few with us. It was our ability to show these weapons to the Honduran military that resulted in our being able to convince them to protect us and let us stay a while inside Honduras. But our first contacts were not easy.

When I arrived in Honduras for the first time, the first people we met were local civilian officials, who took us to the Honduran army base at Arenales, in the province of El Paraíso. The first thing the army did was take our weapons and ask us who we were. We explained we were guerrillas known as MILPAS and had been fighting against the Sandinistas for over a year, but we had just been attacked by a large Sandinista force, were short of guns and ammunition, and needed help. We asked them to let us set up a camp. At first they held us, probably while they investigated or asked for instructions. But within a couple of days they gave us back our weapons and let us establish what was to become our first base camp. It was near the town of Capíre inside Honduras.

Very soon after that we were visited by a former Guardia Colonel, Enríque Bermúdez. That was in mid-1981, and after talking to us he said he could help us with some money and arms. We began building our base, which we called Base Ariel, on the farm of a Honduran peasant named Alvarenga. During those first weeks we were also visited by an Argentine army colonel named Villegas and by several Honduran officers. We were soon joined by three other MILPAS groups that had come out. One was under Irene Calderón and a second led by Encarnacíon Baldivia, *Comandante Tigrillo.* They had arrived in Honduras before us and had been disarmed and sent to San Pedro Sula. All of them were former Sandinista revolutionaries from the MILPAS of *Dimas,* who had been killed by then. I suppose the Hondurans really weren't sure what to make of them, since they probably couldn't believe that former Sandinistas had been fighting against their one-time comrades for almost two years. But when we arrived and they found we were not former Sandinistas and yet had been doing the same thing, apparently they changed their minds and brought them to our base on the Alvarengas' farm, which was when we first came together. For a few months we continued to act like three groups, each under its own leader. But by early 1982, with the establishment of the Fuerza Democrática Nicaragüense (FDN) and its general staff, we were assigned a former Sandinista, *Comandante Ismael,* as our base commander.

Still, each group kept its own leader. The other two were made up mostly of former anti-Somoza Sandinista revolutionaries who had been Milpistas under *El Danto* and then joined *Dimas*'s new 1979 guerrilla rebel group when *El Danto* was killed. *Dimas,* the true founder of the Nicaraguan Resistance, was in turn murdered in an ambush laid for him by his cousin and comrade Mamerto Herrera.[4] But his death did not cause his men to quit. Instead they had broken into smaller groups, stayed together, and kept on fighting. It was one of these smaller groups under Irene Calderón that had been the first to send some men to Honduras from Nicaragua looking for some help and sanctuary.[5] Men from the other two groups had soon followed. But unlike us, they had been suspect because of their Sandinista origins and had not been as well treated by the authorities of that country, who probably found it hard to believe that a group founded by a top anti-Somoza Sandinista field commander like Pedro Joaquín González, *Dimas,* had almost immediately begun fighting fiercely against the revolution in Nicaragua. As a result of this Honduran distrust, the first groups had been removed to the Honduran north coast. It was only after we arrived that the Hondurans realized there was a real war going on against the Sandinistas and decided to bring them back to the border to join with us. In addition to Irene Calderón's group there was a larger one under *Tigrillo*, a former anti-Somoza Sandinista guerrilla commander who had also quickly become disillusioned with the Sandinista revolution and taken up arms against it. Both had left Nicaragua looking for help.

Between us we established our first base camp. At first we didn't even have a food supply. I remember that for the first several weeks we ate what we could hunt and often had monkey for dinner. When you're hungry enough, anything tastes good. A lot of monkeys were to die before some of us were able to get jobs on local Honduran farms and make enough money to buy more normal food for the group. But the news of our presence in Honduras quickly reached the High Command of the Honduran Armed Forces and the American Embassy in that country, and just a short while after our arrival in Honduras we were visited by Colonel Enríque Bermúdez, a former officer of Anastacio Somoza's Guardia. Bermúdez promised us some military help and also some money to help to feed us. A few weeks later he brought us $2,000 so we could buy food. We were not especially happy about his Guardia background, but our needs were overwhelming, and we decided that if we were to continue our struggle inside Nicaragua against enemies who seemed to have a bottomless source of guns and ammunition we would have to take help from whoever offered it. Looking back, it was the first step in our joining into an alliance with them.

We named our first camp Base Ariel. Soon after Bermúdez's second visit, several other former Guardia arrived, and we began

Staff meeting between Argentine intelligence advisors and FDN officers, at 5a Escuela, Honduran Armed Forces (HAF), Tegucigalpa, 1983. Standing right, Colonel Enríque Bermúdez, FDN. From left to right, seated, Argentine Colonel Villeda, Ricardo "Chino" Lau Castillo, Argentine-trained *Comandante Fiero*, and *Diablo* Morales, FDN. Courtesy Luis Moreno Payán, *Mike Lima*.

receiving training in new weapons from them in preparation for the military assistance to come. The first arms that reached us were fifteen M-14 minirifles like those of the American army. *Tigrillo* was anxious to return to Nicaragua and continue the struggle, so we immediately gave some of them to a select group of his comandos, as we called our combatants. We also armed a few of our own guerrillas and sent them back inside Nicaragua on reconnaissance missions to scout out military objectives for future attacks.

We continued to call ourselves Milpistas among ourselves throughout the war. At first we also continued to call our organization the MILPAS, but we had begun the process that was to put us under the mantle of a larger umbrella organization. Base Ariél itself remained a peasant MILPAS operation, and those who had come together to create it, the followers of Pedro Joaqúin González, *Dimas*, the commandos of *Tigrillo's* force, and my own forces, never deviated from these origins. Although our forces and social base support systems continued to expand rapidly, we remained almost exclusively peasant campesino in origin and makeup. But even as we remained homogeneous, we also began to receive support from an umbrella organization that had been created in exile by former Somoza Guardia, known as the Legión 15 de Septiembre, named for Nicaragua's independence day. In 1982 the Legión was renamed the Fuerza Democratica Nicaragüense (FDN).

By the end of 1983 the FDN had grown to over 9,000 comandos, about half inside Nicaragua. Almost all were peasants under the field command of former Milpistas.[6] We had also come to control very large regions of the national territory of our country, in large part because the military assistance we were receiving from the government of President Reagan, which had been approved by the United States Congress, had allowed us to stand up to the Sandinistas. I myself had gone back inside early in 1982 to resume my own struggle together with those we had left inside. My group had grown to about 60 men by then. Soon it grew to about 120, then almost 600. We called ourselves the Salvador Pérez, after one of our heroes, then we became the Diriangens after one of Nicaragua's Indian heroes of the Spanish Conquest. Each time the force grew, I was reelected its commander.

Perhaps an explanation of how and why I was "elected" would be of interest. Ours was a guerrilla force that had emerged from the peasantry in the mountains, not a conventional army. We did receive a lot of American help, but half or more of our guns and ammunition we captured from the Sandinistas or were given to us by sympathizers. Almost all our other support came directly from the peasants—food, medicines, intelligence, proselytizing, recruits, shelter, the evacuation of wounded, guides, and so on. The comandos were just the armed part of our movement.

Display of captured EPS weapons and equipment, including SAM antiaircraft rockets, mortar rounds, mines, radios, hand grenades, and other items. Courtesy ACRN.

By the end of 1984 we had grown to include several task forces, one of which was the Salvador Pérez. Under the name Regional Command Diriangens, we had about 1,500 comandos. But we were able to fight for one reason only, because we were supported by two other Resistance groups, each bigger than we were. We had a corps of *correos* numbering about 2,000 persons, mostly unarmed, who were our link to our largest group of supporters, our *base social* (social support base). The *base social* had a number of committees in each *comarca* (rural community) directed by a *comarca* chief. If you added up the number of peasants in these committees that collected our food, kept an eye on the Sandinistas and let us know where they were and what they were doing, spread our message, helped us bring people together for meetings, rescued our wounded and helped our sick, hid us when we needed help, led us from place to place, and brought us clothes, boots, and medicines, and so forth, then our active support base consisted of most of the peasants in the mountains, as well as a lot of other supporters in the region's small towns, and numbered in the tens of thousands. They were really the ones in charge. For example, any time we wanted to take a military action we would always consult first with the *comarca* chief, who had a veto.[7]

Between them, the *correos, comarca* chiefs and *base social* ran a house-to-house network in every *comarca,* and a *comarca*-to-*comarca* network that covered the entire countryside throughout the mountains. Often it was a *comarca* chief who suggested a military action by us and we almost always complied, since without the chiefs, *correos,* and *base social* we could not have survived, much less grown. Not only that, but since we ourselves were a product of the peasantry, the lines of control ran from the bottom up, not the top down. Just as *comarca* chiefs were elected by the peasants, commanding officers were elected by their troops. That is why, as a senior commander, I was actually a democratically elected official.[8]

Our struggle continued to prosper until the American Congress suddenly cut off our assistance in 1985 for the first time. I had been in and out of Nicaragua and knew how important this help was and began wondering why it had really been cut off. It was apparent that the Americans working with us were very surprised at the growth of our organization and our capacity for struggle. In fact we had proven ourselves to be a real army of great ability and considerable nationalism and patriotism. As a result of our growth we had come to be a real and dangerous threat to the Sandinistas and their revolution. Our *base social* was especially large, including as it did almost all the *campesinos* or peasants in our part of Nicaragua, and our ranks were swelling fast, often with young deserters who chose to desert from the Sandinistas' ranks in order to become members of the popular Resistance movement we had constituted. Most of these young men were either military reservists or youths who had been forced, usually against their will, to join the Sandinista's militia units. We had even begun to believe we could actually win the war.

But this first cutoff of American assistance made me realize that the Americans were not helping us for our sake. They were giving us help for their own reasons as part of the cold war. They did not want us to win the war, but were just using us to bring pressure on the Sandinistas and did not really want us to overthrow the Sandinista government. Not many of us understood this, but for me it was the only good explanation of the 1985 cutoff. Later cutoffs obeyed the same pattern. Every time we began to do too well, Congress would cut off our aid. We could and did continue to fight and grow even when we didn't have American help, but the cuts were always damaging. Regardless, we were able to keep up our struggle until we managed to force the Sandinistas to submit to free elections, which led, if not to the Nicaragua we had hoped for, at least to one that was much better than the revolution. But that was to happen only much later. In between, from 1985 to when we laid down our guns in 1990–1991, there was a lot of war to be fought, and I spent most of it inside Nicaragua or on the general staff in Honduras.

I won't talk too much about my own experiences during the remainder of the war, but a couple of incidents do stand out. One took place in 1986. Sometimes we would dress in Sandinista army uniforms and act like them on missions. Sometimes they did the same to us. Once being dressed like a piri (comando pejorative for Sandinista soldier) saved my life. We were setting up a road ambush on the highway between Wiwilí and Los Chiles in Jinotega and I was waiting for some of my men to bring me an RPG (rocket-propelled grenade) when I heard and then saw an IFA (a Soviet-made military) truck come down the road. My men raced to bring me the RPG, and I had just fired it, hitting the truck, when six more IFAs, loaded down with Sandinista troops, roared around a curve and drew up behind the first one, which was in flames. My men quickly pulled back—we were heavily outnumbered—but when I turned to run I twisted my ankle badly and fell. Before I could escape, the piris were all around me, and a firefight started. All I could do was lay low and pretend to be a wounded piri. The battle lasted almost all day, from about 9:00 a.m. until maybe 5:00 p.m., all the time with me mixing inside the

Soviet-made ZIL truck of the Nicaraguan Ejercito Popular Sandinista attacked by troops of *Comandante Dumas,* Task Force Pancasan, Regional Force Jorge Salazar, near Posa Redonda, Santo Domingo, Chontales, mid-1983. An RPG has set it ablaze. The burst of a second RPG can be seen to the right. Photo by Peter Bertie, a Canadian journalist killed in combat shortly thereafter. Photo courtesy of Luís Moreno Payán, *Comandante Mike Lima,* FDN.

Sandinistas' ranks trying to pass for one of them. You can imagine how scared I was that they would discover me, but they never did. Finally, as it started to get dark, the piris moved on and I was able to crawl about a hundred yards and hide in a grove of trees. Luckily I had hidden my ICOM (pocket-sized tactical) radio and was able to call my men to let them know I was still alive. But they had already withdrawn to safe havens, and I had to walk—twisted ankle or no—almost fifteen kilometers to rejoin them.

In my second experience, I was less lucky. In 1987, after almost seven years in combat, counting my first two as a Milpista and five with the FDN, I stepped on a mine and almost lost my leg. Thankfully, I was able to make it to Honduras and get medical attention, and I don't even limp now. But I couldn't go back into combat, so I became a general staff officer. I was first made chief of operations, then of psychological warfare, and began spending much more time in contact with the Americans, Hondurans, and the political side of the Nicaraguan Resistance. This involved a number of trips to other countries, especially the United States, and once to attend a Nicaraguan Resistance Assembly in the Dominican Republic. During the assembly in the Dominican Republic I was the FDN/ERN's political director. Talking to the civilians at the assembly, I realized they were really just a kind of cover for us. They actually had no voice in our military operations and couldn't even coordinate what we were doing. And yet at the same time they were very important in getting us help, even though the Americans didn't always listen to them. It was during these and other contacts with Resistance political leaders, Americans, and others that I began to realize we would never be allowed to win our war. The Sandinistas had not been able to build the revolution they wanted, but neither could we depend on enough support to stop them permanently. By early 1988 I had come to the conclusion that we had to negotiate an end to our conflict. We had to begin looking for a peaceful settlement of the war.

Even as I was reaching this conclusion, the Sandinistas were still trying to strengthen their hold on the countryside and the nation by taking more and more reprisals against people who disagreed with them or jailing anyone who didn't agree with their political programs. Their confiscations of businesses and productive enterprises were destroying the economy of the country. This ever-increasing pressure, especially on young people, their persecution of religious institutions, their denial of basic liberties like freedom of expression and assembly, were measures that pushed thousands upon thousands more Nicaraguans into our ranks or into exile outside the country. And yet, even as the Sandinistas continued to sack the country at will and were still receiving thousands upon thousands of tons of military equipment every month from Russia and Cuba, the government of United States chose to withdraw the little assistance it had been giving us and to initiate a dialogue with the Sandinistas, using as its instrument the governments of Central America. The Americans' objective appeared to be to pressure the Sandinistas into negotiating a peaceful end to the conflict in exchange for demobilizing our forces, without even consulting us.

In 1985 and again in 1987 and 1988, much to the surprise of both our American allies and the Sandinistas, our war had continued even without external military assistance, because with or without foreign help we were still very highly motivated and also able to supply ourselves from the stockpiles of our enemies and feed ourselves from what our massive social support base, impoverished as it had become, was still able to give us. In fact, in some ways we felt even more than before that we were the authors of our own decisions and were able to advance even further toward the heartland of the country. By doing so we were able to demonstrate both to our enemies and our friends that we could, even without foreign aid, continue the struggle to the very end, even if our objective was to capture Managua and reestablish a durable democracy for all Nicaraguans. It was this realization, even when American military help was renewed and before it was finally withdrawn for the last time in 1987, that convinced the Sandinistas that we had sufficiently advanced in our own struggle to force them to submit to a free electoral process. This is what forced the Sandinistas to accept the peace process known as Esquípulas II and its aftermath. I was sure that Esquípulas was really an American-sponsored process. The United States is simply too important in Central America for the entire region to oppose what it wants. And in this case the United States wanted the war over. We and the Sandinistas were both in their way.

Shortly after Esquípulas I remember we found ourselves launched on a negotiating process. It was a process in which I participated. For the first time we met with the Sandinistas at Sapoa on the Costa Rica–Nicaragua border. The first step was a cease-fire. It was not easy, but we did our best to try to honor it, even though the Sandinistas continued a lot of their military operations. The Americans brought a lot of pressure on us, as did the Hondurans. Both had been helpful before, but now they began pushing us to negotiate faster. Actually the process took the better part of the next two years, and many comandos died before the process ended. In fact, it was not until the 1990 elections, which the Sandinistas lost, that we really moved to negotiate the most important things, disarming our forces, establishing safe-haven areas inside Nicaragua, deciding what our comandos and their families would need to restart their lives.

As it turned out, much of what we thought we had negotiated in good faith was never delivered. Instead of turning to us, even though we were the ones who got her elected, the new Conservative president Violeta Chamorro decided to let the Sandinista army and police keep their guns even while we were giving up ours. She also let them keep as personal property most of what they had grabbed during their revolution, so the Sandinista leaders ended up rich. The enclaves we thought we had negotiated were not fully respected, the farms we had been promised were mostly not given to us, and the army and police carried out reprisals against our comandos and their families. An unarmed group of observers from the Organization of American States [CIAV/OAS] was all that stood between us and them. They did a magnificent job but couldn't really protect us, and hundreds, perhaps thousands, of our people were killed. What especially made us sad was that by and large the Americans abandoned us, and a lot of international human rights organizations that had been very active denouncing everything we did during the war lost all interest and did nothing to protect us from the Sandinistas.

As a result of the Chamorro government's failure to keep its promises, some of our former comandos took up arms, becoming known as Re-Contras. The Sandinistas quickly reacted by tolerating and probably by organizing a countermovement called the Re-Compas. At one point armed groups that mixed the two together even appeared and were known as Revueltos. The frustrations that led to the appearance of these groups may have been understandable, but it was never the right way to go, and I did what I could to help limit the violence. Some of the groups were legitimate descendants of our forces, many were Sandinistas in disguise, others were just bandits taking advantage of the lack of justice or a real government presence in the mountains. This fighting was not to end until well after the next election.

The new government did establish an Institute for Repatriation, and I became its deputy director, a subcabinet-level job. But almost all our employees were Sandinistas, and they manipulated most of what happened. The government received international funding to help war victims, both soldiers and their families, and to assist war wounded, but the vast majority of it went to the Sandinistas. Very little reached our people. When the money flow slowed, the Institution was closed. I was offered another government post but decided that in good conscience I could not keep on, given the way things had been going, and left the government to go into business. I was not even ready to get involved in politics, even though in reality the former Resistance could have become a major influence if it had been organized. A political party, the Partido de la Resistencia (PR), was formed by some former comandos and civilians and did participate in the 1996 election. But it turned out to be a minor party, not a major force.

I myself am still the president of the armed Resistance's veterans organization, the Asociación Cívica Resistencia Nicaragüense (ACRN) and am in touch with many of my former comrades in arms. But mostly now I dedicate myself to my business. For me that is easier now that Nicaragua has had a second election and finally has a government that has been establishing better control over the army and the police and that is sympathetic to those of us who fought, to our families, and to the peasants in the mountains. When I look around at what we accomplished, finally I can be happy. Almost all the current government is made up of Nicaraguans who shared during our war our opposition to the Sandinista revolution. In fact many of our former comandos or members of the civilian Resistance are in positions ranging from cabinet ministers to low-level employees. Even more important, most if not all the violence against our people has stopped, the government is for the first time ever concentrating on helping the peasants of the mountains, and there is at least hope that from now on, as long as Nicaragua remains a democracy, we will be able to participate fully in our country's life. In fact, despite problems from 1990 through 1996, today I can almost say Nicaragua has a Resistance government and that we won the war. As to myself, I may yet someday get involved in public life. But for now I am happy just to be running my own business, without having to fear that if I succeed it will be taken from me. And for the first time in its entire history, Nicaragua is a real democracy. Was it worth twenty years of my life? Yes, I believe it was, because now we have hope for the future.

9

SARIS PÉREZ,
ANGÉLICA MARÍA

A BIOGRAPHICAL SKETCH

Saris Pérez, *Angélica María*, was one of the best known Contra woman warriors. When the Sandinistas began their final push against Somoza in 1975, she was a child of seven. When they began their revolution she was an innocent of eleven. By fourteen she was a battle-hardened combat veteran, having gone from innocent to warrior at a tender age indeed. *Angélica María* was both a winner and a loser in the process. She spent almost seven years at war and carries shrapnel in her body and bullet scars in her arms to prove it, and yet considers herself lucky because she survived and landed on her feet. Most Americans might consider washing dishes in a Miami Burger King failure. But for a mountain peasant woman from Nicaragua who spent most of her adult life at war, merely being alive, free, and in Miami is a resounding success story.

□ □ □

FROM PEASANT TO COMANDO
TO EXILE
Saris Pérez
(as told to the editor)

My full name is Saris Emilia Pérez Baldivia. Both my mother and my father were from the Baldivia family from the area of Lake Apanás in Jinotega and I grew up there. I was born in Managua because my mother was having problems, but I spent almost all my life in Jinotega. My family and I are all Catholics, needless to say. A few in my family claim Spanish blood, particularly on my grandmother's side. But most of us, just like most Nicaraguans, are really Indians, although we try not to say so because in Nicaragua to say you're an Indian is not a good thing.

I was born in November of 1969, so I was only ten years old when Somoza fell. None of my closest family had been with the Sandinistas, although several uncles had. But no one in my immediate family. I also had some family with the Somoza Guardia. One was my father's uncle Jesus and another was his uncle Jacobo, who was killed while in the Guardia. But they were distant parts of my family and lived outside the mountains. My father was from the mountains of Jinotega, the town of Asturias to be precise, and my mother from the same place. I have never been married but have been *acompañada* [accompanied, meaning had significant others] and have five children. My oldest son is fourteen years old.

When Somoza fell my father was a supervisor on a hacienda named El Embocadero owned by a family named Rodríguez. He also had his own small farm, which is supposedly the inheritance he left to us. It's fairly small, really. I remember that he raised lettuce, cabbage, beans, corn, and a little coffee. I guess you could call us coffee growers, although certainly not on a very big scale. My family was all Liberal, without a single Conservative, at least as far as I remember. We lived on the hacienda itself on the east end of Lake Apanás, not too far from the lake's hydroelectric plant. Our home was a hut the owners of the hacienda provided, with one room and a small kitchen.

The war between the Sandinistas and Somoza took place while I was still just a little girl, but I do remember some small battles toward the end that I saw personally, but not in a lot of detail. The first thing I remember happened before the fall of Somoza. It was when *Los Chavalos* ("The Kids"), the first Sandinista guerrillas, arrived in the mountains near our home. They began convincing people to identify with them by wearing Sandinista patches on their shoulders. They also told everyone they were going to help all the peasants, that Nicaragua was going to be a democracy, and that it was going to be more prosperous. The first combat I remember was in the city of Jinotega. I was there with my mother during the battle when the Sandinistas captured it and spent most of three days face down hiding in the warehouse of the Estradas, a famous coffee warehouse. It was then that I learned what bombs are and what gunfire sounded like.

Once in a while I would sneak a look outside, and several times I was watching when the Guardia killed some Sandinistas and when the Sandinistas killed some Guardia. That is the first image I have of war, people killing each other. Neither side cared whether the people they killed were civilians or soldiers, babies or old people, innocent or guilty. One time I almost died myself. There was a great deal of trauma involved. I watched several times as the Sandinistas grabbed Guardia who were disarmed and poured gasoline on them and lit them on fire, or simply shot them. Both sides would challenge people by asking them which side they were on and often confused them with their questioning. They would ask: "Who are you and whose side are you on?" Most people didn't even know who was who. So you would say: "I'm on your side," without even knowing which side they were on. Then they would ask: "Are we Guardia or Sandinista?" People often made mistakes and when they did the people questioning them would throw a grenade into their house and kill them. There were a lot of people killed that way, and a lot of other people were wounded. But we survived. After they captured Jinotega the Sandinistas put us in trucks and sent us to Las Lomas carrying white flags. After a while there, they just told us to go home. The liberation of Managua came only eight days later. But during those final days Matagalpa and Estelí, above all Estelí, were heavily bombed. I remember hearing a few big explosions.

The second time I saw a battle we were fishing down at the lake [Apanás]. We had gone fishing because we were short of food. At first it was just four or five shots. But the worst part was when an airplane arrived and began some bombing from the air. There was a small post with about seven Guardia nearby, and it was attacked by the Sandinistas who were cleaning out the Guardia from that area. When the aircraft came we ran. It was just a small airplane, but they started throwing out barrels that were on fire. They dropped most of them in the lake, so they didn't really do much besides kill fish. I also heard some small bombs go off, almost like hand grenades. It wasn't really a big battle, but I do remember that they killed some of the Guardia.

My third brush with war was less a battle that a political confrontation, but it was terribly important to me. So much so that usually I don't like even to talk about it. It happened a while after the Sandinistas liberated, or pretended to liberate, Nicaragua. It was after their literacy crusade began. They began teaching us in school that now that the Sandinistas were in charge our world was going to change. They talked against the church, against families, against the Americans—we hardly knew who they were then—and praised Fidel Castro, Cuba, and the Russians. My mother pulled us out of school and had some fights with them over what they were teaching.

One day a group of Sandinistas came by and threw a hand grenade into our yard. I was watching when it happened. My mother was picking some chayotes (a kind of squash) and the grenade exploded right next to her and tore her insides apart. It also killed my three-day-old baby brother. I knew the people who killed my mother. They were not soldiers but were sent by the

Sandinistas. They were distant relatives, a nephew, a cousin, like that. That was about a year and a half after the alleged liberation of Nicaragua. I had just celebrated my twelfth birthday. I was terribly angry and had all sort of childish fantasies of revenge. That day changed my life completely, but I didn't imagine how much, or that the changes were going to start just twenty-five days later. I still had my brothers and my father. But my father really wasn't very responsible.

The date of my mother's death was December 23, 1980. When my mother took me out of school because of the politics of the literacy campaign, for the Sandinistas that was unacceptable. I was in the fifth grade in primary school. It was not that we had done anything to resist them at that time. My mother just didn't think like they wanted her to or like what they were teaching. We were peasants and didn't normally think along those lines, certainly not at the beginning. People did make comments about how they didn't like some things that were happening, that life was tougher than before, and complained that the army was forever going from house to house looking for arms, those sorts of things. Anyone who had a .22 rifle or a pistol lost it, and lots of people were unhappy about that. My family, for example, had some hunting weapons that were all taken away by the Sandinistas.

After my mother died an uncle on her side came for me and my brothers. His name was Adrian Manzanares, and later he became a Contra and called himself *Polo*. He wound up a *comandante*. Anyhow, he arrived and took my brother Julio and me from the hacienda where we were living to the mountains where he lived, a farm he had bought in the mountains near San José de Bocay. My brothers didn't like it there and wanted to go back with my father, but my father only wanted to keep his oldest child, so my oldest brother left and the younger brothers stayed with my uncle's family, his wife, their children, and him. My father came back after a while, some months later, and took the smallest with him too, but left me there, and I began to wonder what my life was going to be like. What I was going to do. To be honest, I was also a brat, and they used to punish me a lot. I was also having nightmares about what I had seen.

Once when I was in San José de Bocay, a few months after my mother was killed, I saw small group of *chilotes* (green ears of corn; slang for Milpista). I remember watching them and thinking how neat they were and how much I would like to join them. That was the first time I learned that there was such thing as milpistas. My uncle was farming in the region where the *chilotes* were operating, and my first personal experience with the *chilotes* came a few months after that, when I had already been up in the mountains for a while, so we're talking about the first few months of 1981. One of the big problems up in the mountains was that the Sandinistas had a very hard time getting the weapons away from the peasants way up in the mountains. Instead the peasants started giving their weapons to the *chilotes,* and the first ones I met were already using them to fight against the Sandinista revolution.

Most of them were from the Sobalvarro family. *Johnny* was one. His real name was Armando. Their leader was *Rubén*, Oscar Sobalvarro, whose war name at that time was *Culebra*. Actually the group of *chilotes* I met called themselves the Culebras after him. I had met him when he was still a civilian, because the Sobalvarros had a farm right next to my grandfather's farm. The Culebras never did go around in big numbers but instead broke up into small groups so they would be safer. But it is my impression that by the time I first met them they may have had as many as eighty people with them in the mountains.

The next group I met was that of *Tigrillo* when they passed by my house. There were not too many fighters with him but I remember that one of them was a woman fighter by the name of *La Chaparra* ("Shorty"). I think she was the very first woman fighter because she had already been with the *chilotes* for quite a while when I met her. Her war name at that time was *Yamaliet*.[1] She was one of those who started at the very beginning and continued fighting throughout the war, even though one of her brothers was captured and another killed. She was one of the very first comando fighters.

Once the *chilotes* began fighting in earnest, my uncle decided to go with them. He had been providing them with help before but finally decided to become a guerrilla himself. The *chilotes* did not have uniforms. They used whatever kind of clothing they had, and for arms they used hunting weapons or rifles, whatever they could capture, FALs from the Sandinistas, 12-gauge shotguns, .45-caliber pistols, whatever they could get. They even sometimes used .22-caliber hunting rifles. Sometimes they wore white shirts, sometimes they were cream-colored, sometimes they were just really dirty. When I first met them they were all wearing rubber boots and ordinary civilian pants and civilian clothes. When I first met *La Chaparra*, she was carrying a pistol that was so old I wondered if it could even be fired, and it was the only weapon she had. She was the first woman comando I met. There may have been others but for me she was the first.[2]

I was still a child, just twelve years old. But you have to understand that country peasant girls like me in those days were much more innocent than city girls. We didn't even know what adults talked about. The thing I can remember best is that when I first met *Tigrillo*'s group I really liked their weapons. I also liked the idea there was a woman with them. It was then that I first got the idea to become a guerrilla. I was angry about my mother's death, and my idea was to join them, get myself a gun, and go kill the people who had killed her. I didn't say a thing to anybody, not even my uncle or at first even to the Culebras that came by. After all, what where they going to think anyhow? I was just a little girl.

There were Sandinistas around the area too. They even had a small base nearby because they had begun taking farms away from anybody who had a little bit of money and using them for themselves, and they needed a base to keep control over the properties they had taken. The base was called La Rivera. It was an army base, not a state security base. We called them compas (short for *companero*, or comrade). We didn't call them *los Cha-valos* anymore.

But that time I didn't actually do anything. It was only after I saw the first really big group of comandos, about 80, that I decided to act. Like the first group I had seen before, it was also under the command of *Tigrillo*. It was, to be exact, New Year's Day of 1982 when they came by. This time they were wearing blue uniforms and they were very well equipped.[3] Each one was carrying a brand-new FAL rifle. They all had packs, web belts, comando knives, and brand-new jungle boots. I thought, that's the way to go to war. I wasn't sure where they were coming from but they said they were coming out of their bases in the mountains of Nicaragua. They came into our region, into our part of the mountains, and began establishing their safe areas there. The group stayed around my uncle's house only two days and left on the second of January.

I decided to go with them. I packed up some food and clothing in a backpack that I already had, a sheet to sleep on, and a few personal things and simply walked over to their camp. It was all very simple. They just let me join them. I stayed with them for the next several months. While they were at our house I had talked with several of the guerrillas about whether not I should go with them. But I didn't ask their permission, I just told them I was going with them. My grandfather got very upset by my decision and argued with me, saying I really didn't know what I was getting into or what might happen to the people I left behind, but I went anyhow.

He was right about what might happen to those I left behind because the Sandinistas came and captured him and held him for about three days at their base in San José de Bocay. Then they took him to another base where they had even more troops. When they got into the second base, they hung him upside down by his feet for several days because they thought he had sent me to fight with the Contras. As far as the Sandinistas were concerned, anybody who was not with them was a Contra. Anyone who was not actively helping them out or anybody who didn't agree with every one of their moves and did not support them, as far as they were concerned, they were free to kill. Once I joined *Tigrillo*'s group, the first small group (squad) I joined was led by a member of the Zeláya family (another of the major highland's clans) who had become a guerrilla with *Rubén*. He called himself *Iván* and was to become a top *comandante*. But then he was just another *chilote*. His family was from down around Jinotega. When I reached their base, there was another woman comando whose war name was *Darling*. She was with a group led by a commander named *Relámpago* ("Lightning"). I don't remember her last name, but I do remember she was one of the very first *chilotes*.

After I went with *Tigrillo*'s group, more and more people kept joining us in the mountains. I remember that within a very short time we had almost 700. For four months in the mountains I was a guerrilla but wasn't armed. We were mostly around the area north of Jinotega. We moved almost every day, and sometimes every night as well. During those four months we had three different battles. There were three of us civilian women, the very first women to join *Tigrillo*'s group. At first we were kept busy carrying food to the troops. I remember once that I was carrying a big bowl of cooked beans and rice up to the soldiers when the Sandinistas opened fire and shot the pot of beans right out of my hands. Beans went everywhere! That was my introduction to combat, and it was really too bad because I remember they were very good beans.

A few months later they took me to their base in Las Vegas, which was actually in southern Honduras. There was another group of men there I didn't know, already in training. Las Vegas was like almost any military base. When I first arrived it was fairly small, but we built it into a large one. We went through a course of almost seven months' training. At Las Vegas there were no differences between those who were armed and not armed. If you said you wanted to fight, they asked you if you knew what you were getting into. If you said yes, they would describe combat. If you still wanted to go, they would then say okay. There was no forced recruiting or anything like that. After we arrived in Honduras, my commander was named *Yankee*. I don't even remember what his real name was or where he was from, just that he was killed later in the war.

My father was still back in Nicaragua at the time. When the Sandinista army started forcibly recruiting people, they grabbed him and forced him to enter the Sandinista army. But he drank a lot and began to talk in favor of the Contras. My oldest brother was running at that time to escape from the Sandinista army, and when he was drunk my father began saying "if you keep me here I'm going to run away and join the Contras." So instead they took him out and shot him. They put thirty bullets in him altogether and then took his weapon and put it on his chest and took pictures of him and said he had died fighting for his country against the Contras. But the truth is that the Sandinistas killed him. There was a rabid Sandinista who was a member of my father's family and who was there and gave the orders to kill my father. I believe he was killed in late 1983. By then I was already an armed comando with the Contras.

After training I joined *Mike Lima* (Luís Moreno Payán) at Base Ariél. That was almost at the end of 1983. *Mike Lima*'s people came to the Las Vegas base to talk to *Rubén*'s people, who were right next to us. At that time he had only about sixty men with him. But there were so many people arriving at the base that the growth was very fast and there were armed people all over the place. Supposedly those with *Mike Lima* were a mixture from different groups. There were other groups, too, like the Sagitarios and the Zébras. The Zébras were the only one that was mostly former Guardia, and a lot of us were nervous around them.[4] There were so many people it's hard to remember. But I remember that almost everybody in the mountains started either supporting the Contras or going to the bases for training.

After completing training everyone was allowed to decide which group they wanted to join, within reason. I joined *Mike Lima*'s group because I thought he would be a good commander. You have to remember that our army was made up entirely of volunteers, and we were under no obligation to fight or even to stay, except of course when you were inside, and then you were not allowed to desert. No one could say you had to be a fighter. Only those who wanted to be combatants became combatants. Those who didn't had no pressure put on them to join. And even after you were a combatant, if you didn't want to go to the war but wanted to stay in the rear base, you could do that too. The problem was if you stayed behind you had to work in the kitchen or do laundry, and I didn't want to do either one.

I remember one time while I was at Base Ariél with *Mike Lima* some officer came and told me early one morning that I had to go make tortillas. I followed his orders, but I wasn't happy. One of my commanders saw me and came across to my table and looked at me and said: "Do you want to be a comando or a cook?" I said I wanted to be a comando, not make tortillas. He said: "Then go back to bed," which I did. I remember that his war name was *Pollo* ("Chicken"). Later that day another officer came and asked me whether I wanted to fight or stay behind. I said I wanted to fight. He said fine, then don't ever go back to the kitchen, which made be very happy. At the base our life was fairly happy. We would dance almost every night, which is something I very much enjoyed doing. You have to remember I was just a young girl, although I still like the bands today. But at the base those who were fighters were fighters, and I wanted to be a fighter.

I stayed with the Arieles for a while and then became a member of the Diriangéns and went inside Nicaragua and into combat with that group, with a task force commanded by *Mike Lima*. My immediate commander was *Sereno*. I also fought under the command of *Cinco Pinos* for a while. I never did know their real names. It was about three months after I finished training. There were lots of women with my task force, 14 or 15 as I remember among about 160 comandos.[5] One who went in was in my squad. Her name was named *Judy*, but she was the girlfriend of the commanding officer, so we called her *La Retopina* [unprintable]. Just before we left some of the commanders came over to see us off. That was the first time I'd met Enrique Bermúdez, *Comandante*

Column of FDN (Contra) from Task Force Cinco Pinos, inside Nicaragua. *Angélica María*, the woman comando whose story is told in this chapter, was serving in this unit at the time. The FAL rifles, uniforms, and Caribbean pines in the background indicate it was taken in the Segovian mountains, circa 1983. Courtesy ACRN.

3-80, "Negro" Chamorro, and a couple of the other top leaders of our army.

Infiltrating into Nicaragua was very tough. We left at night and had to fight just to get across the border through the Sandinistas' border defenses. Then we had to fight our way all the way to our area of operations, because each task force was assigned a specific area in which it was supposed to operate. But the toughest part was getting across the border. The rest was relatively easy. Once in our zone of operation we moved constantly, but we were fed by the local peasants and had a lot less problems. One of the hardest things was that we had to carry everything with us. For example, one time we had 81-mm mortars, and I had to help carry the mortar, ammunition for it, plus my own rifle. Other times I carried machine gun ammunition.

My rifle was a FAL with a black plastic stock. There were others that had wooden stocks, but I had one of the better ones. I'd carry it, 500 rounds of ammunition, six hand grenades, an extra uniform and pair of boots, and a compass that someone had given me. I didn't know how to use it but I carried it always. I also carried a first aid kit and food for the first couple of weeks. Besides our personal items we carried things for comandos who were already inside. My pack was so heavy that if I tried just to pick it up today it probably would knock me over. But I was young and very enthusiastic and could carry it for days on end. It was never easy, but I could do it. Today I could not even begin to do that. Those packs were really heavy! The advantage we had later when we got AK-47s was that we did not have to carry in very much ammunition for them because we could capture almost as much as we needed. But when we had the FALs we had to carry in all our own ammunition. In addition, we also carried our personal items. For example, of each of us carried a comando knife and a plate, knife, and fork for eating. We also had toothpaste, soap, and, in the case of the women, Kotex, which was sent to us by the general staff.

That first time we infiltrated it took us twenty-three hours of constant combat and running to get in across the border, fighting constantly. But I loved it, I suppose because I kept thinking that I was going in to avenge my mother. But I really did like it. If I hadn't liked it so much I would have left the ranks of the combatants, but I did enjoy it. I also began asking myself other questions. How could we get the Sandinista Front out of power? How far were they going to go doing what they were doing to us? The more I thought, the more I wanted to fight. The only alternative to surrendering and letting them have the country was to fight, and that's why I wanted to do it. I was just a simple infantry fighter in the front lines, a guerrilla fighter, one of two women who were front-line fighters in a group [company] of sixty.

It was incredible how fast our forces grew and how many Contras we had in our area. We were supported by all the local population. We had more than enough food given to us by the peasants to eat all we wanted every day. We had safety zones within our areas of operations where we were especially safe. But almost anywhere inside our area of operations we had lots of support from the civil population and were constantly in contact with them. The civilians would come looking for us and bring us food. They might kill a cow for us. They would bring us information. They would come tell us where the Sandinistas were, what they were doing, where they were going, which groups of Contras they were chasing, and so forth. They were our connection to everything.

After we got into our area of operations on my first mission, we rested for a few days and then attacked a place called El Cuá. There were a lot of people living in the area, and most of the people in my unit were from there as well. In that sector there were a lot of other people fighting besides us. *Tigrillo* was one of them, as well as the MILPAS of *Pichardo* and *El Venádo*.

My first combat was an ambush. I was scared but managed to control myself. Anyone who says they aren't scared is lying. With so many bullets flying around, you never know when there would be one with your name on it. I also knew what a bullet could do to someone. But I fought nonetheless. Mostly I just shot my FAL and watched the comando next to me to see what he did, because I wasn't about to stay fighting all by myself. We had a signal already prepared for when we should withdraw, so we would know when to retire. Three men on our side were killed, and I believe at least four were killed on the Sandinista side. We were actually probably better trained than the Sandinistas were. They were mostly just a bunch of young kids. After that, I was in so many different battles that it would take three days just to list all of them.

After a few months I went back to the base in Honduras and they sent me to a leadership course, and then back into Nicaragua with another unit as a small unit leader [roughly squad leader]. That's the way I went through the war, going into Nicaragua to fight and then returning. On one of my returns I went to the paramedic school, which I found very interesting. When I finished the paramedic school I was assigned to another task force named the Nicaráo and went back inside for a very large operation known as Operation Maratón. I didn't like being a paramedic as much as being a combatant, so after that operation I went back to being a front-line soldier up in the mountains.

On my next trip back to base they sent me to still another school on how to be a radio operator. That was when I joined *Comandante Rubén*. I became his personal radio operator up in the mountains after his earlier radio operator had been killed. I was selected because I was also a front-line combatant and knew about war. By then *Comandante Rubén* had his own base. After a while I went back into Honduras again, helping to escort several hundred new men, and then rejoined *Mike Lima* and became a basic training supervisor [drill instructor]. I trained all the front-line soldiers, not just the women.

I remember that at that point there was a Guatemalan army officer who began teaching a Ranger course. I was the only woman who went to it. I had my doubts that I would be able to go through the training, but *Rubén* said I was perfectly capable, so I accepted the assignment. I was the only woman they thought could do it, and I did. The Ranger course was tough. We had to run through some very difficult obstacle courses, and there were lots of problems with barbed wire, mine fields, and night operations. There were eighty students, my number was 43, and only half of us made it through. We graduated on Holy Week. They didn't give us diplomas or anything. All they did was have a parade. But they did invite the TV and some newspapermen from the United States, Central America, and everywhere, so I imagine even some Sandinistas came to watch us graduate.

The only time after that I left my main unit, the Diriangens, was to go for a short time with "Chele" Douglas. But I didn't really enjoy it as much as I did my own unit, so I went back to mine. Altogether I spent five years with *Rubén*, and his brother Danielo was my direct commander for the rest of the war. Up until that time I had been wounded a few times in combat, but never badly.

Saris Pérez, *Angélica María,* wearing her Ranger beret just after graduation from the Guatemalan Escuela Caibil (Ranger School). Courtesy Saris Pérez.

There was one combat experience I remember especially. It happened on a special patrol when I went inside with *Campeón*. It was one of the few times I went in after Ranger school without *Rubén* or his brother. You need to remember that it was all voluntary and we didn't always have to go with the same people if someone else wanted you to go with them or you wanted to join with someone else. I tried to avoid staying in the base. So instead of going back to Honduras I went inside with *Campeón*. That was in 1987. We got into a very difficult fight at a place called Cerro Helado. The battle started at 5:00 in the morning precisely. I remember the time so well because just before we had been in another battle and I had taken a radio from one of the Sandinistas who was killed. I was listening to music on the Sandinista's radio, and they announced the time just as the shooting started. I had to run and leave the radio behind. The battle lasted for four hours and didn't end until about 9:00 in the morning. We lost two men while according to our intelligence sources we killed seven of the Sandinistas. We didn't actually recover the bodies so we weren't certain.

By then I had decided that I just wanted to be in the infantry at the front and was tired of doing special jobs. I didn't want to be a paramedic, take people meals, or be a radio operator. But during the battle at Cerro Helado all the officers in my unit were killed so I took command and did a good enough job that *Rubén* offered me a field promotion to *comandante*, but I told him I didn't want to have responsibility for others. I said that when I decide to run away I want to be free to run by myself. But I did have the chance to become a *comandante* if I had wanted.

I remember that the men used to brag that they were never scared. Maybe they weren't. But I was every time I went into combat. I supposed some might think that means women are too scared to go into combat, but I think it just means women talk differently and say what we really feel. Anyone who is in combat is afraid, unless they are very foolish. I got along very well with my male companions in combat. The relation between men and women in combat is perfectly normal. It's only those outside of the war who think it's strange. Sex really doesn't matter very much. In my case I usually had a *liga*, who was like a husband, and all the other comandos respected us as if we were a married couple even though we really were not. It was fairly informal, of course, because if either one of us wanted to change partners there was really no problem. Sometimes someone's companion would get killed. But that wasn't a problem of sex, that was simply a problem of combat. I lost one of my companions who was named *Félix*, who said he was a Guardia and told me had been trained in Argentina. His family is from Ocotal.

Returning to the question of women in battle, there really wasn't anything a woman couldn't do in combat. The men and women were the same, period. Both of us sometimes cried. Both of us sometimes ran. It really made no difference what your sex was, we were treated the same. There was no difference because I was a woman. I can't speak for the whole army, but they treated me just like they did everyone else. I did my guard posts, I ran for food, I did everything the men did. There also was no difference in the training.

Women in the combat units were expected to act and work just the same as a man. If a woman wanted to go the combat route, she had to carry her own load. It was a guerrilla force, and there wasn't anything else to do. You went to the bathroom and took baths along with everyone else. Nobody really paid any attention when you satisfied your needs or whether you had clothes on or not when you took a bath. Baths were too rare, and nobody was looking to see what you had. It was perfectly normal. No one was looking to see if that woman was skinny or if that man was naked or what. We just took our baths, because as soldiers and guerrillas we had no choice. If we had been divided into sections of women and men and not mixed into the same units, then I suppose there might have been more of a problem and more attention paid to sex. But we were all mixed together in a military force and no one really paid very much attention one way or another about things like that

We did have sex, of course. But for that we had contraceptives. Many of us took a shot that they began giving us in 1993. It was called "deproprobera" or something like that. I remember that it worked very well. They told us that they were going to give us vitamins and some of the women believed them, but not very many. They didn't force us, they just asked who wanted it. I told them yes. One of the reasons I did it was because when you have children and are a combat soldier, it's difficult when you go back into combat and have to leave them behind. Many of the women comandos when they had children would decide to stay back and not return to combat. Others who went back couldn't find anyone they trusted to leave their children with and worried about them constantly. There were cases where babies left behind died. I thank the Lord all of my children survived.

Probably my worst experiences during the war came toward the end. We were coming into Nicaragua from Honduras in 1988, near the end of the war, when I was finally badly wounded. I was still with the Regional Force Diriangens. The Sandinistas had

Two unidentified women FDN comandos, one with a baby in her arms, head for the front during March 1988 multibattalion attack by the Sandinista army against the FDN's last bastion in the Bocay wilderness that immediately followed the last U.S. congressional cutoff of lethal aid to them. Brown, *The Real Contra War*, chapter 12. Photo courtesy HAF.

spotted us about 3:00 p.m. the day before. We got away, but started being bombarded more or less continuously by rockets and artillery, and one of their patrols was following us very closely. For most of the day all that was between us and them was a hill. At 5:00 a.m. we had a short skirmish with them, and my commander *Jimmy Léo* said we had to head up the mountain to try to escape, but, if we had to fight, we had to fight. As I reached the top of the mountain a Sandinista came up in front of me from the other side. I fell backward and so did he, but someone behind me tossed a hand grenade and the piris shot an RPG at us, which exploded next to me and threw me farther down the mountain. I woke up with three bullet holes in my legs and shrapnel in my arms. Three comandos had carried me out, or they would have killed me up there. We lost sixteen comandos altogether. The precise location was a place we called La Pita de Ventillo, which is at the very top of the mountains. It took me three months to recover from my wounds, and I only survived thanks to the paramedics who were with us.

But despite my wounds I stayed inside with the forces because I wasn't about to go to Honduras or give up my rifle. Others helped carry my pack and gear. I just carried a pistol. Once I was recovered from the wounds I went back to the infantry, although I never did completely recover and still have inflammations. The day I was wounded was the first day when the first meetings took place between the Sandinistas and Contra commanders in Sapoá. I stayed inside the combat zone when we finally arranged a cease-fire and was wounded again that same day. We were in an area around a place called La Vígia. During the three months of the supposed cease-fire the Sandinistas attacked us several times. I never saw a Sandinista as worried as one officer who came to see us after one of the attacks. He promised that if the cease-fire worked they would not fire their 105-mm artillery at us. But what he really did was give me the impression that actually the Sandinistas did not want to keep fighting. He was very senior, although I don't remember his rank. After that I went back to Honduras and said I had done my part and wanted to stay out. I was assigned to

the general staff as a human rights officer, then to the G3 operations section and worked as a map coordinator until we laid down
our arms.[6] By then I was pregnant with my son Javier.

I demobilized in the security zone of Yalí, but I don't remember the exact date, although it was in 1990. After demobilizing I
went to work in the town of Waslála, then moved to Jinotega and
tried to get my father's farm back for my brothers and me, but
that didn't work. So then I decided to go to Managua, where I
found a job as a maid. By then a number of the *comandantes* were
in Managua and *Rubén* invited me to work in an office with them,
so that's what I did. I became the telephone operator in the offices
of the ACRN and then went over to the OAS [CIAV/OAS], where
I worked as a radio operator.

When I look back on my life I see it as interesting. I liked the
war, I liked the rifles, I liked the fighting. I did not like demobilization at all because it brought bigger problems of all sorts. They
gave almost no help to the former combatants. I wasn't interested
in money, but I did have to restart my life and didn't get any help
to do that. The second thing I didn't like about demobilization
and disarming, mostly disarming, was that we laid down our guns
but the Sandinistas didn't, so after that they did anything they
wanted to do to us. In my own case I received threats by telephone, they attacked my house, they tried to kill me two or three
times when I was trying to get my father's farm back because they
wanted to keep it. That proved impossible anyway for the simple
reason that all the courts and all the judges were Sandinista ap-
pointees and would never give anything back to anyone who had
opposed them regardless of what happened during the elections
in 1990.

I finally left Nicaragua as an exile and came to Miami on July
30, 1996. I had tried for six years to get my life started again in
Nicaragua. While I was working for international organizations
the Sandinistas didn't bother me. But afterward they began to
screw with me. They stole things from me and attacked my house
and me. They even stole a pickup from my house that belonged
to *Rubén*. They persecuted me because they knew I believed in

human rights and wanted to put Sandinista violators in jail and knew what I was talking about.

I think there is going to be another war in Nicaragua because they have not made a good peace. People are suffering, above all the peasants. It's always the peasants who pay the consequences of other people's ideas. They have to support them, they have to support poverty, they have to support manipulation by people like the Sandinistas, then they have to support their exploiters. It's always the peasant who is abused. If the people in the city go on strike the people hurt are the peasants because they can't ship their crops. If the hospitals don't have medicine they give what they do have first to people in the cities and the peasants do without. It's all very sad. In Nicaragua today people say there is no war now, but that is only true in the cities. There is still a war going on in the mountains, except that now the Sandinistas have all the guns and keep killing people so others have to try to protect themselves. But since it all is happening deep in the mountains people don't see it and think there is no war when there is.

I thank the Lord that since I arrived in the United States I've done fairly well in the sense that I have received no more threats, have my papers in order to become a resident, have a job, and my *liga* and children are safe. I could have expected just the opposite had I remained in Nicaragua. I have to work and pay for my house, just like everyone does here. I have no intention of going back to Nicaragua because I think it would turn out very badly for me. All I hope for now is to be left alone and allowed to live here in the United States in peace.

10

SALOMÓN OSORNO COLEMAN, COMANDANTE BLASS

A BIOGRAPHICAL SKETCH

Comandante Blass, whose real name is Salomón Osorno Coleman, is an ethnic Miskito Indian who was born in the hamlet of Kum on the Rio Coco in the region of Waspám on the North Atlantic of Nicaragua on October 6, 1954. He received both his primary and secondary education through high school in the Nicaraguan Mosquitia. By the time he graduated, he was already an active Indian combatant in the war against the Sandinista revolution. In 1987 *Blass* was elected General Commander of YATAMA, the Miskito Indian Resistance (Contra) army and led this second largest of all Native American armies of the twentieth century (only Emiliano Zapata's was larger) into combat from then until 1990. After more than ten years at war he resettled himself and his family within Nicaragua. He did advanced studies at the Instituto Centroamericano de Administración de Empresas (INCAE), Harvard's Central American School for Business Administration in 1991, then went to the Catholic University in Managua and received a dual degree in law and social sciences in 1999. He is the president of the Miskito Indians' veterans' organization YAAD (Yatama Aiklakla Almok Daknika). *Comandante Blass* writes from two perspectives, his personal worldview and that of his Miskito Indian people. In his case even more than others, his cultural origin as a Native American assures that the two are inextricably intertwined.

□ □ □

MY PEOPLE, OUR WAR:
WHY I FOUGHT AGAINST THE
SANDINISTA REVOLUTION
Salomón Osorno Coleman

A Brief Geographic and Demographic Description of the Mosquitia

Because the Nicaraguan Mosquitia and its peoples are poorly known outside of Nicaragua, before discussing our reasons for engaging in guerrilla activities against the Sandinista revolution and the problems we have had even after the revolution ended, I think it would be useful to provide a brief description of the region in which we live. Geographically, the Mosquitia is situated on the Atlantic coastal plains of Nicaragua along the country's Caribbean coast. With a total land area of 61,320 square kilometers, it occupies 47 percent of the national territory. It has a mostly hot tropical climate, although there are some hills in a region we called the Three Mines (*Tres Minas*) in which it is a little cooler and which are physically more like the central mountain region than the coast. Rainfall is quite heavy, ranging from two meters in the north to as high as six meters a year in the extreme southeast. As a consequence, more than 95 percent of all the riverine waters of Nicaragua flow through the Mosquitia, giving it the country's most important river system. All these rivers empty into the Atlantic Ocean into what is known as the Caribbean Sea. Despite its size the Mosquitia's population is relatively small. It has only 370,000 inhabitants, representing just 6 percent of the nation, making it the most lightly populated region in the country. The Mosquitia's social structure is well defined and based on multiculturalism and many ethnicities, with numerous components having their own identities, languages, land tenure systems, local government patterns, and means of economic activity.

In addition to being the home to most of Nicaragua's rivers, the Atlantic coastal region also has many open areas, swamps, lakes, and wetlands that contribute to an impressive variety of economic activity in the region. There are also in the Mosquitia extensive wet tropical forests that are important to its economic potential and also are the key to the conservation of its ecosystems and the biodiversity of its animal and plant life, including in particular those with food value, commercial importance, or scientific potential. In addition, the region has the country's most important gold deposits in the mining region around Rosita, Siuna, and Bonanza, which make it important because of its natural resources.

Indigenous Presence in the Mosquitia by Ethnic Group

The most important indigenous people of the Nicaragua Mosquitia are the Miskito Indians, who number about 170,000. Most live in small communities along the banks of its rivers, in particular the Rio Coco, along the Caribbean Coast from Cabo Gracias a Dios in the north to the banks of the Rio Grande de Matagalpa and Laguna de Perlas in the south. There are also Miskito communities in the municipalities of Rosita, Siuna, and Bonanza, the mining district, and at Waspám, Bílwi, and Prinzapolka. Important settlements include Wankí, Tasba Ráya, Raudales de Jinotega, Llano Sur and Llano Norte, and along the Prinzapolka and Matagalpa Rivers.

The Sumu Indians are the second largest indigenous community, numbering about 15,000, and live in thirty-two communities located along seven rivers, the Bambana, Tunki, Pipis, Uly, Waspúk, Khwahbúl, and Bocay. There are also some 1,000 Rama, a fast disappearing tribe, who live in five small communities south of Bluefields known as Rama Kay, Wiring Kay, Tursuani, Cane Creek, and Punta Gorda. The fourth major ethnic group are the Garífuna, of whom about 1,500 live in Nicaragua in seven communities located around Laguna de Perlas: La Fé, Orinoco, San Vicente, Wawa Shang, Marshall Point, and Brown Bank. The remainder of people in the Mosquitia all are either Spaniards[1] or descendants of black Africans who arrived after the wreck of a slave ship taking blacks from Africa and who escaped into the bush when the ship ran aground.

Political Divisions of the Mosquitia and a Recent Change in Its Name

Until 1987 the entire Atlantic was included in one department, or province, known as Zeláya. That year the National Assembly approved Law 28, known as the Statute of Autonomy for the Atlantic Coast of Nicaragua, which divided Zeláya into two regions, North and South. The North Atlantic Autonomous Region, or RAAN, has its capital at the city of Bílwi, better known as Puerto Cabezas. The Caribbean lies to the region's east and the South Atlantic Autonomous Region, or RAAS, to its south, with the dividing line along the Rio Grande de Matagalpa. To the west of the RAAN lie the departments of Jinotega and Matagalpa, which hold Nicaragua's largest indigenous populations.[2] The RAAS has its capital in the city of Bluefields, with the RAAN to its north, the Caribbean to the east, the department of Rio San Juan to the south, and to the west Chontales. This region has the largest population of black Creoles.

The Early History of the Mosquitia

To understand why my people fought against the Sandinista revolution, it is important first to understand our history and origins, because they are what created our ethnic identity and led to the development of our particular cultural, linguistic, political, and religious characteristics. The people of the Atlantic regions differ in culture and origins from the rest of the people of Nicaragua, something that the elite governing class and the rest of the country have not wished to understand and chosen to ignore.

When in 1502 Christopher Columbus visited the Atlantic Coast of Central America, he found it already inhabited by Miskito and Sumu Indians. After his visit, the Spanish conquered Pacific-Coast Nicaragua. But they never conquered the Atlantic.[3] Despite their military and religious efforts, the Spanish were unable to conquer the indigenous population of the region, which remained unconquered throughout the colonial period. The first important foreigners to establish themselves in the region were the English in 1633. In 1641, the wreck mentioned earlier took place, and the escaping blacks very quickly intermingled with the native American Indians. The region then became important to the English, who regularly used the people of the Mosquitia as their allies against the Spanish, which was made quite easy because of the cruelty with which the Spanish traditionally treated the Indians on the Pacific Coast. This history also facilitated alliances between the Miskito Indians and pirates who attacked the Spanish. In the seventeenth century English, Dutch, and other pirates freely used the territory of the Atlantic Coast as a refuge and a center of operations for incursions against the Spanish settlements on the Pacific Coast, in particular to the south and Rio San Juan and as far inland as Granada.

In 1687, as a consequence of extensive contact between the Miskito Indians, the English, and the pirates, the region developed a very close relationship with the outside world based on exchanges of goods, the availability of arms, and other mutually beneficial trade. It was for this reason that in that year the English decided to support the creation of a Miskito kingdom, fashioned roughly on the English model. That year the first Miskito monarch, King Jeremy I, was crowned as king of the Mosquitia, and England recognized the Mosquitia as an independent community under English protection. The dynasty lasted until the nineteenth century, and the English used it quite ruthlessly to exploit the natural resources of the region, neither leaving permanent benefits for the people nor paying taxes. As a consequence the Miskito kings were really just puppets of the English and had neither economic nor political power, and the English exploited this to extract the riches of the region.

It was not until 1860 when the Zeledón–Wyke Treaty was

signed in Managua that England renounced its protectorate, which allowed Nicaragua to create the Miskito reserve. But even then it took an additional thirty-four years, and it was not until 1894 that Nicaragua actually drew the Mosquitia into its national territory, doing so by military occupation of Bluefields. To justify this annexation by force, Nicaraguan military authorities, under the direction of Liberal President Jose Santos Zeláya, called a Miskito convention to ratify a treaty of annexation of the indigenous communities. The evidence indicates that although ratification was obtained, this was done against the will of the indigenous participants, who were forced to sign the treaty. Among other things, the Nicaraguan authorities used intimidation, inadequate translations, large-scale distribution of alcoholic beverages, and bribes to convince Miskitos to sign. The legitimate representatives of the indigenous communities were not present, casting doubts on the legal validity of the ratification, which is also replete with defects. There is no doubt that this forced incorporation of the Mosquitia into the nation violated the rights and traditions of the indigenous population. There is also little doubt that it was not sufficient to lead to either transculturation or assimilation. But even though neither took place, from 1894 to 1987 the Nicaraguan state refused to recognize the ethnic diversity of the nation and regularly claimed Nicaragua was a mestizo country.[4]

As a consequence of these historical events, the indigenous peoples of the Mosquitia found it necessary to come together to support a single regional organization with clear and defined objectives for the purpose of demanding that their historical rights be recognized, based as they are on 1,000-year-old experience and on natural law. This is why ALPROMISU came to be created.

The Sandinista Revolution—Hope Turns to Despair

ALPROMISU was created in the small towns or city of Waspám in the same municipality on the Rio Coco in 1973, and in the community of Sisín, by a group of tribal elders and ministers of the Moravian and Catholic churches from that municipality.

Its roots can be found in the marginalization of the Indian people of the region and their treatment as citizens of the lowest class in cultural, economic, and social terms by both the Spanish mestizos and Chinese business people of the region, as well as by others who were not themselves indigenous persons. The objective of ALPROMISU was to demand from the government and other sectors of society recognition of the historic rights of the indigenous communities of the region, including political rights. When the Sandinista revolution succeeded in mid-1979, most of those who had been exploiting the region left. But rather than recognizing and honoring the rights of the indigenous peoples, the Sandinista government merely became the new exploiters of the region's natural resources and used the Atlantic Coast to find positions of command and decision-making responsibilities for their own mid-level leaders. This quickly began to create resentment among the local population.

It was during the first few months of the Sandinista revolution that a second organization was created to replace ALPROMISU. Known as MISURASATA, the acronym for Miskitos, Súmus, Ramas, and Sandinistas United, it was created in Puerto Cabezas on November 11, 1979, founded in hopes that with the Sandinista revolution the indigenous peoples of the region would be able to change their ways of life, improve their standards of living, and become full and equal citizens of Nicaragua. We believed we would be able to vote, to obtain benefits from our own natural resources in a more equitable manner, and would be treated differently and better than we had been by the governments that preceded the Sandinistas. We made this assumption because the Sandinistas had preached social justice and equality and spoken so often about the need to solve the problems of the poor that we felt they would also solve the problems of the indigenous peoples of Nicaragua.

To our great regret, once they gained power the Sandinistas demonstrated that their message had simply been a form of propaganda designed to help them win the war with the support of the people and that they had no intention of keeping their promises. What they established instead was a Communist–Marxist government principally committed to defending the interests of the senior *comandantes* of the Sandinista movement and dedicated to promoting the interest of international communism. It was because of this that a new conflict emerged between the Sandinistas and the indigenous peoples of the Atlantic Coast.

It became clear very quickly that the primary objective of the Sandinista Front was to implant Marxism in Nicaragua. They had joined in the creation of MISURASATA only because they wanted a mass popular organization to promote their objectives. But the system they were attempting to implant clashed directly with the culture, beliefs, and traditional customs of the people of the indigenous communities, and it soon became clear that MISURASATA would not support their objectives. As a consequence, the Sandinistas quickly began to call it an organization in the service of the American CIA and charging that it was dedicated to separating the Atlantic Coast from the Pacific. They also began calling it a counterrevolutionary organization and even accused its leaders of being Somocistas; they began applying punitive measures against those of its leaders not prepared to go along with the Sandinistas' plans.

As these punitive measures became more and more drastic, they produced a conflict of expectations between the governing Sandinistas and the indigenous peoples of the Atlantic. Among the active measures applied by the Sandinistas in their efforts to control the situation in the Atlantic, they put many of the Miskito and Súmu leaders of MISURASATA in jail, closed its principal offices in the administrative capitals of the municipalities of the region, prohibited all meetings by Miskito Indians, and flew army troops in from Managua to reinforce those already in the region. The purpose of all these measures was to threaten the indigenous peoples and force them to accept the social and political programs the government wished to impose on them.

In April of 1980 the conflict turned violent. The Sandinistas imposed a state of siege in the region, and army troops moved into the indigenous communities. MISURASATA, the indigenous peoples' umbrella organization, was decapitated by the jailing of many of its remaining key leaders. Those who escaped fled across Nicaragua's northern border into Honduras or southward into Costa Rica. A few young men went into the mountains. This spread the conflict throughout the region, and news of confrontations between the Sandinistas and the indigenous peoples of the Atlantic reached even the international press. The [Moravian] Church later tried to mediate the conflict but could not find acceptable grounds for negotiation between the two parties because of the level of repression by the Sandinista army and state security.

My Personal Political and Military Participation

At first my own participation during this period was ambiguous. In November of 1980, even though the conflict between my peoples and the Sandinista revolution was already under way, I became a member of the youth branch of MISURASATA. But it soon became obvious to me that the Sandinista revolution was on a collision course with my Miskito people, and I decided to abandon attempts to cooperate with them and instead fled, together with thirty-four others, including Stedman Fagoth, at that time the principal leader of MISURASATA, to Honduras. When we arrived we immediately contacted other groups that were already in that country, that is to say other Miskito Indians who had preceded us. That was on May 9, 1981. We fled because of the unyielding persecution of my people by Sandinista state security and their repression of all the indigenous peoples of the Mosquitia.

At that point I abandoned the peaceful approach to struggle and joined the ranks of the new guerrillas, as then not even named, made up of young Miskito Indians preparing to fight against the Sandinistas militarily. After a short period of training, in December of 1981 I participated in my first action, the occupation of Sandinista positions in the communities of Raití, San Carlos del Rio Coco, and other positions they had taken on the upper Rio Coco. The Sandinistas called these skirmishes Operation Red Christmas and used them as a pretext to force the peoples of the upper Rio Coco to abandon their homes and all their worldly goods. The Sandinistas then burned their homes and killed their domestic animals. All those peasants who had been unable to escape fell into the claws of the Sandinista People's Army and were taken to concentration camps, which with great irony were called Tasba Prí, a Miskito word meaning "The Promised Land," a name that became a bitter joke among the peoples of the Atlantic. Most of those who escaped this Sandinista People's Army [EPS] sweep crossed the Rio Coco and became refugees in Honduras.

In 1982 I became the S-4 (logistics chief) of the Leymus Region, comprised of Sisín, Sandy Bay, Slima Lila, Waspám, Kum, and Livinkrik (Living Creek), which was my home territory. This operational region covered more than 12,000 square kilometers and was garrisoned by Sandinista People's Army frontier guards.

Comandante Fermán, brother of Salomón Osorno Coleman, with AK-47, Miskito Indian YATAMA, seeking cover beneath savanna grasses in an open area of the Mosquitia circa 1987. Courtesy YAAD.

From then until 1985 I was also a field commander, leading a unit of 120 guerrillas, and spent all my time fighting inside Nicaragua. In May of 1985 we held an all-Indian assembly in Rus-Rus to create a new organization known as KISAN, for Kus Indian Sut Aslika Nicaragua. I was elected a member of the overall general staff of the Indian guerrilla movement and became its chief of Operations in 1986. Even though I had this headquarters position I also continued to be a field commander and returned to battle as the commander of a unit of 500 guerrillas. In July 1987, at a second all-Indian assembly in Rus-Rus, I was elected chief of the general staff of a successor organization to KISAN known as YATAMA, for Yapti Tasba Nana Masraka Asla Takanka, which means Children of the Mother Earth. YATAMA was also occasionally known as the Atlantic Front of the Nicaraguan Democratic Resistance, but we operated entirely separately. I continued to hold that position until the end of the war.

In March of 1988 I was a senior participant in the cease-fire negotiation at Sapoá, Nicaragua, together with the senior commanders of the other Nicaraguan Resistance armies and their political directorates, and signed a cease-fire agreement as representative of YATAMA. Following the signing of the agreement I became part of the technical commission responsible for its implementation and served in that capacity along with Nicaraguan Resistance Comandantes *Aureliano, Toño, Fernando, Rubén*, and, of course, their senior commander *Comandante 3-80*, Enríque Bermúdez. In 1989 I headed up a YATAMA negotiating team that went to Washington, D.C., to meet with representatives Ricardo Wheelock and Jose Guzmán of the Sandinista Front in the offices of the OAS. Following this, in March of 1990, I headed up a military delegation of YATAMA that went into Nicaragua to look for enclaves to which our troops would be willing to return, and also in 1990, in May to be precise, I signed a cease-fire and disarmament agreement between YATAMA troops and the government of Violeta Chamorro in Managua. I finally laid down my own arms on the June 20 at the cease-fire enclave of Bilwaskarma on the Rio Coco, together with the last group of armed YATAMA troops.

John Blacker
David Randolp
Hank Sasfe
Tom Slater
Esto screen responsable
noticia del Dpto del Estado
que se informaron con
Voluntario en el chofer
de la Casa Blanca.

Inconbes con
Alfred Sankford

Roger Balandin Marzo 85

Franco Stiman 5 10 -92
I mrio Valunyule 7 0 Oct

Domingo 24/3/85
Hable por telefono con
un amiga en Managua
Nicaragua.

EMBAJADA AMERICANA
CASA GRANDE
R/c WINSTON GUTIERREZ

LUNES 25-3-85
HABLE POR TELEFONO CON
MI TIA EN MANAGUA NICA.

25-3-85
ATACA BASES DEL FDN
EN LODOSA Y LAS BEGAS.
UNDIERON UN BOTE CON
CARGAMENTO DE PROVICIONES
POR FALTA DE ZISTASTE
CIA MILITAR NO MANDAR
PATRULLAS DE RECONOCIMIENTO
QUEMA DEL HOSPITAL DE
LAS BEGAS POR UN IMFI
LTRADO DEL F.S.L.N.

Pages from personal diary of Salomón Osorno Coleman, *Comandante Blass*, concerning March 1985 visit to Washington, D.C., naming eight Americans officers with whom he met in the White House. Bottom right note of March 25 contains comments on a concurrent Sandinista army attack on FDN Resistance camps at La Lodosa and Las Begas [sic] inside Honduras. Much of diary is in Miskito. Private collection.

Unidentified YATAMA Miskito Indian fighters checking the plunger circuits of a Claymore mine that failed to detonate. Inside the Nicaraguan Mosquitia, November 30, 1986. Courtesy YAAD.

For three years after I disarmed I worked full time on the process of reinserting the combatants and their families back into civilian life. Mostly this involved working with the government and international organizations responsible for the demobilization and reinserting of the combatants, their families, and those who had been displaced during the war into Nicaraguan civil society. This turned out to be a very difficult process for a number of reasons. The former combatants of the Resistance returned to Nicaragua believing that they had won the war and therefore returned with a sort of triumphalist mentality. They did not accept or fully understand that the triumph also was a consequence of the elections of 1990 and of processes set in motion by the peace agreements reached by the Central American nations in Esquípulas, Guatemala, in 1987. It was, after all, the sacrifices of the com-

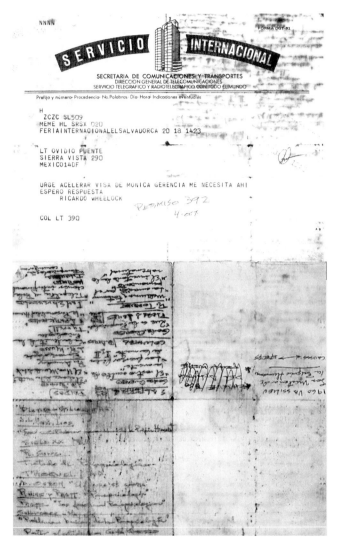

Telegram from Ricardo Wheelock, later chief of Sandinista army intelligence, to "Pepe" Puente requesting help with a visa. Ricardo was the chief Sandinista negotiator with whom *Blass* met in Washington, D.C., in 1989. Ricardo's brother Jaime was one of the Sandinista revolution's nine comandantes and directed the Sandinista's agrarian reform efforts. The brothers joined the Sandinista Front in the mid-1970s toward the end of the anti-Somoza revolution. The pen and ink notations on the back of the telegram were made by Carlos Fonseca Amador, apparently as part of his research for an unpublished study, "Historia de Nicaragua." Both the telegram and Fonseca's manuscript are in a private collection.

Unidentified Súmu Indian woman with children, awaiting forced evacuation by U.N. High Commission for Refugees (UNHCR) from Bocay to an unprepared open-air camp deeper inside Honduras, 1989. During the first week after evacuation, death rate among Súmus over 60 and under 2 years of age reached 90 percent. It is not known if this woman survived.

batants that had forced the Sandinistas to the table and made it possible to hold real elections. But once those elections had been held, it was no longer necessary to continue the war, and changed circumstances required that we lay down our arms. And yet even though that was necessary, it was not understood by our troops. The second problem was the trauma caused by the war itself, especially its impact on those who were militarily organized and accustomed to carrying arms and engaging in combat operations. Without going into an excessive amount of detail, our troops simply were not prepared for peace.

As a consequence we had a number of serious problems up to and including death threats directed at us by our own people, a situation that was exploited politically by our Sandinista enemies, who attempted to use our own troops to sow discord in our ranks and to gain political advantage by creating a lack of confidence in us among our people. Our former combatants thought that all their needs and problems could be resolved almost immediately and that the reason this was not done was that their leaders were not competent. Our Sandinista opponents and others took advantage of this lack of understanding of the problems involved to incite uprisings against us, which added to the difficulty of our job.

Nonetheless we were generally successful in persuading our combatants to rejoin civil society and successfully attained their reinsertion. We did this primarily by organizing various training courses to help them reenter the civilian economy. These included workshops on such things as agricultural and fishing cooperatives and others. One of the objectives of the workshops, in addition to teaching economic activities, was to change the guerrilla mentality into a civilian mentality with the objective of establishing some form of sustainable and independent development process in the region. We were helped in this by a number of international organizations that assisted us with several small but high-impact projects immediately and then larger, more complex ones that involved even more change.

But there was an even greater and more dangerous problem

that arose because the soldiers of all four Resistance forces⁵ found themselves confronted by the still-armed police and army of the former Sandinista government when the new government did not restructure its security forces. This caused a particularly complex problem and a great deal of unhappiness among former guerrillas from throughout the Nicaraguan Resistance, and this had tragic consequences. Among those consequences were the murders by police, army and Sandinista-armed cooperative activists of hundreds of former combatants of the Resistance, including a number of *comandantes*, a situation that provoked the rearming of thousands of former comandos of the Resistance.⁶ This in turn forced the government of Nicaragua to look for some way to reestablish peace and to assure the safety of the former Resistance fighters, their families, and the former members of their social base support structures, including both those of the Nicaraguan Resistance and of YATAMA. The government's first attempt to reestablish peace involved the creation of new peace and verification commissions. But these were unable to carry out their obligations because of a lack of collaboration on the part of the army, the police, and criminal elements from within the Sandinista Front who, to this very day (1998), continue to freely walk the streets of the Mosquitia with absolute impunity because no one has been prepared to investigate their acts or to apply legal penalties to them.

In response to the very serious security problems in which we found ourselves involved after we laid down our arms, we created a new association known as YAAD, or YATAMA Aiklaklabra Almuk Daknika, Miskito Indian for the Association of Ex-Combatants of YATAMA. A nonprofit private organization, its mission is to provide legal representation for the former combatants and their families before the government and national and international organizations and to work on their behalf in the promotion of their social, cultural, and economic interests. I was elected president of its board of directors, a position I continue to enjoy today. In that position I have direct responsibility for two radio stations, one known as Radio Miskut and the other as

Radio Bílwi. The first is a short-wave station and the second FM, operating from Puerto Cabezas, or Bílwi.

Radio Miskút has existed for a number of years and served us during the war against the Sandinistas as our principal means of communicating information to the population of the Atlantic Coast and even into other regions of the country about the political situation in Nicaragua. It was quite successful in promoting our armed struggle against the Sandinista regime and also provided us a voice through which we could denounce the many atrocities committed by the Sandinistas against the people of Nicaragua and particularly against the indigenous communities of Nicaragua's Atlantic Coast. Today it is serving us equally well as our principal means of communicating with the indigenous communities of the Atlantic and other sectors of the population, providing us with a means of also giving them a social service. It has played a particularly important role in the process of reinserting the former combatants and has a number of different programs addressed to various sectors of the population, including programs concerned with protecting the natural environment, the rational use of natural resources, public health, hygiene, programs of communal development, antidrug messages, and the promotion of our indigenous culture.

My Transition from Indigenous Guerrilla Commander to Law Student

Even though I continue to serve my people in a number of capacities, after my three years assisting with the reinsertion process I chose to return to school. In 1993 I therefore began studying at the Catholic University of Nicaragua to obtain a university degree. It had been more than ten years since I had been in a classroom, and when I sat down with the other students I found it difficult. Among the many difficulties I encountered was the very different class of persons and classmates, as well as professors, with whom I came to deal in the university. They were especially different from those who had fought alongside me in the mountains and plains of the Atlantic. I am also the only Miskito Indian law student at the university, and all my classmates come from quite different social classes and very different environments. Nonetheless, and despite all of the sacrifices required, if God wills it I will receive my law degree within a very few months. [He succeeded in 1999.] Overall, the transition from indigenous guerrilla commander to legal professional has been, to say the least, difficult.

Nonetheless, even though I am entering into a new life in many ways, I consider myself still committed to my people and to my many former comrades, especially those who fell during the war. My hope is that once I have my law degree in hand I will be able to provide them with the professional services for which I have been prepared. It is also my intention to reenter the political field as soon as I have obtained my degree, which I hope will strengthen my leadership position within the Miskito community and help me in future regional or national elections to gain a position from which I will be able to help the indigenous communities of the Atlantic Coast and support the new leaders of our communities and the region.

We, the indigenous peoples of the Atlantic Coast of Nicaragua, along with all of the indigenous peoples of the Americas at the beginning of the new millennium, are faced with the enormous challenge of recovering our historic rights over our land, our culture, and our traditional customs, so we can live dignified lives as equals with the rest of the people of the Americas. This requires that our standards of living be raised in both the social and economic senses, and that we began to play political roles in the public life of every country, to include serving as officials at all levels of the government of every state of the Americas in which there are groups of indigenous people.

To conclude this short essay, in addition to discussing my personal experiences, I have tried to explain that for me, as a Miskito Indian, I merely form part of a centuries-long historical struggle of my people. It is important that our friends, and particularly the person who has this short essay in his or her hands at this mo-

GUERRILLAS

226

ment, understand that we indigenous peoples are not opponents, nor are we resistant to cooperating with those of the other races that inhabit this planet with us. Quite the contrary, we are normally hospitable and friendly and seek to maintain close relations with all those who treated us as equals created by God, just as they were. But to those who seek to humiliate us, enslave us, steal our lands from us, or treat us as the lowest class of citizens, we are implacable enemies and will struggle constantly against anyone who does not respect us as equals. Those who fail to respect us will be treated as we treated the Sandinistas, as enemies.

PART III
THE DANGERS
OF PEACE

11

Ambassador Myles R. R. Frechette, an American Diplomat

A BIOGRAPHICAL SKETCH

Myles Frechette was born and raised in Chile and received his university education in Canada. He is completely bilingual and bicultural in English and Spanish and is an especially adept mimic of various Spanish accents. After a short career in business, he joined the U.S. Foreign Service and made diplomacy his career. After numerous assignments, he became Coordinator for Cuban Affairs in the Department of State, where I was his deputy for two years. Blocked by the Cuban-American community from immediate assignment in Latin America, Frechette was appointed Ambassador to Cameroon. He was later assistant U.S. Special Trade Representative in the Office of the President with special responsibilities for negotiating free trade arrangements in the Americas. From that position he was appointed ambassador to Colombia, about which he writes here. Since retired, he is a consultant on foreign trade at Hill and Company and lives in the Washington, D.C., area.

□ □ □

COLOMBIA: THE WAR THAT
WILL NOT END

Myles R. R. Frechette

Inspired by "Che" Guevara's and Regis Debray's thesis of the revolutionary enclave, or *foco*, guerrilla movements were born in most countries of Latin America in the 1960s. Most failed and passed into history long before the Berlin Wall fell in 1989 or the Sandinista Liberation Front was defeated at the polls in 1990. But some lasted longer. In Guatemala the signature of the peace accords on December 29, 1996, ended thirty-six years of armed conflict. The longest, bloodiest, and most intransigent of these has proven to be that of Colombia, which began in 1946 and continues to this day. Colombia is a very large and populous country. Its area of 1,141,748 square kilometers, about 600,000 square miles divided into thirty-three departments, is four times the size of California. Its population of 37,422,721 in 1997 was only a little smaller.

The Colombian Guerrillas

In Colombia as of 1998 three guerrilla groups continued armed conflict. The Fuerza Armada Revolucionaria Colombiana (FARC) was formally organized in 1966, the Ejército de Liberación Nacional (ELN) was founded in 1964, and the Ejército Popular de Liberación (EPL) in 1965. In the early years the FARC was supported by the Communist Party of Colombia and had connections with the Soviet Union. The ELN was supported by Cuba, and the EPL looked for orientation to the People's Republic of China. But the roots of violence in Colombia lie in economic inequality and predate "Che" Guevara by many years. The fact is that armed conflict has been underway in Colombia almost with-

out interruption since 1946. The FARC, Colombia's oldest guerrilla group, actually began as peasant self-defense groups during
the early 1950s.

What I would like to discuss here are four things: first, the
origins of the guerrilla movements in Colombia; second, some of
the efforts that have been made there to end armed conflict; third,
what the situation is as of 1998; and fourth, I would also like to
suggest some of the reasons why Latin America's longest running
armed conflict, that of Colombia, continues.

The origins of this conflict lie in agrarian unrest, land title
disputes, rent disputes, and problems of squatting that are not
new in Colombia. In 1928 the so-called banana strike over these
issues was brutally suppressed by the Conservative Party then in
power. Small rural self-defense groups that included communists
were formed in the 1930s. Also in the 1930s, with the stirrings of
industrial development and urban growth, unrest developed in the
cities.

On April 9, 1948, Jorge Eliecer Gaitán, a Liberal Party populist politician, was shot to death in Bogota. This led to rioting and
violence in Bogota and other Colombian cities. Although this
event is known today outside of Colombia as the "Bogotázo,"
popular frustration was in fact expressed all over Colombia. But
this was only one significant episode within a period known as
"'La Violencia," which lasted from 1946 to 1966 and primarily
affected rural Colombia. Close to 200,000 Colombians died during "La Violencia."

When a Conservative was elected president in 1950, Liberal–
Conservative party hostility expressed itself in three years (1950–
1953) of extreme violence nationwide. It was during this period
that significant rural self-defense forces allied with the Communist Party came into being in the upper Magdalena River valley.
These rural armed groups are considered the beginnings of the
FARC, which is today Colombia's largest and most important
guerrilla organization.

The ELN began among some Colombians who went to Cuba
on scholarships after the 1962 missile crisis. The ELN officially

came into being on July 4, 1964, in what is known as the Magdaleno Medio and Santander Department. Composed largely of disaffected middle-class youth, it attracted even some members of the Catholic Church, such as Father Camilo Tórres, who joined the ELN and died in 1966 in his first armed action. The ELN was almost wiped out by the army in the 1970s, but in the 1980s it regenerated under Manuel Pérez, also known as "El Cura" Pérez. The ELN operates in economically rich areas of Colombia. This produces revenue and also serves its long-term strategy of disrupting or controlling areas of vital economic importance. The ELN frequently blows up oil pipelines despite the environmental damage caused by the oil spills.

Another group, the M-19, began in 1972 composed of disaffected members of the ANAPO (Alianza Nacional Popular), a political movement begun by general and then dictator (1953–1957) Gustavo Rojas Pinilla. But it also included some people expelled from the FARC. It was strongly nationalistic and hostile to U.S. interests and advocated greater social equality. However, like the ANAPO, the M-19 was never clear about its specific goals. It engaged primarily in urban terrorism and never succeeded in rural areas. The M-19 was known for spectacular actions. Early in its existence it stole Bolivar's sword. In 1979 it stole some weapons from a military installation in Bogota itself. In 1980 it kidnapped a number of diplomats during a Dominican Republic Embassy reception. In 1985 it attacked the Palace of Justice in Bogotá, an action that ended in a bloodbath. It specialized in kidnapping, bank robbery, and symbolic assassinations. On March 9, 1990, some 900 M-19 members turned in their weapons and ended their guerrilla operations.

The EPL went to the field in the lowland areas of Antioquia Department in December 1965. It operated primarily in rural rather than urban areas. In January 1991 2,000 EPL "guerrilleros" turned themselves in. In 1996, 275 more gave up their weapons and entered the government's "reinsertion" program. However, a dissident group, although tiny, is still active. Two reasons contribute to the fact that the EPL never acquired the importance of the FARC or the ELN: The EPL never had access to external financing, and it did not develop economic links with narcotraffickers.

The Situation in 1998

The guerrillas in Colombia number between 10,000 and 15,000, and they operate in the majority of Colombia's departments in the *cordillera*, or central mountain chain, and to the west of the *cordillera*. They also operate in the plains and rain forests of some of the departments that lie east of the mountains. There are over sixty FARC "fronts." The ELN has about forty "fronts" and the EPL fewer than ten, of which fewer than five are active. There are also fewer than 200 guerrillas operating in Valle del Caúca and Caúca Department, who call themselves the Jaime Bateman Cayón group. They are remnants of the M-19, named for an M-19 leader who joined that group after being expelled from the FARC. One Colombian study released in 1996 concluded that guerrilla activity reduced Colombia's gross domestic product by 4.1 percent and that over the previous five years Colombia had lost productivity and materiel totaling $12.5 billion.

Some Colombians believe the goal of the guerrillas is the total takeover of Colombia. Others believe they seek autonomy or semi-autonomy in parts of Colombia where there is little government presence. Still others believe the guerrillas have abandoned ideology for political banditry as a way of life because they have access to a lot of money from kidnapping, various forms of extortion, and, in many cases, their involvement with narcotrafficking (about two-thirds of the FARC's "fronts" and about one-third of the ELN's "fronts" are associated with narcotrafficking in some way). But those Colombians who have dealt with them, such as government negotiators, members of the Catholic Church, and members of the National Conciliation Commission, believe the senior guerrilla leadership still conserves its ideology.

Today in Colombia there is an intense desire for peace shared almost universally. On October 26, 1997, during the gubernatorial and mayoral elections, Colombians voted overwhelmingly in favor of national peace talks in a nonbinding referendum. All the guerrilla groups have said publicly that they support a peace process that could begin once Colombia's new government comes into office on August 7, 1998. Within Colombia an important actor moving the peace process forward is the Commission of National Conciliation, founded in August 1995 and headed by the Episcopal Conference of the Catholic Church.

For its part, the government proposed a peace process in 1997 and introduced legislation, approved by Congress on February 3, 1998, that establishes a National Peace Council whose function it is to "advise and consult" on behalf of the government in pursuit of peace. The same law establishes peace as a "permanent and participative" policy of state. On February 8, 1998, the government issued a presidential directive stating that only the central government can conduct peace negotiations. Earlier, in September 1997, the government received support for its peace initiative from the governments of Mexico, Spain, Venezuela, and Costa Rica, now called the "Friends." At the November 1997 Ibero-American Summit, President Sampér asked President Fidel Castro to facilitate peace talks. Finally, during a trip to Moscow in March 1998, Foreign Minister Mejía announced Russia wanted to join the "Friends."

Previous Attempts at Peace

This is not the first time negotiation with the guerrillas has been tried in Colombia. Nor is it the first time other governments have helped. Mexico hosted two rounds of unsuccessful talks between the government and the guerrillas in 1991 and 1992. President Alfonso López Michelsen (1974–1978) made an attempt at negotiation with the guerrillas, but it didn't prosper. Colombian and foreign analysts agree that the Colombian military was unwilling to cooperate. President César Turbay (1978–1982) took a different approach. His government tried force, but that tactic did not end guerrilla activity, and human rights violations by both the armed forces and the guerrillas increased. President Belisario Betancúr (1982–1986) offered the guerrillas democratic reform (thus fulfilling some guerrilla demands) and a truce leading to dialogue and an eventual peace pact.

Guerrilla demands made to the Betancúr government included amnesty for political prisoners, national dialogue, democratic reforms, a truce, and pacification. In response the Betancúr government took several steps. On September 8, 1982, it held a multi-party political summit to discuss political reforms. On September 19 of that year a peace commission was formed. On November 19, an amnesty law was passed. Additional steps took place later. Between March and August of 1984 truce agreements were signed with the FARC, M-19, and the EPL. Also in 1984 and 1985 bills were introduced in Congress to lock in democratic reforms. In the end, however, little came of this process in terms of achieving peace. Neither side could guarantee nonviolence because neither side had full control of its subordinates. Nevertheless, the efforts to achieve peace through negotiation continued through the presidency of Virgilio Bárco (1986–1990). The M-19 disavowed the Betancúr government efforts as betrayal, and in 1985, in its most spectacular but also its last significant action, it attacked the Palace of Justice, an action that earned it public rejection. As I mentioned earlier, almost all of the M-19 turned in its weapons in 1990.

The FARC hoped to launch its own political party as a result of President Betancúr's initiative. This party, launched in 1985, is called Unión Patriotica (UP). It assembles former guerrillas, communists, and other leftists for legitimate political activity. It ran a presidential candidate, Jaime Pardo, in the 1986 elections, as well as mayoral candidates, taking advantage of the 1985 constitutional amendment, part of the Betancúr political opening, which provided for direct election of mayors. Interestingly, in subsequent years former M-19 members proved more popular in the polls than UP candidates. Navarro Wolf, an M-19 member who abandoned violence, got 13 percent of the votes for president in 1990.

One sequel to the political activity of the UP, which also affected other guerrillas who attempted to "reinsert" themselves in society, was that many were killed by right-wing elements and narcotraffickers turned rural landowners. Between 1985 and the end of 1997, 3,000 UP members have been murdered. (Jaime Pardo was assassinated in 1986 and Bernardo Jaramillo was killed in 1990. Both were UP presidential candidates.) Of the 5,897 guerrillas formally demobilized between 1990 and 1994, 340 had been killed as of August 1997.[1]

Guerrilla Activity

Guerrilla activities have continued in recent years. In 1994 there were forty-one guerrilla attacks in Colombia, the highest number in Latin America, with damage to economic targets such as petroleum pipelines. The guerrillas also continued to derive much of their income from violent acts, including extortion, bank robbery, and kidnapping. There were 1,378 reported kidnappings in 1994, a 35 percent increase over 1993. Foreigners were far from immune. For example, during 1994 the guerrillas held eight kidnapped Americans, the largest number in any country in the world. In 1995 there were seventy-five guerrilla actions in Colombia, an 85 percent increase over 1993, and at least four kidnapped Americans were held. Two more kidnapped American missionaries were murdered by the guerrillas when the guerrillas had a chance encounter with the army. In 1996 thirty-six more foreigners were kidnapped by guerrillas, and they also continued to hold the four kidnapped Americans. Of course, kidnapping of Colombian citizens remained high and included the brother of former President Gavíria, Juan Carlos Gavíria.

In 1996, although the number of guerrilla actions declined from seventy-five in 1995 to sixty-six, attacks on the Colombian army increased. On April 15 at Puerres in the Department of Nariño, thirty-one conscripts were killed. On August 30 at Las Delicias in Putumayo, twenty-seven soldiers were killed in an attack and sixty taken prisoner. They were not released until almost a year later, when they and ten Colombian Marines were set free in the presence of international observers. On September 6 at La Carpa in Guaviare Department, twenty-two more soldiers were killed.

In 1997 guerrillas threatened officeholders, candidates, and election workers as "military objectives" and tried to intimidate voters into not voting in the October 1997 gubernatorial and mayoral elections. As part of this effort, they killed or kidnapped 200 candidates and elected officials and forced 2,000 candidates to withdraw from political campaigns. Despite this violence the government carried out elections in the vast majority of municipalities, and Colombians voted in large numbers. Guerrillas were responsible for over 23 percent of the extrajudicial killings in Colombia in 1997 and carried out well over 50 percent of the 867 reported kidnappings. Americans continued to be held by the guerrillas. Since 1980, eighty-five American citizens have been kidnapped in Colombia, and twelve of them have been murdered in captivity.

Why have the guerrillas not succeeded, and why is a peace process so difficult? I suggest several reasons. First, Colombians continue to be loyal to the two traditional parties, the Liberals and the Conservatives, and, despite the levels of violence in some areas, guerrilla activity has had little impact on the lives of most Colombians. Second, political parties on the left have had little success in attracting the electorate to programs for radical social reform. The guerrillas have survived largely because Colombia is a very large country and more than one million square kilometers of its land mass lacks government presence. This is the area in which the guerrillas have been particularly active. In addition, despite the lack of external financial support in this decade, the guerrillas have good sources of income from kidnapping, various forms of extortion, and the association of many guerrilla fronts with narcotrafficking. Third, it has always been difficult for the guerrillas to cooperate with one another or to speak with one voice. This dispersion is still an obstacle, despite the creation in the 1980s of two groups intended to help the guerrillas speak with one voice—the Coordinadora Guerrillera Simón Bolívar and the Coordinadora Guerrillera Nacional.

There are also nonguerrilla armed groups that form a sort of counterpart to the guerrillas, known as "paramilitaries." The increased numbers and armed actions of such "paramilitaries" in recent years makes it necessary to include them in peace talks. It will be necessary to establish some way to guarantee the safety of those guerrillas and paramilitaries who reject violence, bearing in mind what happened to guerrillas who have been "reinserted" since the 1980s. In recent years it has been difficult to determine what the guerrillas want from a peace process. Authoritative statements by the guerrilla leadership are several years old, and there is no way to determine who now speaks authoritatively for specific guerrilla organizations, let alone all of them. Once guerrilla and paramilitary goals are known it will be necessary to discover whether these are acceptable to Colombian civil society and, particularly, to the economic and political elites.

What Is New?

There are three new elements in the present peace process in Colombia that inspire hope among Colombians: first, the overwhelming desire by key actors and by civil society for peace; second, the recognition that this process may take many years and extend beyond the term of Colombia's next president; and third, the existence of a National Conciliation Commission and a "permanent" government institution such as the National Peace Council. These are clear signals of awareness that the peace process will take time, but there is general Colombian eagerness for and acceptance of international support for the peace process. One lesson the violence in Colombia should teach all of us is that no matter how long it takes, one must never lose hope. Peace is always a prize worth pursuing.

12

Major General
Ian Douglas,
a United Nations General

A BIOGRAPHICAL SKETCH

The next essayist, Canadian paratrooper and General Ian Douglas, was the first chief of staff of a United Nations military observer force in Central America, ONUCA (Organizacíon de Naciones Unidas en Centroamerica), which had as its original mandate the disarmament and demobilization of the armed Nicaraguan Resistance, the Contras. A paratrooper by trade, at the time of his assignment Douglas was already on the United Nations' military staff. ONUCA did manage the supposedly voluntary disarmament and mobilization of the Contras. In theory, at least, it then acted as an observer force to assure that the peace accords under which this had taken place were honored. General Douglas has applied the lessons he learned to later missions in Bosnia-Herzegóvina and Africa.

His conclusion that peace is not just the absence of war, although not new, is important, and his comments reinforce much of what the former revolutionaries and guerrillas who have spoken earlier have had to say. They also suggest some ideas on solving other conflicts. As Ambassador Frechette has pointed out, a failure to understand these lessons may have been responsible for the continuation of "La Violencia" in Colombia for at least an extra decade.

□ □ □

UNITED NATIONS PEACEMAKING: LESSONS LEARNED

Major General Ian Douglas

It is always a pleasure to discuss something I deeply believe in, the process of international peacemaking, from my perspective as a practitioner in the field. Although relatively new on the world scene, international organization involvement in peacemaking, peacebuilding, and peacekeeping have already become very complex topics. All I ask is that you bear with me as I to try to condense into a short essay a two-week course taught at Canada's Pearson PeaceKeeping Center, which, in itself, is too short. The focus of the course is on three subprocesses—disarmament, demobilization, and reinsertion—that take place at the end of civil conflicts. We call this DDR. The course also covers peace operations in general. Perhaps this short discussion will generate more questions than answers. But at least I hope it gives the reader a basic idea of the philosophy of peacemaking as we see it and some appreciation for the many kinds of activities one must engage in in connection with peacemaking, peacebuilding, and peacekeeping efforts. My own peacekeeping experience began in Central America in 1990. Since then my efforts have mostly taken me to Africa, with an important side trip of several months to Bosnia-Herzegóvina. There are important differences between the societies of Central America and Africa, but I have found that the basic problems underlying many conflicts in both regions have fundamental similarities.

In preparation for this presentation I reread, among other things, the recent study by Timothy Brown of the Hoover Institution, *The Causes of Continuing Conflict in Nicaragua,*[1] and several papers on peacemaking problems in Africa, in particular studies by Peter Locke of the BICC (Bonn International Center for Conversion) in Germany and Richard Cornwall of the Institute of

Security Studies of South Africa and chapters on "The Results of Military Downsizing" in *The Failure of the Centralized State: Institutions and Governance in Africa.*[2] These excellent studies, all of which are used in our Canadian course on peacemaking, have among them one particular similarity that stands out. In case after case, the countries in which international involvement in a peace process has become necessary have been countries in which national leadership has traditionally acted within closed patrimonial governmental systems. In Africa, as described by British expert Paul Richards, too often they have had individual leaders who catered only to sycophants from within their own power bases in the military and to the elites in urban centers, while ignoring, and in many cases actually crushing, the aspirations of the majority population in rural areas. Although he does not go so far as either Locke or Cornwall, Brown's description of the oligarchical elite of Nicaragua and of its historical attitude toward the peasantry and his comment that "neither the poor nor the nation seem to rate overly high in most Latin political value systems"[3] are worth keeping in mind when approaching peacekeeping operations. They remind me personally just how often, when up country in Liberia or Sierra Leone, I heard talk of the Monrovia or Freetown syndromes, the capital city syndrome if you will. In Africa they often use more earthy terms than Brown does, but the meaning is the same. It has become quite clear to me that, whether in Africa or Latin America, too many countries are run for the benefit of a handful of the elite, many of whom, especially in the case of Africa, have their families living in the United States or perhaps the United Kingdom, and not for the benefit of the many, and most especially not in the interests of their poor rural farmers, the campesinos in Latin terminology.

It thus has become clear to me that there are parallel cancers within the systems of some Latin American states and those of much of Africa. This seems to me best demonstrated by a number I often used to describe the distribution of wealth in many African states: 2:98, that is to say 2 percent of the people control 98 percent of the wealth. Brown, talking about a different region, uses two numbers that may be more precise in the Latin American context, 5:95 or 6:94, meaning that 5 or 6 percent of the people control 94 or 95 percent of the wealth. But neither describes a situation that is equitable or permanently acceptable in the modern world. In Nicaragua, the Freetown or Monrovia syndromes of Africa can be called the Managua, Granada, León syndrome, but neither is sustainable.

As shallow as the analogy might seem to some, and I understand things have changed significantly in Nicaragua particularly since the 1996 election, the building of systems that look after the population as a whole, not just the few, must be the baseline for any successful peace operations. At the United Nations and in Canada, to describe the political bottom line of the process required to accomplish this, we use an ideal process we call the "continuum model," based on the processes described by Brown and others. It is a means of illustrating a first essential point—that a durable peace can only be attained by following a progression of political stages.

A second essential point we also teach, the economic bottom line if you will, is one I have extolled for years and was pleased to see reflected in my colleague Tim Brown's Hoover essay. The international community must stop just throwing money resources at the problems of conflict-torn countries and societies and start dealing with their leaderships on a businesslike basis. We must play hardball, to use a baseball analogy, with the would-be leaders and elites of these "sovereign states" and use the only argument many of them really understand, the power of the dollar. Conditions for aid and development must be negotiated as with any business deal, with measurable and sustainable social improvements required for hard aid. I promise you this is not a pie-in-the-sky idea developed by a "do-gooder." It is a conclusion based on my experience as a professional soldier involved in the building of peace. I have seen reductions in aid due to budget balancing and the end of the cold war, and concerns in many developed countries with internal economic problems, sometimes known collectively as donor fatigue, have an extremely negative impact on the campesinos of the world, and especially on women and children at the front, or leading edge. And yet this is only to be expected when no amount of help seems to solve the problem. Unless results can be attained, open-ended development flows from the rich to the poor will not be permanently sustainable.

Nicaragua

Let me now leave discussion of backgrounds and bottom lines and go to my introductory experience to peacekeeping operations in Central America. When it began I was assigned to the United Nations as a military staff officer. After eight years of the Contadora political process, there finally was an opening to deploy U.N. peacekeeping troops to Central America in 1989. A rushed three-week technical study mission called for a 250-soldier military observer mission called ONUCA, with a mandate, which was "Mission Impossible." The study did not recommend that ONUCA have a political manager, known in U.N. parlance as an SPRSG, or Special Political Representative of the Secretary General, but did recommend the assignment to the mission of a CMO, or Chief Military Observer, who had never before served on a peacekeeping mission: me.

For those of you who know the borders of Central America, can you imagine 250 soldiers controlling the flow of arms across the Nicaraguan borders with Honduras and Costa Rica, the mission that became our mandate? It would make one smile were it not so serious. Can you, in fact, imagine 25,000 observers controlling those borders, especially the one with Honduras? Even with 25,000 soldiers, absent the goodwill of the parties in conflict, it would still be a "Mission Impossible." We learned quickly that the real aim was to pre-position ONUCA in anticipation of the disarmament of the Contras in concert with an organization called CIAV, the Comisión Internacionál de Apoyo y Verificacíon. We also learned it was to be a joint U.N.–OAS operation, even though neither international organization had a philosophy or concept of joint operations. It was simply a matter of throwing the United Nations into the same pot with an OAS entity called CIAV. At the time we didn't even know who they were.

I remember vividly one afternoon in February of 1990. At around 4:00 p.m. Mark Goulding, then the Undersecretary General of the United Nations for Special Political Affairs, precursor to the Director of Peace Keeping Operations, dropped by to tell me as the chief of staff of ONUCA that he was off to meet with the president of Honduras but would be back around 7:30 or 8:00 p.m. and to ask would I please have ready a concept of operations and a plan prepared for the demobilization of the Contras by the time he got back. Strange though it may seem, and may I add this was the first I had heard that the operation was about to be implemented, we produced both a concept and a plan of operations in the four hours provided. Its quality did not, however, speak highly either of our research or our in-depth planning. At that time I had not even met a member of CIAV and still wasn't even sure what it was. It was only later that the then head of the operation, Santiago Murray, showed up at ONUCA looking for the plan of operations, which had by then become the U.N. plan. To say that the U.N. plan and my own operation were prepared and conducted on an ad hoc basis would be quite an understatement.

Somehow, though, we worked it out, although neither I nor the military under me quite understood what was really going on, except that we had to disarm and demobilize the excombatants of the Nicaraguan Contra. Somehow, it happened. At places with exotic names like Lakiatara, Yamales, Las Colinas, El Valle, La Pinella, El Almendro, Wiwilí, Bilwaskarma, Alamikámba—names that now bring back fond memories—we demobilized 22,373 ex-Contras in May and June of 1990. We also reinserted them back into their geographical home areas. But there was no reintegration. Two words, reinsertion and reintegration, which I would like you to note, and which hopefully will become clearer, were the keys to the eventual failure of the Nicaragua peace process.

It really was a pitiful effort. I do not fault those in CIAV who were responsible for the reintegration part, as they too had little

General Ian Douglas, U.N. ONUCA, congratulating the first YATAMA Miskito fighter (unidentified) to disarm April 1991 at Bilwaskarma, Nicaragua. Soldiers in background wearing berets are from Venezuelan battalion with ONUCA. Courtesy General Douglas.

policy guidance or specific direction and suffered from a severe lack of resources. In neither international organization, neither the U.N. nor the OAS, had anyone taken into consideration a number of rather basic questions. For example, what were the excombatants going to live on when their initial sixty-day supply of reinsertion food, beans, rice, cooking oil, was used up? We simply assumed that it was the hope of grants of land and of help to go back to tilling the soil, things they had been promised in return for disarming, that would cause these hardened guerrillas voluntarily to lay down their guns, demobilize, and return home with hopes that the 1990 election of Violeta Chamorro as president, a victory of the united opposition known as the Union Nacional Opositor (UNO) over their enemies of the Sandinista Front, would lead to these promises being kept. Hope sprang eternal. The former Contras did disarm, sort of. We knew that the weapons they turned in only manifested the poorest quality and represented only a small percentage of the weapons in the region but hoped nonetheless that they were a symbol that perhaps peace and prosperity lay ahead one day. To my sorrow, I later learned that little that was promised was delivered and that in many ways the conflict continued until just recently. If there are lessons to be learned from that experience, it is that disarmament, demobilization, and reinsertion are merely the beginning of a process. If peace is to endure, much more must be done.

These questions once more faced me a few years later when I opened my DDR office as commander of UNIFIL (United Nations International Force in Liberia) in Liberia. UNIFIL was a U.N. version of ONUCA and CIAV in one. Again, no one had budgeted for the operation to last beyond sixty days, nor indeed had it been seriously budgeted for at all, and we faced failure even before we started. And in Liberia, unlike in Nicaragua, there were not even promises of land grants, nor indeed a real government to talk to. This second experience made it even more obvious to me that unless a more holistic approach is taken to DDR operations, they become merely pauses in cycles of violence that restart as soon as a reinsertion assistance package is no longer available. As with ONUCA, we knew in Liberia that for every gun turned in there were one, two, or three tucked away in plastic in the forest. It became very clear to me then, in 1993–1994 in Liberia, that what is required to convert excombatants into peaceful civilians is a very complicated issue that involves the community at large, not just the parties in conflict, and that when, as in both Liberia and Nicaragua, along with excombatants comes a mass of refugees from outside the country returning at the same time, it becomes even more complicated. People must emerge from times of war with at least the hope of a minimal standard of living and reasonable hope for peace and security. If not, peace will not endure.

The Continuum Model

Perhaps it would be useful at this point to outline what we at the Pearson Center call the "continuum model," because without it or something similar it is far too easy to miss essential steps on the road to permanent peace. I will try to cover all its key points, partly for academic purposes, partly just to let you know that all of it is there, but I will concentrate on postconflict peace operations. In its written version, a time line is drawn from the left to the right and an action line from top to bottom, starting with peace, going through war, and arriving back at peace. When filled out with the details of actions taking place in Africa today, it clearly demonstrates how the peace process is working there at this very moment and suggests how it will go on in a continuous cycle that may well take months or even years to complete. The three most useful sets of data that can be plugged into the model are symptoms, participants, and activities at each key stage.

The prevention stage may be the most important in the long run. Very quickly, it has two phases, and to be successful it must be continuous. Regrettably, prevention is not sexy. If successful, it does not get the world's attention, and this is one of its biggest problems. Because it is not sexy, until very recently not very much attention has been paid to this stage of peacemaking by the international community, despite its overriding importance. Thankfully, more recently I have seen some increase in interest in conflict prevention. The Organization of African Unity (OAU) has, for example, just opened an office responsible for conflict resolution with emphasis on prevention. It is set up but not yet working. There is also a study done last year by the United Nations of how this new office can be tied in with international peacekeeping operations. The connection between the new office of the OAU and the United Nations' regional peacekeeping center in Africa bodes well for future cooperation related to the prevention of conflicts. Prevention efforts must go on constantly and always be of concern. There will be failures, let there be no doubt, and wars will happen. In Africa these days these may more and more often be intrastate wars, that is to say, conflicts inside states rather than between countries.

When prevention proves unsuccessful or insufficient to avoid a conflict, we come to the next stage—war. We need not discuss here what war is all about. The model we use does not provide a formula for resolving conflicts, much less a panacea for war. But it does explain where peacekeeping fits in. Hopefully, one can end a war quickly and move on to the postconflict stage. Probably the main value of using a model comes at this point, because it can highlight what must be kept in mind as to how to proceed with peacemaking. Based on my personal experiences, I can almost guarantee failure unless some sort of model is kept constantly in mind. It is at the point at which a war has ended but peace has not yet been achieved that such a model of international peacebuilding and -keeping becomes most important. It is also at this stage that the U.N. has most often become operationally involved, at the ends of wars such as the Contra war in Nicaragua, many wars in Africa, and other conflicts elsewhere throughout the world.

What is the usefulness of a model? The analogy I make is to building houses. You have to pour the foundation before you put the walls up, and put the walls up before you put the roof up. In order to do that you have to take a series of logical steps. Foundation before walls, walls before roof. Analogies only go so far, but this one can make one other point. In Canada you can build a house in June and not put in insulation, but by October you had better put in the insulation or the house will no longer be livable. The point is that you need not slavishly follow a model, but you had best take one into consideration and then adapt it to local conditions, or else you leave out an essential element. What working from a model allows you to do is to make considered decisions and, if necessary, take calculated risks. That's what life, after all, is all about, as opposed to irresponsible and ad hoc decisions, which is the approach that, indeed, the international community has been guilty of.

Before I go any further, a lot of people have been talking here about face-to-face negotiations and how essential they are. I would like to tell a little story. The participation of former Resistance *Comandante Rubén* in this study brings to mind a time when we were doing what amounted to shuttle diplomacy related to the disarmament of the Nicaraguan Contras. It was in early 1990, and we had been flying back and forth meeting first with the Contras and then with the Sandinistas. We had done so perhaps four or five times but were not achieving anything. We would talk with one side, and all they would do was speak badly of the other without discussing anything of substance or accomplishing anything. We decided to get the two sides to meet face to face and convinced the Contras to go to Managua under our protective umbrella to meet directly with the Sandinistas to start direct discussions between the two parties.

What happened was interesting. For the first time, I saw *Rubén* and other Contra *comandantes* in civilian clothes rather than in fatigue uniforms and carrying a weapon. They looked decidedly uncomfortable and felt, I think, distinctly uneasy. We took them in our airplane. Flying from Honduras to Nicaragua, as they crossed the Nicaraguan border they became more animated. By the time we were approaching Managua's Sandino airport, they had started talking rapidly with one another about their experiences, asking each other, "Do you remember this?" and "Do you remember that?" For the first time in eight, nine, or even ten years they were back in their own country without a gun in their hands or the possibility of being killed. The tension again rose rapidly as we got out of the airplane, especially because we were promptly surrounded by the Sandinista army soldiers; and when we went into the negotiating room it was like walking into a walk-in freezer. The atmosphere was cold, even icy. These were, after all, men who had in some cases known each other all their lives and who had, in any case, been trying to kill one another at war for many years. And yet, only about fifteen minutes later, the two sides were talking with one another and even telling a occasional joke. That is not to say that over the next several hours when serious negotiations were under way there was not a great deal of acrimony and heated argument back and forth. There was. But the ice had been broken, and that was the whole point of having them meet together face to face. It is perhaps one of the most important points in the negotiation phase of free continuum models with which I agreed most completely.

But let us move on and talk about the separate stages of the postconflict part of the peace process. The first phase is emergency stabilization. A cease-fire, no matter how tenuous, must be put in place and be sufficiently visible so that all can see that it is working. No matter how tenuous, this is the first signal that peace is in sight. Notice, it may well be weeks, months, or even years before the conflict itself is solved. But absent a cease-fire, peacemaking cannot even begin. It must precede the DDR process, that is to say, disarmament, demobilization, and reinsertion, which are the heart, the very core of the subsequent peace process.

After the stabilization stage, the next stage is disarmament. This need not be real or comprehensive disarming as we often talk about it, and it is a voluntary process. Only defeated forces can be disarmed involuntarily. Here we are talking about a different process. This disarmament process is essentially a confidence-building exercise. You are probably not going to get all the weapons; you are not necessarily even going to get the best weapons; in fact, at best often you will get only the bad weapons and, in many cases, not very many of these. But what is important is that you are building confidence. The purpose is to demonstrate that the war is over, that the machinery of war is being destroyed, and that we should destroy the weapons. The soldiers are becoming civilians, and so on and so forth.

Permit me another anecdote. Another participant in this study, *Comandante Blass*, may even get a chuckle out of this one. I can remember when we went to do the Miskito Indian disarmament and demobilization on the Atlantic Coast of Nicaragua and CIAV gave the first reinsertion packet to the first Indian who went through the line. In it he got a nice shirt, a nice pair of blue jeans, and a number of other things. At one point he held up part of his package, which consisted of two very fancy sets of Playboy bikini underwear. You can imagine the look on the face of this hardened Indian guerrilla fighter when he looked at this Playboy underwear and wondered: "What in the world am I going to do with this?"

Still, after thinking just a few seconds, he accepted them, and we went on with a very human operation quite distant from the ideal or theoretical.

Let me at this point say a few other things. While we use a schematic to represent the DDR process, in practical terms it is a very human process. Those disarming must assemble together with their families, they must be clothed and housed, and medical attention must be provided to them, always with the objective of building confidence; convincing them the war is over is the key. Food is given to those being demobilized. They must also be registered, a census must be taken, and they must be counseled as to what they can expect to go through as part of the peacemaking process. These are measures that ideally are taken at this time.It is often at this point that a special problem emerges, the problem of the child guerrilla. It is a terrible problem that exists throughout the world and can emerge with particular poignancy at this point of disarmament and demobilization. In Liberia alone we had to deal with at least 7,000 child soldiers, defined as armed fighters under the age of fifteen.

Returning to the process, at the point of demobilization, a re-insertion package is normally given to the fighter and his family. The question often arises whether this should be given to the combatant at that point or on returning home, particularly in guerrilla warfare situations. After all, combatants and their families are often returning to their homes of residence along with a large number of refugees. This is a question quite often discussed in considerable detail in relation to demobilization. The answer almost always is that it should be done at the point of demobilization, because one must never lose sight of the fact that the principal objective of the exercise is to build confidence. "The war is over, you are going home, there is light at the end of the tunnel."

What we have learned by experience is that DDR is vital but not sufficient to building a permanent peace. Even as DDR is going on, preparations for a next phase of peacebuilding must be made. Why was peace more fully achieved faster in places other than Nicaragua? I am not entirely certain and believe it is an issue that is important to pursue. I do know that one important factor is that information on what is happening and an explanation of the process must reach down to those at the bottom, down to the working campesinos so that they can clearly see what is happening. And this did not happen in Nicaragua.

Final Comments

Peace, in the long run, must be attained through hard-nosed negotiations. It is simply not sufficient to throw resources at a problem in the hopes they will solve problems that should have been thoroughly discussed between all the parties to a conflict and its resolution. It is particularly important to make sure that presidents or would-be presidents, ministers or would-be ministers, counselors or would-be counselors commit themselves to making any negotiated resolution work before you, as the peacemaker, even begin seriously to do your work.

The peace process in Sierra Leone in which I was involved came very close to being a resounding success and jewel in the crown of the United Nations and the international community. We had macroeconomists from the World Bank on the United Nations team of which I was a part. We had an agricultural team, a government team, a medical team. But the entire process failed because of a lack, during the immediate postconflict stabilization phase of which we spoke earlier, of sensitivity to assuring that the needs of all concerned were met.

In summary, there is no magic formula for peacemaking, -building, or -keeping, and the model we are using here is constantly being discussed, improved, and expanded. But in the end, every time we have discussions we come back to the same conclusion. The most important single thing is to reestablish hope in the minds of those who are in conflict. They must be able to look forward to reforms in the system they have opposed, to the establishment of educational opportunities, to acceptable social programs, and to an opportunity to be heard and to participate in their own futures. It is not necessary to bring conditions up to the level of developed countries. But it is necessary that conditions be offered at a level acceptable to the people of the soil in developing countries. Because only then will they have hope.

In short, if peace is to be durable, what is required is a realistic social contract between the parties in conflict, supported by assistance from the international community, from such organizations as the United Nations. I am well aware that this is easy to say but also know from experience that it is hard to accomplish and even harder to implement. With a holistic approach based on something like our continuum model, with a willingness to take calculated risks, and with a refusal to engage in ad hoc processes, the chances of success will be vastly improved.

I have met many very decent people since I became a peacekeeper, many of them in Central America and Africa. In Nicaragua, I was involved when we collected more than 22,000 weapons and disarmed over 22,000 combatants. I am proud of how that process went because no one was hurt in the process. We did largely stop brother killing brother, at least on a programmed and daily basis. We did not, however, solve the problems of Nicaragua. Even so, while in the long run it was not a complete success, as a soldier of thirty years' experience at the time, what I did is a source of pride because it was still the most positive thing I have ever done in my professional life. That is why I decided to continue attempting to apply the lessons I learned in Central America to other cases.

Because we failed to take into account so much that was important after disarmament, since then I have learned how important it is continuously to urge the international community, the United Nations, and all others who are involved in similar processes of bringing peace to take all-inclusive, holistic approaches to such situations. Unless the real causes of a conflict are addressed and, insofar as possible, solved, the end of war does not necessarily mean the beginning of peace. One must first create hope and then take a long-term bottom-up approach to the process of building peace so that the peace that is built will be durable, not merely ephemeral.

13

Sergio Caramagna, an OAS Peacemaker

A BIOGRAPHICAL SKETCH

Sergio Caramagna is a professional peacemaker with the OAS and has been involved in the peacemaking process in Nicaragua since 1990, most intensively in the Segovian highlands and tribal Indian Atlantic coastal regions, first as director of its office for disabled veterans, then of its verification and investigative office, and then as coordinator general of CIAV/OAS. In 1997 OAS Secretary General César Gavíria appointed Caramagna his representative in Nicaragua, a chief of mission position.

Born in Paraná, Argentina, in 1951, Caramagna is a sociologist educated at the Universidad Catolica de La Plata, Argentina, specializing in the promotion and defense of human rights, conflict resolution, demining, election observation, and reinsertion programs. He is especially adept at dealing with ethnic minorities, marginalized peoples, and the extremely poor. In my view, CIAV/OAS deserves the lion's share of the credit for transforming Nicaragua's once-failing peace process into one that is succeeding, and Caramagna's model for such missions, based on more than nine bitter years of experiences, should be must reading for anyone interested in bringing peace to wartorn regions anywhere.

□ □ □

PEACEMAKING IN NICARAGUA
Sergio Caramagna

I would like to express my appreciation for this opportunity to describe, as part of this study of peacemaking in Central America, my perspectives on the process as viewed from my position as director of the Organization of American States (OAS) office in Nicaragua, and to thank the Hoover Institution, the University of the Americas, and Timothy Brown, who made it possible for me to do so. It is a particular honor to be invited to participate in a study that features so many prominent individuals who have played vital roles in the process of bringing peace and democracy to our Americas. In the next few pages I would like to present to you my reflections and comments on the lessons learned by the OAS in Nicaragua and by its Comisíon Internacional de Apoyo y Verificacíon (CIAV/OAS) on peacemaking in Nicaragua, where I have been working for eight years. While I may occasionally mention persons or organizations, my comments should not be misconstrued as directed at any particular individuals or groups but rather as dealing with the process as a whole. But I will try to speak to you with as much sincerity and directness as possible, an approach made easier by being within an academic environment.

Most people believe Nicaragua's war ended in 1990. But peace in the sense of an end to war arrived in Nicaragua much later than that, quite recently, in the mid-1990s to be exact. It was then that several rearmed groups of various social and political origins, which had been fighting since the formal end of that country's civil conflict, finally laid down their arms. And yet, even as they laid down their arms, these groups continued to identify important economic, social, and political revindications as unachieved objectives. In Nicaragua today, there is also still an ongoing program to remove remaining antipersonnel mines in the countryside. While little noted, Nicaragua remains the most affected country in world by antipersonnel mines still in the soil after a war, with the estimated number of mines remaining in 1998 exceeding 90,000. These two dramatic and difficult problems, unmet expectations and uncleared mine fields, are but the sequels of an armed civil conflict followed by a peace agreement that failed to resolve them, and both the nonresolution of political problems and the enormous number of remaining land mines must give us pause to consider just how difficult, even now in 1998, the path to peace in Nicaragua remains. And yet as dramatic as the remaining problems, difficulties, and danger are in Nicaragua, it can still honestly be said that the country has made major progress toward peace. The Nicaragua of today, 1998, is vastly different from the Nicaragua we found when we began our mission in 1990. Its people have matured politically and its institutions have gained a great deal of strength, and these and other improvements merit full recognition. But a major question remains. Why, seven long and cruel years after a long and difficult war supposedly ended, is Nicaragua still faced with extremely difficult obstacles and problems?

The peace process in Nicaragua was possibly the first of its kind in the Americas. For us there were no precedents, either for how to end the war or for how to deal with the thousands upon thousands of persons, especially mountain peasants, who had been affected and who continued to be affected by its aftermath. Nor indeed did we understand how one might go about healing a country so affected by war that had, with great ferocity, resulted in thousands upon thousands of deaths and an immense amount of material destruction. Although it seems strange in hindsight, there weren't even any precedents for how to identify those who had and had not actually been involved in the conflict.

In the preceding essay, General Douglas made some introductory comments concerning the motivations of those who had engaged in the conflict, discussed the beginnings of the pacification process, and commented on the importance of ONUCA, the United Nations observer force with whom during the years of

1990 and 1991 we shared the difficult mission of bringing peace to Nicaragua.

Just one significant fact may best describe how unprepared Nicaragua was for peace. Two political parties competed for power in Nicaragua's 1990 national elections, and it was understood that the winner would be expected to take responsibility for pacification of the country. And yet neither party even included as a theme in its campaign the pacification and reconstruction of the country, much less the reinsertion into the country of tens of thousands of refugees and former combatants. This simple fact can serve as a yardstick against which to measure how ill prepared the nation's institutions were to deal with this immense problem in the future.

CIAV/OAS was created in response to an agreement reached between the five Central American presidents at Tela, Honduras, in 1989. At that time Nicaragua was represented by President Daniel Ortega. It was that agreement, known as the Telamar Accord, that led to the creation of both ONUCA and CIAV by assigning responsibilities for managing the peace process to two secretaries general, those of the United Nations and of the Organization of American States. In turn the two secretaries general divided their responsibilities, with the United Nations accepting greater responsibilities in Honduras and Costa Rica and the Organization of American States doing so in Nicaragua. It was assumed this would result in the U.N.'s military dealing with the armed Nicaraguan Resistance, with the OAS involved only after they were disarmed.

Then what was expected changed fundamentally. Most of the forces of the Nicaraguan Resistance demobilized neither in Honduras nor in Costa Rica but in Nicaragua, and many times more combatants, combatant family members, and social-base supporters were involved than had been expected. The OAS, the institution intended to be primarily responsible for the process only after reinsertion, was forced to learn on the job how to accomplish a much expanded and largely new mission. There was no manual to explain how to accomplish the peacekeeping mission it had been assigned, much less a model to explain how to advance the suddenly expanded process.

Perhaps the very first lesson we learned in Nicaragua was not to bring prejudices and preconceptions to such a process. For indeed we brought our own biases and fears with us. At the very beginning, officials of international organizations must abandon their preconceptions and come down to earth. In our case it was very difficult to become realistic because the reality we discovered was very different and far more complex than what we had been led to believe by our only previous source of information, wartime propaganda. Reality was much harder than the picture that had been painted in articles or on television screens.

This led to the second important lesson learned. Peace is not simply the laying down of arms. Disarmament and demobilization are not peace. From the very beginning we mistakenly thought that these two steps would be enough, and even later we sometimes continued to confuse disarmament and demobilization with peace. But disarmament, even at its best, is merely an early baby step taken voluntarily by the parties involved, merely a first stage in a process. The most difficult and complex part of the process comes next. We also learned that peace does not arrive naturally. It bursts on the scene. And the very suddenness of its arrival can create enormous difficulties, immense disorders, and the danger of blood flowing once more, largely because in the beginning the individuals, institutions, and international organizations involved in the process invariably seem to underestimate just how difficult and complicated the overall pacification process can be.

In Nicaragua the pacification process was too slow, incomplete, unverified, and unplanned, which had negative consequences and created great hardships and difficulties. To give an idea of these, I need merely point out that within two years of the disarmament of the Nicaraguan Resistance's combatants in 1990, CIAV had in its files the verification, based on the results of detailed formal investigations, of 142 murders of former combatants of the Nicaraguan Resistance and convincing evidence that in 70 percent of these cases the motives were political.

As a consequence of a peace that had not emerged from adequate negotiation or as part of a natural process, the civil institutions of Nicaragua were not ready for its arrival. For example, they were not ready to receive or to provide minimal health, education, or other social services to the returning population of refugees and former combatants and their families. On the other hand, the armed forces of Nicaragua were almost totally intact, but the original mandate established no mechanisms for controlling their actions during the pacification process. This contrasts sharply with what happened in El Salvador. Later agreements reached in El Salvador to end the insurgency there were more effective by several levels of magnitude, and as a consequence the peace process there was far more integrated and balanced because they paid a great deal more attention to the essential factors required for the establishment of a durable long-term peace.

Now to other matters. As concerns the process of reinsertion, from the institutional point of the view of the OAS it was of great importance simply to have been involved in the process, to have discovered a new purpose of its mandate. But we, like too many other international organizations, brought our preconceptions to the effort. Normally, in international organizations we routinely commit an enormous error. We see those with whom we work as the "objects" of our efforts. We talk of quantities, we treat human beings in quantitative terms, and in taking this quantitative approach we also adopt a dehumanized perspective when we plan programs. We plan "tasks," we engage in "programs," but in so doing we too often miss the point. When you change this perspective, when international civil servants think of themselves not as dealing with "objects" but with "subjects," this changes dramatically.

It is only when one looks at the mission of peacemaking as involving face-to-face human relationships with subjects and not just as a program involving objects that the human and social aspects of the problem emerge with great clarity. In terms of peacemaking, regardless of how well intentioned a program may be, if it is not conceived in human terms it will be flawed from the start. The Telamar Accord is an excellent example of this. The accord barely mentioned humanitarian assistance to the demobilized members of the Nicaraguan Resistance, covering the entire issue of humanitarian assistance, food, clothing, medical attention, housing, and reinsertion in just one short line that was barely explained. Telamar gave no evidence of any understanding of how important these things would be if CIAV were successfully to comply with its mandate to reinsert into civil society those combatants who agreed to demobilize. This lack of attention to fundamentals at the beginning was to create major future problems.

In terms of the operation itself, we were also in for many surprises. The first and possibly biggest surprise came when we discovered who the people really were who demobilized and repatriated. It was the first of many challenges to our preconceptions and prejudices. As the former Resistance fighters demobilized in 1990, a dossier was created on each person, on each combatant who disarmed. It was not a dossier designed with the idea of scientific research in mind, but it did include basic information on the identity, age, place of origin, nuclear family, gender, and place of origin of each combatant who laid down his or her arms. It was only at this point that we discovered, and the word really is *discovered,* that well over 80 percent of those laying down their arms were simple peasants, campesinos from the North Central mountain region of Nicaragua. Another 10 percent were Miskito Indians from the northern part of the Atlantic region of that country. Fewer than 20 percent were over twenty-six years of age, whereas more than 80 percent were under that age—to be more precise, between the ages of sixteen and twenty-six. In sum, what appeared before us was an unknown human dimension of the situation of which we had previously been entirely ignorant. It was a human dimension that wartime propaganda had totally misrepresented and that forced us to drastically change our way of thinking and our plans.

When suddenly we found ourselves dealing with subjects and

not objects, with real live human beings, when we found we had to begin to work on the social dimensions of the problem and of our mandate at its deepest human levels, we were forced to abandon the prejudices and preconceptions created by prior propaganda. We were forced to begin to think with greater maturity that the person we once thought of as an object was in fact a subject complete with his or her own personality, beliefs, and personal history, with his or her own problems and difficulties, concerns and hopes. But, and above all, we were forced by this discovery to accept that the former Resistance combatants and their families had, above all, their own culture, and that their culture had its own value.

This taught us, then, a major lesson. It is only after peacemakers manage to overcome their own prejudices and accept reality that communications between them and the subject, not the object, of their mission can deepen and become authentic and effective. The problem is that international civil servants are too often not prepared to accept that a major part of their mandate is to take into consideration how their actions will affect the individuals with whom they deal in their full human dimension, complete with individual histories, social identities, and a basic need to rebuild their lives, to return to the places that gave them birth, to familiar landscapes and communities, to rediscover their families, to confront the drama such experiences so often signify. And yet, especially in terms of peacemaking, accepting this dimension of the situation is essential to success. Once international civil servants have overcome their prejudices, they must abandon any relationship based on treating those with whom they deal as objects in favor of a much more personal relationship between peacemakers and their all-too-human subjects. It is this establishment of real communications that then allows peacemakers to incorporate into their efforts an understanding of the world in which the subject lives. Only after this can programs be designed based on a solid foundation of real understanding of the world in which the subject lives and not on a false ideas based on propaganda or misinformation brought into the equation by the peacemaker from outside. And only after programs are transformed from ones built on foundations of prior prejudices into programs founded on reality can they hope to really succeed, because this change of focus inevitably results in fundamental changes in what one first thought reconciliation should be, in what one imagined should be done to combat poverty, and above all in attitude toward social development.

By changing the process from one of an international organization merely dealing with an object to one that involves its working together with a subject, the importance of the individual and the culture of the subject become the overriding consideration. This new focus brings with it a commitment. International organizations too often differentiate between commitments to individuals and professional obligations to missions. In our view, when you are dealing with communities that have their own culture, they merit profound respect for their historical traditions, and an international organization must never differentiate between its commitment to a community as a culture and its professional obligations. To the contrary, a commitment to deal with persons or communities at the human level deepens the professional obligation. This was certainly the case with the changes in attitude and perspective forced on us by our discovery of the real situation that underlay our program and the humanity of the people we were dealing with. In short, to use a popular expression, before we could do our job right we had to *bajar los zumos*, to clear our heads of the misconceptions and prejudices we had brought with us.

When we talk about reinsertion we therefore are speaking of a process we were forced to create, or re-create, based on new realities we discovered only after we began working. This was particularly true as regards humanitarian assistance. It became obvious that if humanitarian assistance were treated simply as charity, it would be of no lasting value to the communities receiving it or to its individual beneficiaries. We would simply be creating mechanisms of dependency and paternalism that would have been useless in terms of the deeper need of the process to make pacification permanent. This required us to rethink the fundamentals of the program, which initially had been planned to last only about two months.

Let me repeat myself, because our error illustrates so clearly what we learned during the process of pacification in Nicaragua. The original mission of CIAV was expected to last at most two months between June and August of 1990. From August on, therefore, we had to invent how to reinsert the thousands and thousands of former combatants and others who were still in the process of reintegrating into the life of the country from exile, how to transform a mechanistic reinsertion program into a program of human development. One program that illustrates how the process had become two-way was owner-construction of houses.

A great majority of those who demobilized were persons who had nothing, no material possessions, just a change of clothing, a bag of food, and an ID card issued to them by a peace mission. Once we began communicating clearly, we found that they had been promised land and demanded that they receive it. After all, they were peasants. They also insisted on receiving at least a tent under which they could be protected from the weather, from the sun and rain. But soon a program of owner-construction of houses was suggested by former combatants. It proved to be very valuable to the process. It was not a program executed by CIAV or the OAS but one designed in all its characteristics and executed by its own beneficiaries, and they designed and built their own houses with only technical support from CIAV. This was an excellent example of the new philosophy of our mission, that the beneficiaries themselves be involved in their own programs. We also became engaged in a participant-initiated program in support of agricultural production, which, in the regions of Jinotega and Matagalpa in the years after 1991, resulted in record levels of production of beans and rice. Throughout our years of building peace, the construction of schools and health clinics, training and educational courses, and others were also programs in which beneficiaries worked directly and that marked our process.

But the process has not been easy. Neither has it been entirely peaceful. In 1992, two years after the former Resistance combatants demobilized, small groups of former combatants began to rearm and return to the mountains, precisely because of a lack of security in the region. These groups emerged precisely in the regions that had seen the most fighting, the Segovias. They were the first to be known as Re-Contras. The emergence of the Re-Contras in the Segovias should have alerted the authorities that the situation had become dangerous. But it did not. In the communities affected by this phenomenon, not even the most rudimentary governmental presence and services were reestablished after the war. They had no institutions of justice, police, health services, or education. In fact, they were communities in which, from 1979 on, there were no legitimate government institutions functioning. They did not even have institutions with the authority to perform these tasks.

At its very beginning, the Sandinista Revolution had abolished the community's preexisting institutions of government, but it then failed to replace them with any alternative institutions with legitimacy, especially as this refers to the resolution of conflicts and the administration of justice. So for almost twenty years an entire region of the country suffered, from eleven years of war and eight years of less than peace, and was maintained totally at the margin of the nation. In fact, the communities most affected by the Re-Contra had been absolutely marginalized by a state that was highly centralized. In 1992 they still remained, after two decades, absolutely at the margins of the national economy and absolutely at the margins of the culture of the nation. This was to continue to be the case until 1996–1997.

The Final Frontier

The region engaged in this new conflict, the heartland of the Nicaraguan Resistance movement, has been labeled "the forgotten frontier." It is a label that was first used by General Augústo César Sandino, who applied it to the Segovias in 1927. Seventy years later, after the Somozas, after the Sandinista Revolution, after the false peace of 1990 to 1996, the region is still what General Sandino called it, forgotten. In 1993 one Nicaraguan in this region was dying every two days from violence, and the army was having one clash every day with the armed groups. It was also the region of Nicaragua in which we were able to verify the highest incidence of poverty in the nation and which is the poorest in the entire country. These facts well explain the dimensions of the term "forgotten frontier" to those who care to listen.

The Peasants Create Their Own Peace Process

And yet it was from this same region that hope emerged. It was to be exactly the communities most affected by the return to violence from which we were to learn an extraordinary lesson about the capacity for civic virtue of even the poorest of peasants, of Nicaragua's most humble, the campesino sector. Without any outside involvement they were to demonstrate a capacity of spontaneous organization to put themselves on their own feet and an amazing ability to address their own problems. From the communities most in conflict in the mid-1990s there emerged an authentic grassroots-level form of social organization capable of transforming the region, Comisiones de Paz (Peace Commissions). The most fundamental objective of the Peace Commissions the campesinos created was to solve their own basic problems at a local level. To do this they invented a process of pacification that did not flow from the capital downward but rather spread from the community outward. Their most important objective was to defend their very right to life itself against those who threatened them. Their second objective was to promote human rights and to create a means to resolve conflicts locally and then also to generate, by involving the entire local populace at the rural community level, means to engage in self-help projects.

It was for us a surprise to discover the process. At first we did not even know it was going on. But as soon as we discovered what was happening, the OAS began to assist the rural Peace Commissions in their efforts. In fewer than three years the commissions had grown, merged with neighboring commissions, and pacified much of the Segovias. Today (1998) there are well over 100 Peace Commissions in operation, each made up of members popularly selected from the community it serves, with altogether more than 3,000 locally elected members. They constitute the largest, most effective, and most participatory example we have been able to identify of local communities spontaneously organizing themselves to advance their own interests. But from our perspective, they do even more than that. They constitute what may well be the best example we have ever found of institutions that can maintain the peace, that can in fact build peace, and that can successfully engage in an authentic process of national conciliation starting at the local level while being neither managed nor directed by external institutions, much less by international organizations, but through the creativity of the peasantry and managed by Nicaraguans themselves.

Lessons Learned

I would like to conclude with a recapitulation, by describing eight key lessons we have learned from our experience in Nicaragua.

1. The international community quickly forgets countries that have suffered from internal conflicts once the conflicts end. The peacemaking process in Nicaragua did not receive anywhere near the same level of external attention from international observers as the war did. And yet it is when peace agreements are signed that the really difficult work begins, the process of pacification, reconciliation, and reconstruction of the country. International attention must continue until this process is successfully completed.

2. The haste with which the international community insisted on resolving the conflict in Nicaragua and the pressures brought on one of the parties in conflict left substantial holes in the peace agreements. Failure to address all of the key problems at the be-

ginning caused serious problems later during the process of pacification.

3. If the peace-building process is to succeed, those involved must have an objective, honest, and accurate understanding of the populations and people involved in the conflict and must treat them as subjects and participants, not just as objects. If not, the peace process will fail. It is a serious error not to take into account during the entire process the interests and concerns all of the protagonists in a conflict, and the process of peacekeeping must be pursued within the context of the conflict that made it necessary and in direct contact with all the parties that were involved. This is especially true in every country and situation in which there has been a civil war. This is a lesson that can be applied to the planning of any peace operation in which the international community becomes involved. An international organization must abandon its prejudices, forget its preconceptions, set aside its bureaucratic assumptions and arms-length approach to problems, and obtain accurate and honest information about the parties involved in the conflict and the actual situation on the ground prior to planning its operations and becoming engaged. Otherwise it will not successfully perform its mission once it arrives on the scene.

4. During a peace operation it is important to monitor human rights, but there is no need for a human-rights-monitoring organization with a large number of participants or activists. The lesson learned by the OAS was that very few people are needed in the countryside. It was possible to reduce sharply the number of international civil servants involved once demobilization had been completed. In Nicaragua, the OAS was perfectly capable of fulfilling its human-rights-monitoring mission with only seven international civil servants involved in field operations. Together with only nine national, that is to say Nicaraguan, officials, they were able to do the job quite efficiently when supplied with vehicles capable of moving around in the extremely difficult terrain of the mountains and with a system of efficient communications that allowed them constantly to transmit up-to-the-minute information and reports to a central office. All the OAS field officers engaged

in human rights monitoring were civilians and fulfilled their obligations with no military or police support or protection. Indeed, the presence of soldiers and police officers was often counterproductive.

5. Local institutions and individuals must be involved alongside the international mission in the peace process and work together for the peaceful resolution of conflicts. This approach was used by the OAS to resolve various sorts of conflicts, particularly agrarian, community, or political conflicts. The most important instance of this occurred when we were accompanied by institutional representatives and prominent persons in successful efforts to arrange the release, on August 27, 1997, of forty-one hostages taken on El Súngano mountain in Nueva Segovia, including three national congressman, officers of the army, and other prominent individuals.[1] In another earlier instance this approach was also employed to obtain the release of thirty-eight other individuals, including the vice president of the Republic and members of the national assembly in Managua on August 26, 1996.

6. Peacemaking activities of international missions must include as participants nationals of the country in which they are operating. Normally, local missions of international organizations relegate local citizens to secondary positions of administrative or logistical nature. But the gradual incorporation of Nicaraguan nationals at the operational level within CIAV, while taking necessary precautions as regards these national employees, particularly as related to their prior roles during the war, proved to be a major success.

7. Peace missions should be transitory in nature. This is a lesson primarily drawn from the experience of the Peace Commissions. International organizations can best perform their roles during the emergency stages of stopping a war and in the immediate aftermath of a conflict. But their primary objective should be to work themselves out of jobs by helping create conditions under which the country itself can maintain the peace. They play important roles during the pacification stage, but their principal objective after dealing with the armed phase of conflict should be to

develop institutions and conditions that will allow the country to continue the process on its own. If international organizations do not do this and do not work as much as possible through national institutions, the national system will not be able to sustain the peace process once they leave, leaving behind what at best will be only a very fragile peace.

8. International organizations should never proceed more quickly than the natural pace set by civil society. It is vital first to gain the goodwill of all those who firmly believe in peace, reconciliation, and democracy as the most important of permanent values, because it is the people themselves who in the end must resolve their own problems. International organizations should not propose solutions. International organizations should never say what must be done. They should only accompany a national society as it advances at its own pace. Each country must resolve its own conflicts on its own terms and apply its own solutions to its own problems.

Perhaps lesson 8 is the biggest lesson learned by the OAS from its experiences in Nicaragua. It is one we did not fully learn until we uncovered the capacity for organization of those Nicaraguans who were, after all, the real principal protagonists in the process of war, pacification, and reconciliation. The final goal must be to help a country build a sustainable peace not dependent on international organizations but founded in the capacity of the nation itself. The OAS is proud to have accompanied the Nicaraguan people through the process.

14

Timothy Charles Brown,
Editor

AN AUTOBIOGRAPHICAL SKETCH

In fairness to the other contributors, readers deserve some personal background on me, the editor, as well. Although born in Kansas, I was raised in Nevada, and took my B.A. in International Relations at the University of Nevada. My professional experiences include Marine service (ten years), diplomatic service (twenty-seven years), and academia (eight years), most recently as a research fellow of Stanford University's Hoover Institution (since 1994). I earned a Ph.D. in 1997 from New Mexico State University with a dissertation on the Nicaraguan Contras. Experiences directly relevant to this study include professional tours of duty in Nicaragua, Honduras, El Salvador, Guatemala, Spain, and Mexico; as deputy coordinator for Cuban affairs and country officer for Paraguay/Uruguay during their insurgencies; and shorter tours in Guatemala and Panama. I also have a home in Costa Rica. In terms of guerrilla and other limited wars, I served in Vietnam, did counterinsurgency work with the Philippine Rangers and Thai Border Patrol and Rural Development teams, was a NATO advisor, covered the Sergeant

Brunswyk rebellion in Suriname and *independentiste* violence in Caribbean France, and from 1987 to 1990 was senior liaison in Central America to the Nicaraguan Resistance and ONUCA.

□ □ □

THE CHILDREN OF SANDINO: A VIEW FROM THE RADICAL MIDDLE
Timothy Charles Brown

Latin America has a well-deserved reputation as a region of unjust and inequitable societies. Although conditions vary considerably from country to country, in general each is dominated directly or indirectly by a traditional and usually tiny elite, often descended from Spanish colonial-era elites, that dominates it socially, economically, and politically. Although some countries have been far more successful than others at softening the consequences of such control by the few, this is still almost as true of Costa Rica as it is of Paraguay. One need only read Samuel Stone's *The Heritage of the Conquistadores* or contemplate the family connections between several of the participants in this study to catch a glimpse of just how closely intertwined these elites can be, even across national borders.[1] They have kept their grips on real power thanks largely to defensive mechanisms erected by these same elites against both external and internal competition. Their external defenses are largely economic and commercial, the internal ones political and societal. It was the relative impermeability of these defenses and the organized disenfranchisement and poverty of the masses they engendered that created the conditions for violent revolutions in this century. Stated another way, it is the unwillingness to share the "Three P's," *Prestígio, Podér y Plata* (Prestige, Power and Prosperity) of Latin America's neocolonial oligarchies that created the conditions that made the region's violent revolutions possible, if not inevitable. The revolutionaries merely took advantage of what the elite had wrought.

The several armed conflicts discussed above, from Sandino's wars in the 1920s and 1930s against Nicaragua's Conservative government of the time and the American Marines to the Contra war of 1979–1996, took place within relatively restricted parameters in terms of both time and space, and each had both unique qualities and similarities with the others. In their own ways, every revolutionary and guerrilla who speaks here bases his or her arguments on the injustices and inequalities produced by elite monopolies over the Three P's and justifies his or her actions in essentially the same way. Each claims to have acted to right what they saw as grievances so serious and so set in politicosocial concrete that only armed violence could redress them. From "Pepe" Puente's support for Fidel Castro and the original Sandinista rebels to *Fermán Cienfuegos*'s quarrel with the exceptionally inequitable economic class divisions in El Salvador to the reactions of *Comandantes Rubén* and *Blass* against Sandinista land seizures and attacks on the identities of the highlands peasantry and Miskito tribal Indians, all the participants couch their reasons for taking up arms in such terms. But the two sets of participants, revolutionaries and guerrillas, also describe what were two very different kinds of struggles.

Eduardo Sancho, *Fermán Cienfuegos*, accepts without question, in fact almost revels in, the description of the revolutionary struggle in El Salvador as one generated and directed by a small and self-selected intellectual elite, of which he was a member. "Pepe" Puente, Plutarco Hernández, and Alejandro Martínez, although less categorical than Sancho, in essence say much the same of their struggles. They themselves self-identify as members of the radical revolutionary elite that led the Sandinista rebellion against Nicaragua's Somoza dictatorship, and their reasoning is founded in intellectual analytical processes. Their main argument is that the true Sandinista elite did not then survive to direct the subsequent social revolution, leading to its failure. The perspective is, then, cognitive and vanguardist. In sharp contrast, the former Nicaraguan Resistance members, the Contras if you will, are all peasant highlanders or Native Americans. Their descriptions of why they fought, although similar in terms of their founding in the redress of grievances against a closed and unresponsive politicosocial system by violent means, are couched in terms of identity and survival.

The differences between the two forms of armed rebellion are the reason that the first part of this study was divided into two sections, one of revolutionaries and a second of guerrillas. The revolutions discussed in the part I were elite driven, from the top down. The guerrilla conflict discussed in part II, the Contra war, was peasant and tribal-Indian driven, from the bottom up. The nature of their leaderships and prosecutions reflect this sharp difference. In the first case, that of elite-generated revolutions, although the social conditions for revolution may have existed before, the eruption of armed conflicts largely was caused by the deliberate decision by a few to exploit those conditions for the purpose of establishing a new status quo based on ideological principals, usually Marxist. By way of contrast, the Miskito Indian and highlands peasant rebellions were reactions against efforts to build precisely just such a new status quo on the ruins of their traditional systems, social structures, and identities.

There is a second dimension to the problem. In each conflict discussed here, there was extensive external involvement, which usually deepened and lengthened the conflict. But the extent of the organic links between those on the left, Cuba's 26th of July Movement, Nicaragua's Sandinistas, El Salvador's Faribundo Martí Front, and Mexican leftists, has never, insofar as I can tell, been discussed so candidly by those who were direct participants in the process. One of the biggest surprises, especially for those reasonably well acquainted with the historic view of these conflicts, is the extent of Mexican involvement. It is no secret that Mexico strongly sympathized with many anti-American revolutionaries in Central America, from Sandino to the Sandinistas. But the depth and detail with which several participants describe its proactive participation with money, guns, professional training, logistical support, and even troops is new. "Pepe" Puente's discussion of how Mexican army officers ands troops fought, and sometimes died in combat, against the U.S. Marines in Nicaragua in Sandino's 1928–1933 war has not, to my knowledge, been previously revealed, nor has the extent to which Mexican officials and labor unions provided money, transportation, and arms to

Fidel Castro. A second surprise is the extent to which the Salvadoran FMLN and Nicaraguan FSLN were involved in mutual support. The $15–18 million in cash sent by the FMLN and the return of, according to *Fermán Cienfuegos* of some 83,000 guns, by the FSLN put numbers to a long suspected but rarely publicly documented linkage, but the direct involvement of the Panamanian armed forces in the transport of arms has not previously been publicly confirmed by those most directly involved.

Revolutionary Cuba's role in actively supporting several Central American revolutions has long been alleged. But never before have actual participants described in such vivid detail the extent to which Cuba was involved in operational planning, political manipulation, or the provision of training, arms, financial support, advisors, and even troops in the field during the final push against the Somozas. And neither have the extent of People's Republic of China involvement nor the collusion of the Costa Rican and U.S. governments in efforts to overthrow Somoza been described so directly by those best placed to know. Nor, to my knowledge, has it ever before been publicly documented.

Although the roles of the United States and the Soviet Union in exploiting these conflicts in their own national interests have been more fully discussed on the record, never before have both radical revolutionaries and prodemocracy Resistance combat veterans come together in one book to accuse the United States of so much. All of them accuse several successive American administrations of simply exploiting conflicts in the region to advance diverse political agendas of both left and right. Alejandro Martínez's not only claims that it was the Carter CIA that tried to recruit him to head up a nascent American-supported Nicaraguan paramilitary movement even before Reagan was inaugurated but also accuses Carter of having caused the problem in the first place. This supports and even partly documents both the editor's own findings in a separate study that dates Carter-era involvement with what was to become the Contra project even further back, to early August of 1980, and the conclusion that Carter, not Reagan, was the real father of the Contras.[2] *Rubén*, Martínez, and

Tigrillo, each in his own way, then accuses the United States of having deliberately fine-tuned its assistance to the Contras to assure that they could neither win nor lose, perhaps a politically defensible approach but an exceedingly painful one in terms of additional bloodshed. The problem was then compounded by both the Bush and Clinton administrations—Bush by shoving the Contras pell-mell into a fatally flawed disarmament and demobilization agreement that left them exposed to massive reprisals by their still-armed Sandinista enemies; Clinton by then failing to ensure that the massive U.S. mission in Nicaragua demand the Nicaraguan government honor its commitments to the United States' erstwhile Contra allies and that it channel sufficient assistance to them to ensure their safe reintegration back into Nicaraguan society. To their shame, as *Rubén* and many others in separate discussions have painfully noted, those international human rights organizations that were most critical of the Resistance during its 1979–1990 war were hermetically silent when it came to even greater human rights violations committed against the Contras during 1990–1996 after they laid down their AKs. The American Latin Americanist academic community, which during that time had also been exceptionally loud in its condemnations of the Resistance, remained equally silent.

In fact, it was precisely the failure of the United States, of academe, and of the human rights establishment to treat the Contras the same way they did the Salvadoran and Guatemalan guerrillas that caused, prolonged, and then failed to resolve fairly the conflict there. The laudatory comments by *Fermán Cienfuegos* about how the U.S. Congress, the FMLN's lobbying office in Washington, D.C., and the pro-FMLN partisanship of President Bush's Assistant Secretary for Latin America made certain the FMLN got a fair deal stand in stark contrast to American abandonment of its erstwhile peasant and Indian allies in Nicaragua.

Further, it was precisely a combination of this American indifference and the clear ideological biases of both the American academic community and the international human rights establishment, as well as their willingness to suspend their critical judgment during the conflict in Nicaragua, that transformed what was wartime Sandinista propaganda into the conventional wisdom that *Rubén* labels *La Leyenda Negra de La Contra*, The Black Legend of the Contras, that misled both the U.N. and the OAS so badly that their missions in Nicaragua initially failed. Both U.N. General Douglas and especially Dr. Caramagna of the OAS make this in fact central themes in their essays and conclude that the biggest mistake an honest peacemaker can make is to believe such Black Legends. Although both Douglas and Caramagna are much too diplomatic to say so directly, I can only conclude that it was the failures of both the human rights establishment and academe to honor their ethical obligations to be objective and nonideological in favor of supporting political agendas that prolonged several of the conflicts, but most especially that in Nicaragua.

The Sons of Sandino

Perhaps most fascinating of all was the discovery by the participants while they were on the podium at the University of the Americas in Puebla, Mexico, during a Hoover-sponsored seminar of just how much they have in common. Their "*¡Hijo de Puta!*" exclamations after it ended were heartfelt expressions of shocked realization of this. Each had risked his life in a cause, and yet each quickly agreed that their similarities are far greater than their differences. Each also realized he was not alone in deciding to lay down his AK-47 in favor of nonviolent participation in Latin America's ongoing but peaceful democratic revolution.

Even more, every one of those participating traced his or her personal or professional roots back to Nicaragua's legendary rebel, General Augústo César Sandino. Whether it is "Pepe" Puente's father carrying water to him in Mexico's oil fields, or *Don Alejandro* seeing that Sandino was safe in the Segovian mountains, or *Rubén* explaining that one of the peasant's grievances was unhappiness over how Pacific lowlands Marxists denigrated the name of Sandino—in whose army the Contras' fathers but not those of the 1979–1990 FSLN directorate had fought—even though they appropriated his name, it is the image of Sandino that unexpectedly comes to form the spinal cord of this study. When Sergio Caramagna closes his own study of the process of peacemaking by referring to Sandino's description of the homeland of the Contras as Nicaragua's "forgotten frontier," he perhaps inadvertently labels all those who present here as legitimate children of Sandino. Outside that circle lie both their traditional hard-right neocolonial oligarchical opponents and their hard-left international radical enemies. From the region's armies, which should be demilitarized if not abolished, to its still hardline radicals willing to use violence before reason, both these extremes lay beyond the pale of this study. Within its circle stand people dedicated to struggling against Latin America's tradition of unjust and inequitable societies and who will continue to struggle to change this, but who are now dedicated to advancing their causes through the ballot box, not out of the barrel of an AK-47. Opponents of both the extreme right and extreme left but still dedicated to making basic, revolutionary changes in their societies, they then are of the radical middle.

APPENDIX

On following pages are photocopies from Costa Rican passport 8-043-357 of Alejandro Martínez confirming he traveled to the United States late in the Carter presidency. Martínez says he was invited to Washington, D.C., by the CIA to discuss paramilitary aid to the Contras. The American Consul in San José, Costa Rica, initially refused Martínez's visa and, to alert other Consuls to his decision, inserted a special handwritten note to that effect on page 40 of his passport. The Ambassador immediately intervened at the urging of the CIA Station Chief and the Consul reversed his decision that same day, 13 January 1981, issuing Martínez a most unusual three-month, one-entry B-1 visa valid for business travel only [visa 00364, page 17. Tourists receive B-2 visas; most business travelers receive dual B-1/B-2s]. Martínez traveled immediately and was admitted to the U.S. on 15 January for business purposes only, as confirmed by Immigration Service admission stamp 060 MIA 26 [also page 17]. [Courtesy of Alejandro Martínez]. Ronald Reagan was inaugurated on 20 January 1981 and did not issue his first, now-declassified Presidential Finding authorizing covert paramilitary aid to the Contras until eleven months later on 24 December. Since by law prior to engaging in covert operations such a Finding must be signed by the President and formal notifications made to select committees of Congress, Martínez's trip would have taken place pursuant to an earlier but still secret Finding by Jimmy Carter.

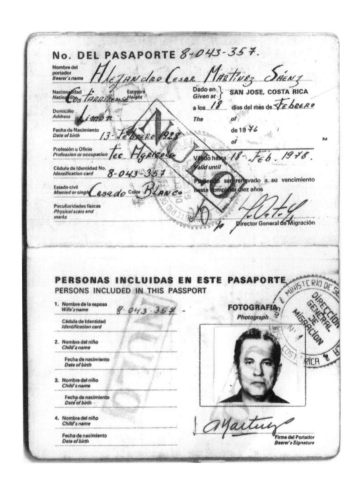

Ministerio de **VISAS** idad Pública
DEPARTAMENT DE MIGRACION
REPUBLICA DE COSTARICA

VISA 03282

Bueno para salir del país de ida y cualquiera. Esta visa caduca al los treinta días San José 21 ABR. 1982

JEFE DE MIGRACION

Nº 03605

THE UNITED STATES
OF AMERICA
NONIMMIGRANT VISA

SAN JOSE
B-1   14 JAN 1981
ONE
12 ABR. 1981
BEARER(S)

Karl E. Boh... IMMIGRATION
DIA 26
JAN 1 5 1981
ADMITTED

...ER RETIRADO
por cualquier Delegado de Migra-
ción o a su ingreso a Costa Rica y
ENTREGARLO al DEPARTAMENTO DE
MIGRACION EN San JOSE.
Fecha 21 ABR. 1982

NULO

6848

EXPEDIDO
en
Fecha 18 FEB 1976

COSTA RICA
JUAN SANTAMARIA
26 MAR. 1976 2
SALIDA
MIGRACION

END NOTES

Chapter 1

1. Comando (one *m*, not two, Spanish style) was the Contra combatant's term for themselves and is used throughout this book to refer to individual Nicaraguan Resistance fighters. The better-known term Contra, for counterrevolutionary, was a pejorative propaganda label that stuck.

2. I am not unaware of the implications of this early date, which dates the first U.S. government contacts with those who were to become the Nicaraguan Contras back to the Carter administration's time in office.

3. For discussion in detail of the identity and roots of the Nicaraguan Resistance movement known as the Contras, see T. Charles Brown, *The Real Contra War: Highlander Peasant Resistance in Nicaragua* (Norman: University of Oklahoma Press), 2000.

Chapter 2

1. Confirmed by Jaime Wheelock in his *Nicaragua: El Papel de La Vanguárdia* (Buenos Aires: Editorial Contrapunto, 1986), p. 50, and by

Tomás Borge at several points in his *La Paciente Impaciencia* (Mexico City: Editorial Diana, 1989), pp. 164–178, 184, 187–188, 192–214.

2. Oral history, José Obidio Puente León, Mexico City, May 15–18, 1998. Videotape interview, conducted by the editor in Spanish. This and all other translations in this study, unless otherwise noted, are by the editor. Private collection.

3. Manuel Jirón describes "Pepe" Puente as the first Mexican internationalist to enroll in the Sandinista cause, as the only living link between Augústo César Sandino and the FSLN, and as the single person who knows best each of the Nine Comandantes who conducted Nicaragua's 1979–1990 socialist revolution. Manuel Jirón, *Quién es Quién en Nicaragua* (San José, Costa Rica: Editorial Radio Amor, 1986), p. 457.

4. The mural formed a striking background for the oral history, and José Obidio's children's names made for some strange dialogue during its filming. "Was that Marx in the phone? No, it was Sandino saying Stalin will be late for dinner," or "We're having a birthday party for Mao, and Lenin and Fidelia will be there. Want to come?"

5. A Mexican army officer who later served with Sandino in Nicaragua, Andres Garcia Salgado, claims that at one point Pórtes Gil, then governor of Veracruz and later president of Mexico, was called to Mexico City by President Plutarco Elías Calles and told Cárdenas's support for Sandino had to stop or the United States would invade Mexico because of it. Andrés Garcia Salgado, *Yo estuve con Sandino* (Mexico City: Editorial Colores, n.d.), p. 57. "Pepe" Puente, who later met him, says Garcia confirmed that he and other Mexican army officials had served with Sandino and that some Mexican army personnel had died in combat against the American marines in Nicaragua.

6. One instance of this is discussed briefly in the United States Coast Guard's official history of the period, *Rum War at Sea* (Washington, D.C.: Government Printing Office, 1964), pp. 124–125, by Commander Malcolm F. Willoughby, which identifies the ship being used to transport Mexican Army troops to Nicaragua as "El Superior." In *Sandino en Yucatán 1929–1930* (Mexico City: Secretaria de Educación Publica, 1988), p. 55, Carlos Villanueva reports that Sandino arrived in Progreso, Yucatán, on July 11, 1929, aboard "El Superior," which is identified as a Mexican government vessel.

7. Noél Guerrero, not Carlos Fonseca Amador, is considered by both "Pepe" Puente and Tomás Borge as the real founder of Nicaragua's

Sandinista Front. Puente, interview of October 1999, and Borge, *La Paciente,* pp. 138–40. Borge claims that Guerrero disappeared in 1963 and became "lost in the increasingly dense jungles of Mexico City," *La Paciente,* p. 140, but I had an extended discussion with Guerrero in Mexico City in October 1999 and found him lucid and active despite his eighty-four years (he was born in Leon, Nicaragua, in 1915). Guerrero said he has been in personal contact with Borge for many years. He said that he became a Communist in Nicaragua as a youth and was active in clandestine operations for decades both there and in other countries. Guerrero confirmed he had worked closely with "Pepe" Puente's father in Mexico in the Mexican petroleum workers' union, the STPRM, and then with "Che" Guevara in Cuba. He also confirmed meeting the Puentes in his Mexican jail in 1956 and that the Puentes also met Fidel Castro and his group at the same time. Further, Guerrero confirmed his 1960 meeting with "Che" and the Puentes in Guevara's Cuban Central Bank office, and "Pepe" Puente's description of the ill-starred Sandinista Bocay expedition of 1963; it was he who issued the orders for the group to divide.

8. During a February 1999 visit to the Museum of the Revolution in Havana, I was struck by a plague honoring Lázaro Cárdenas that occupies a place of honor at the entrance to the salon honoring "Che" Guevara.

9. Today the *Granma* stands in a glass enclosure in central Havana just behind the main building of the Museum of the Revolution. It is a major attraction.

10. As of 1999, Zabalú owned and managed a posh tourist steak house in a suburb of Havana. I visited it in February of that year and had an excellent dinner.

11. Edelbérto Tórres Espinosa is also mentioned repeatedly by Tomás Borge in *La Paciente.* He and his son, Edelbérto Tórres Rivas, were both important figures in recent Nicaraguan history. For a biographical sketch of Tórres Espinosa, see Jirón, *Quién es Quién,* 459–461. For an idea of the son's thinking, see Edelbérto Tórres Rivas, *Crísis en el Podér en Centroamerica* (San José, Costa Rica: Editora de la Universidad de Costa Rica, EDUCA, 1989).

12. APRA, Alianza Popular Revolucionaria Americana, is a hemisphere-wide socialist but not Marxist–Leninist revolutionary movement that originated in Peru under the leadership of Victor Raúl Haya de la

Torre, who had visited Central America often and once taught in Costa Rica.

13. Alejandro Martínez, whose own story appears as chapter 4 in this book.

14. Fonseca appears in the Mitrokin KGB archives under the code name GIRODOLOG (Hydrologist) as "a trusted agent," Christopher Andrews and Vasili Mitrokhin, *The Sword and the Shield: The Mitrokhin Archives and the Secret History of the KGB* (New York: Basic Books, 1999), p. 363. "Pepe" Puente noted during our November 29, 1999, telephone interview that from the Soviet perspective Fonseca no doubt did seem "a trusted agent."

15. Carlos Fonseca Amador, *Un Nicaragüense en Moscú*, which was published in Managua on May Day, 1958, by Editorial Artes Graficos. I purchased my own copy that same year from a bookstore run by a Canadian, across the street from Managua's Gran Hotel.

16. Tamara Bunke Bider, better known as Tania La Guerrillera. Born of East German Communist parents who fled to Buenos Aires, Argentina, during World War II, she returned to East Germany as a youth and was educated there. Bilingual in Spanish and German, and with knowledge of French and Russian, her relationships with "Ché" Guevara and Carlos Fonseca Amador are detailed in *Tania—the Unforgettable Guerrilla* (New York: Random House, 1971), pp. 16–17, 39, 70, 74. Some believe she was an agent of the East Germany's STASI intelligence service and Guevara's case officer in Bolivia, if not before.

17. Identified in KGB archives as Manuel Ramón de Jesús Andara y Úbeda, code name PRIM, he received Line F sabotage training in Russia in 1965 and was then sent in 1966 to head a sleeper sabotage team in Ensenada, Mexico, targeted against the United States. Andrews and Mitrokhin, *The Sword and the Shield*, p. 363. In a telephone interview on November 29, 1999, "Pepe" Puente confirmed that Andara did travel to Moscow in 1965 and return to Ensenada via Mexico City in 1966. Puente recalled that when he passed through Mexico City en route to Ensenada, Andara gave him a camel hair coat and a pair of gloves but refused to part with his Astrakhan hat.

18. At the time, Ticabus was the main international bus line serving Central America and Panama. The next-door safe house would have been on Calle 9, a main artery near the city center.

19. Harold and Alejandro Martínez are from a Conservative family

from Rivas in southwest Nicaragua. For a short biography of Harold see *Nicaraguan Biographies: A Resource Book* (Washington, D.C.: Department of State, 1988), p. 83, which also discusses the FRS, Raudales, and the later Marxist–Conservative split within the FSLN.

20. For example, Nolan begins his excellent work on Sandinista ideology with this version of the founding of the FSLN. David Nolan, *FSLN: The Ideology of the Sandinistas and the Nicaraguan Revolution* (Coral Gables, Fla.: University of Miami, 1984), p. 1.

21. Calle 23 is a main artery in the Vedado neighborhood of downtown Havana. Borge also places the FSLN's safe house in Havana in Vedado.

22. Tomás Borge tells the cover story version in *La Paciente*, 139–40.

23. The Rio Coco originates inside Nicaragua, where its course extends for over one hundred kilometers before it turns east to form the border with Honduras.

24. Guerrero did not confirm during our October 1999 conversation whether he was acting under orders or on his own, but he did confirm he issued the order to split up the group and called it "a terrible mistake." At the time Puente's father was a top labor advisor to Fidel Castro in Cuba, work he continued until just before his death, and "Pepe" Puente went on to be the key liaison between the Russians, Cubans, Mexican Communists, El Salvador's FMLN, and the Sandinistas, among others. Victor "El Mejicano" Tirado, later one of the Nine Comandantes, had been introduced into Sandinista ranks by Andara. It seems highly unlikely that Guerrero, who was then working closely with the Cubans and Russians, would have made such a fateful decision on his own.

25. She was actually Noél Guerrero's Honduran mother-in-law, and it was her Comayagüela, Honduras, home that had served as his group's safe house prior to the 1963 Bocay disaster. Guerrero is still married to her daughter Vilma.

26. According to "Pepe" Puente, Victor "El Mejicáno" Tirado was recruited into the Sandinista Front in May 1963 by fellow Mexican radical Manuel Andara, who then himself left for Moscow in 1965. Telephone interview of November 29, 1999.

27. For a short biography of Pablo Úbeda, see *Nicaraguan Biographies*, p. 15.

28. Plutarco Hernández Sancho, the ambassador of Costa Rica to Moscow in 1999 and the author of chapter 5 in this book.

29. A posthumous ghosted "autobiography" of Pomáres was published ten years after his death. Germán Pomáres Ordóñez, *El Danto: Algunas Correrías y Andánzas* (Managua, Nicaragua: Editora Nueva Nicaragua), 1989.

30. Jirón, *Quién es Quién*, pp. 19–23.

31. "Nago," short for Abdenago. "Chelita"'s real name was Graciela.

32. The Mitrokhin KGB archive indicates that the Cuban DGI (Dirección General de Inteligencia) had "expropriated" the lead role with the Sandinista Front (code name ISKRA) from the KGB early on, much to the KGB's displeasure. Andrews and Mitrokhin, *The Sword and the Shield*, p. 385.

33. Shot in Cuba many years later along with General Ochoa.

34. Confirmed by Hernández. Oral history, Plutarco Hernández S., San José, Costa Rica, September 8–9, 1997. Private collection.

35. Hernández confirmed this in his oral history.

36. Eduardo Sancho, Fermán Cienfuegos's father, is the brother of Plutarco Hernández's mother. Fermán confirmed the story in an interview in San Salvador (oral history, Eduardo Sancho Castañeda, *Fermán Cienfuegos*, San Salvador, August 14, 1998, private collection), but put the total they gave the FSLN at $18 million, about 10% of the FMLN's capital. A senior Costa Rican security official who was present at the time and in charge of airport security for the exchange in Costa Rica also confirmed it in a separate interview. Audiotape. Private collection.

37. According to Costa Rican investigative archives and dozens of other sources, most arms reached the Sandinistas directly from Cuba, with over 4 million pounds arriving in 437 cargo flights, although cover stories were put out claiming they were from Panama, Colombia, and Venezuela. See especially *Informe Sobre el Tráfico de Armas*, Comisión de Asuntos Especiales, Costa Rican National Legislature, May 14, 1981. About 3,000 pages.

Chapter 3

1. His descriptions of Sandino's abilities, ideas, and movements coincide in most regards closely to what José Obidio Puente heard from his father.

2. Videotaped at his small farm on the slopes of El Súngano mountain on February 4, 1998, with invaluable assistance from the Organiza-

tion of American States, which called him to my attention and provided a vehicle and an escort. Salvador Talavera, formerly an FDN, or Contra, field commander under the pseudonym *El Chacál* and director in 1998 of the most important agricultural cooperative in the region, Cooperativa Agropecuario 3–80, also assisted with follow-up inquiries. The cooperative is named after the late Contra Chief of General Staff, Colonel Enrique Bermúdez Varela, whose nom de guerre was *3-80.*

3. El Súngano is a mountain just opposite El Chipóte mountain, where Augusto César Sandino had his main headquarters during much of his war with the U.S. Marines. Both are near the Segovian mountain town of Quilalí. In this case it is also used by the peasants as the name of their community, which they often term *comarca.* Unlike the line or market-centered villages of Pacific lowlands Nicaragua, which was Nahua in the pre-Columbian era, the peasants' settlements in the Segovias are scattered farmsteads without central cores, the pre-Columbian settlement pattern of their ancestors, who were South American Chibchans. It is one of the societal markers that marks the sharp ethnohistoric division between the Chibchans of Nicaragua's mountains and the Nahua of its Pacific lowlands.

4. Milpa is an Indian word for cornfield.

5. Meaning solid-walled structures. In earlier days it was the custom to estimate the size of a town by the number of its solid buildings, which were the homes and/or businesses of the wealthy. Churches, government structures, and huts or mud and wattle structures were not counted.

6. The San Albino mines are just a few miles from El Súngano.

7. This would have been Sandino's first trip to Mexico that was also mentioned by Puente, not the better known second one when Puente's father met Sandino.

8. The reader may have noticed how names and places begin to repeat. Rúfo Marín was also the name of a later FSLN guerrilla leader, and José Obidio Puente's group tried to occupy Wiwilí years later.

9. Don Alejandro was able to identify several of these men from photographs I showed him in a book on Sandino officially authored by the first Somoza, Anastacio Somoza Garcia, *El Verdadero Sandino, o El Calvario de Las Segovias* (Managua: Editorial y Litografia San José, 1976). Somoza's book, although heavily documented, has been widely decried because of its authorship. Don Alejandro, although unable to

read the text as he is unlettered, identified and named many of those listed in the legends of photographs included in the book and, in one instance, identified two Sandino staff officers but said the legend had their names reversed.

10. *Botas de hule*, rubber boots, which is also urban Nicaraguan slang for peasant, the equivalent of the English despicatives "nigger" or "greaser."

11. Known as the yellow house, or Casa Amarilla.

12. *Chilote*, green ear of corn. Slang for Milpista, or one of the original 1979–1981 anti-Sandinista guerrillas of the Milicias Populares Anti-Sandinistas (MILPAS), who took up arms well before the United States was involved. The MILPAS in turn were mainly former anti-Somoza Sandinista Segovian peasant guerrillas from a unit of the 1963–1979 Sandinistas Liberation Front known as the Milicias Populares Anti-Somocistas (MILPA).

Chapter 4

1. The Vírgen de Los Angeles is the patron saint of Costa Rica.

2. Followers of Costa Rican President Rafael Ángel Calderón Guardia.

3. A Spanish colonial-era fortress just inside Havana harbor next to the more famous El Morro. In 1999, during my most recent visit to Cuba, La Cabaña was a major tourist attraction.

4. In 1998 La Cabaña became a tourist attraction, especially for its nightly re-enactment of the Spanish colonial ceremony of firing a sunset gun at the close of day. The cell block Martínez lived in now welcomes hundreds of tourists daily.

5. The military base is near Havana and the Russian electronics intelligence center at Lourdes, which was home to a Soviet brigade during the 1970s and 1980s, and was still the world's largest such site in 1999, when it remained under Russian direction.

6. The U.S. and Soviet governments publicly claimed at the time of the Cuban Missile Crisis that all Soviet missiles had been removed from Cuba. While not admitted by either government at the time, it has since also been confirmed that there were also nuclear warheads in Cuba during the crisis. Martínez's eye-witness account is consistent with persistent rumors that contrary to these claims not just missiles but also

warheads were left behind. More recently a story began to circulate in Havana that subsequently Kruschev became so concerned Castro might try to use the warheads that he sent a Speznat (Soviet Commando) unit into Cuba and removed by force against Cuban opposition those that remained.

7. Mostly from Cuba. Added up, the Costa Rican Legislature's Special Investigative Commission identified 473 cargo flights, most directly from Cuba, carrying an estimated 4 million pounds of arms and other military stores. *Trafico de Armas*, 1981.

8. Other non-Marxist FSLN officers began organizing similar opposition movements at the same time, especially among a Segovian peasant guerrilla movement known as the Milicias Populares Anti-Somocistas (MILPA). Timothy C. Brown, *The Real Contra War: Highlander Peasant Resistance in Nicaragua*, chaps. 1–3.

9. This has been substantiated by numerous Costa Rican participants, including the then Minister of Public Security and Costa Rican security officers. Oral history, Juan José "Johnny" Echeverria Brealey, San José, Costa Rica, November 15, 1994, videotape; oral history, Carlos Manuel Zúñiga Duran, San José, September 1997, videotape; interviews, Echeverria Brealey and Zuñiga Durán, 1997. Private collection.

10. According to then CIA deputy director for operations (DDO) for Latin America, "President Carter signed a series of Presidential Findings in the fall of 1980, authorizing CIA covert action, and the Central American Task Force (CATF) had been formed to implement them." Dewey Clarrige, *A Spy for All Seasons* (New York: Scribner's, 1997), p. 196. These have not yet been fully declassified.

11. On page 17 of Martínez's Costa Rican passport, number 8-043-357, there is a three-month One Entry Non-Immigrant B-1 Visa, number 003605, issued by the U.S. Embassy in San José, Costa Rica, on January 13, 1981. The same page also contains a U.S. Immigration Miami entry stamp dated January 15, 1981. A B-1 visa is for business only. Had his trip been for pleasure he would have received a B-2 tourist visa. Ronald Reagan was inaugurated January 20, 1981. See appendix.

12. The exact street address, although known, has been withheld for reasons of privacy.

13. Names withheld, although several are known to have been involved later in the "Contra project."

14. A number of these officers provided extensive verbatim testimo-

nies to that effect to a special commission of the Costa Rican National Assembly. See *Trafico de Armas*.

Chapter 5

1. A second highly reliable Costa Rican source (identity reserved) claims to have met Fidel Castro in 1948 when some Cuban revolutionaries were living in La Marseillesa Pension (boardinghouse) in Barrio La Merced, San José, Costa Rica. Although this does not fully coincide with other accounts of Fidel's movements, it is consistent with reports that he was in the region in 1948 as a member of the Caribbean Legion and the April 1948 Bogotázo popular uprising in Colombia, although there are no reports that he fought in support of José "Pepe" Figueres Ferrer during Costa Rica's 1948 war.

2. Manuel Jirón, *Quién es Quién* (San José: Editorial Radio Amor), pp. 206–211.

3. Hernández is thus the nephew of President Calderón Guardia on his father's side and first cousin of later President Calderón Fournier.

4. Because both Figueres Ferrer and Calderón Guardia had sons who became presidents of Costa Rica later, both patronyms and matronyms are used to distinguish between fathers and sons.

5. According to Hernández, Mora was a regular visitor at his home in Barrio La Merced, Costa Rica, as was "Pepe" Figueres. Oral history, Plutarco Hernández, San José, September 1997, videotape, private collection.

6. Benemeritos de La Patria are national heroes.

Chapter 6

1. Drawn from a in-depth oral history interview with the subject. Oral history, Eduardo Sancho Castañeda, *Fermán Cienfuegos*, San Salvador, El Salvador, August 14, 1998. Audiotape. Private collection.

2. In separate conversations, the total was put at about $184 million, of which between $15 and $18 million were given to the FSLN between 1977 and 1979. While an extraordinary sum to generate through kidnappings and other "recuperations" *Fermán Cienfuegos,* the military commander of El Salvador's FMLN during the period when it was collected up, publicly confirmed this amount in 1998 in Puebla,

Mexico, during his presentation. "Pepe" Puente told me in September 1999 that $184 million is correct and that he personally had managed much of this money for the FMLN, investing large amounts in several countries and arranging for Plutarco Hernández to carry about $15 million in cash to Costa Rica for the Sandinista Front.

3. Altogether, according to Eduardo Sancho, an estimated 83,000 small arms were provided to the FMLN by the FSLN.

4. Then Colonels Jaime Abdúl Gutiérrez and Adolfo Majano. Extensive discussions of solutions to El Salvador's problems took place in my home in San Salvador. The reported closeness of later General Gutiérrez to the United States may stem from this.

Chapter 7

1. For a short biographical sketch see *Nicaraguan Biographies*, 44–45. Encarnación's brother Francisco, *Dímas de Tigrillo*, is also listed.

2. Named after a Nicaraguan heroine. In 1948, Rosendo Argüello, a Nicaraguan Independent Liberal who had fought alongside Costa Rica's José Figueres and then become chief of Figueres's presidential guard, also chose the name "Compania Rafael Herrera" to differentiate his unit from the Caribbean Legion. Charles Ameringer, *The Caribbean Legion* (University Park: Pennsylvania State University Press, 1995), p. 80.

3. In January of 1984 the Rafaela Herrera Regional Command had 1,943 comandos officially enrolled in its ranks and was the largest formation in the FDN. Status of Forces Report, Cuartel General General, Fuerza Democrática Nicaragüense, February 2, 1984. Private collection.

4. Oral history, Encarnación Baldivia, *Tigrillo*. Matagalpa, Nicaragua, June 8, 1998. Videotape. Private collection.

5. By June 10, 1987, according to Sandinista army records, 6,441 Sandinista army officers had been trained in Cuba, another 1,143 in the Soviet Union, 120 in East Germany, and 56 in Bulgaria, for a total of 7,356. "Resumen de Oficiales Preparados el E.P.S, 6-10-87," Hoover Institution Archives.

6. *Tigrillo*, wildcat. The *tigre* or *tigrillo* is admired by the peasants for its independence and ferocity, so it was a good name. It also had historical connotations. For example, then U.S. Marine Captain and

later General "Chesty" Puller, when fighting in Nicaragua against General Sandino, earned from the peasants the nickname "El Tigre de Las Segovias."

7. The author of chapter 8.

8. By then, González had been killed.

9. The doctor was Alejandro Ortega, pseudonym *Dr. Javier.* Subsequent to the war he became a medical doctor with the Organization of American States. The rescue operation, in itself a fascinating saga, was recounted separately to me by Dr. Ortega in August of 1998.

10. *Comandante 3-80* was Colonel Enríque Bermúdez, the Resistance's top military commander. *Rigoberto*'s real name was Tirzo Moreno. He was a former Somoza-era Sandinista guerrilla who had served with Germán Pomares, *El Danto. Aureliano* was Manuel Rugáma, a medical doctor who became the field commander of the Regional Force Segovia. He was killed in an unexplained ambush in Honduras after the war ended. *Nicaraguan Biographies*, pp. 48, 52.

11. Lethal aid included weapons, munitions, and purely military items. Humanitarian assistance was not included, although the line between the two was not always easy to distinguish. When is a radio military and when a civilian? A truck? A pair of boots? and so forth.

12. *Franklyn,* also known as *Franklyn 16*, Israel Galeano, brother of *Tiro al Blanco. Rubén,* Oscar Sobalvarro, who tells his own story in chapter 8.

13. The predecessor to the eventual author of chapter 13.

14. When I went to La Concordia to ask *Tigrillo* to go to the Third Congress of the Americas, he agreed only if I first helped him burn his bean fields so he could get his crop in. It became an example of hands-on scholarship.

15. "Compa" stood for *compañero,* Spanish for comrade. There were even mixed groups of comandos and *compas* known as *Revueltos,* with their common denominator being peasant origins. In February of 1997, twenty-seven groups were still operating in the province of Jinotega alone, with a total of 236 combatants. "Consolidación de Grupos Armados Departamento Jinotega," Programa de Seguimiento y Verificación (PSV), CIAV/OEA, Mes Febrero 1997, private collection. In February of 1996, another twenty-one groups with twenty-one combatants were reported active in Matagalpa. "Cuadro de Grupos Armados Departamento Matagalpa," Mes de Febrero 1996, P.S.V., CIAV/OEA. Of these groups, eight had leaders using the nom de guerre *Culebra,* and at

least one was a Galeano clansman. Private collection. The last important disarmament of such groups took place in March of 1998, although a few reportedly still remain. By then it had become difficult to differentiate between groups with legitimate grievances and simple bandits.

16. Named after the *Pablo Úbeda* discussed by "Pepe" Puente in chapter 2.

Chapter 8

1. Pomares, *Algunas Correrias*, p. 159. His comrades, including then active Marxist revolutionaries José Obidio Puente and Plutarco Hernández, who was *El Danto*'s comrade and sometimes commanding officer for over twenty years, both of whom appear in this book, are convinced he was assassinated under order of radicals within the FSLN. The intellectual author they name is Humberto Ortega Saavedra, later commanding general of the Sandinista People's Army, the EPS.

2. For short sketches of Oscar and three of his brothers, see *Nicaraguan Biographies*, p. 56.

3. The following essay combines remarks made by Sobalvarro to the Third Congress of the Americas, Puebla, Mexico, March 1998, and during an extensive oral history interview on December 13, 1994, in Managua, Nicaragua, conducted by the author. Private collection.

4. He is incorrectly identified in *Nicaraguan Biographies*, p. 35, as Mamerto Torrera.

5. Irene Calderón is the most controversial figure in early Resistance/Contra history. He disappeared from their ranks in 1983 after returning to Nicaragua independently. Rumors of what then happened to him ranged from allegations that he defected to the Sandinistas to claims that he was killed by them. He was quietly released from a Nicaraguan military prison in 1994, four years after the government had claimed all former Resistance prisoners had been freed. Today he lives quietly in Nicaragua but thus far has refused to tell his story.

6. A Status of Forces report in February 1983 puts the number inside Nicaragua at 4,299 (Estado de Fuerzas, Cuartel General General Fuerza Democrática Nicaragüense, 2 de Febrero de 1983. Private collection). By the end of the year this had grown to 8,104. (Estado de Fuerzas, Cuartel General General Fuerza Democratica Nicaragüense, January 2, 1984. Private collection). These were only those comandos

officially enrolled in the FDN and provided weapons and training. The actual number of combatants, including recruits still inside and armed *correos*, or intelligence support activists, was several thousand more.

7. This often caused confusion and tensions. Both the Guardia and their American counterparts at headquarters often assumed the FDN was organized like a professional army, from top down and under tight command and control. In fact it was organized from the bottom up, with control in the hands of the peasants, not the general staff.

8. Assumptions by outsiders that the FDN/ERN was a conventional army were the foundation beneath concerns outside Nicaragua about the role of former Guardia Nacional at the top headquarters level. In fact, they functioned mainly as an administrative staff. Although the top command could and did plan operations, it could only suggest, not order, actions and had little authority over officer selection beneath its own ranks. Toward the end, it lost even this authority to a council of commanders elected from below with the authority to appoint or remove members of the general staff. It was this council that elected Sobalvarro chief of staff in 1989.

Chapter 9

1. *La Chapárra*'s real name is Elisa María Galeano Cornejo. Oral history, Elisa María Galeano Cornejo, *La Chapárra*, November 30, 1994, videotape. Private collection. The Cornejos, like the Galeanos, were a large highlander clan that supported the Resistance.

2. Not further identified.

3. The blue uniforms were actually work clothes purchased from Montgomery Ward. Earlier photos of the Contras show them in these uniforms. Private collection.

4. The first Zébras were formed on July 23, 1979, in Choluteca, Honduras. They, not the Legión 15 de Septiembre, were actually the earliest exile Guardia organization. A copy of their initial personnel roster is in a private collection.

5. An estimated 6 percent of the comandos were women, and they served alongside the men in mixed-gender units. About 3,000 women fought as comandos, and over 1,000 were killed in action. Brown, *The Real Contra War*, chapter 8.

6. The Contras were probably unique among guerrilla armies in

that they had specially trained human rights officers with each unit of sixty or more.

Chapter 10

1. As used here, "Spaniard" is a despicative for Pacific lowlands Nicaraguan.

2. This is a surprising statement coming from a Miskito, because it recognizes the peasants of those two departments as Indians rather than Spaniards. This is the thesis I have endorsed in several articles; see, for example, "Nahuas, Gachupines, Patriarchs and Piris: Nicaraguan History Through Highlands Peasant Eyes," *Journal of Popular Culture* (Summer 1997). It is also partly endorsed by Jeffrey Gould in his *To Die in This Way: Nicaraguan Indians and the Myth of Mestisaje, 1880–1965* (Durham: Duke University Press, 1998).

3. For a discussion of this, see Brown, *The Real Contra War.*

4. See Gould, *To Die.*

5. Contrary to popular opinion at the time, there were several independently organized and led Contra armies, not one. The largest, with about 80 percent of the total, was the FDN; the second largest, YATAMA, with about 10 percent. The third largest was the Southern Front of Edén Pastora. The fourth, the Floyd Wilsons, was black English-speaking Creole. There were also the *Súmus de Las Montanas,* a Súmu Indian task force, and an internal front. There is also evidence that a few MILPAS continued to operate independently and that at least one MILPAS group was still active as recently as 1996. Periodic U.S. support was given only to the first three and the internal front. The Sumus, Floyd Wilsons, and MILPAS were given arms and military supplies by the FDN secretly, without U.S. knowledge.

6. Many were documented by CIAV/OAS in a series of public reports. See CIAV/OEA Nicaragua, Programa de Seguimiento y Verificación, "Informes estadisticos de denuncias por Homicidio: Desmovilizados de la Resistancia y familiares," Managua, and *Nicaragua: La Frontera del Conflicto* (Managua: CIAV/OEA, 1995). Resistance Human Rights offices reported the number of murders was about 3,000, more than three times the number CIAV documented. Because not one single perpetrator identified by CIAV was ever prosecuted and those who filed charges were often themselves assaulted or killed, the Resis-

tance Human Rights offices claimed that after a while the peasants simply stopped reporting murders and other serious violations to CIAV. Although this difference could not be fully resolved, I found considerable evidence to support the Resistance's number over CIAV's far more conservative one.

Chapter 11

1. Excepting the narcotrafficking connection, this history would seem to parallel postwar periods of violence against former FMLN guerrillas mentioned by Fermán Cienfuegos and against former Resistance comandos mentioned by various earlier authors.

Chapter 12

1. Brown, *Causes.*
2. James S. Wunch and Dele Olowu, eds., *The Failure of the Centralized State: Institutions and Governance in Africa* (Geneva: Institute for International Studies, 1995).
3. Brown, *Causes*, p. 15.

Chapter 13

1. The home *comarca* of Don Alejandro Pérez Bustamante. See chapter 3.

Chapter 14

1. Samuel Stone (Zemurray), *The Heritage of the Conquistadores: Ruling Classes in Central America from the Conquistadores to the Sandinistas* (Lincoln: University of Nebraska, 1990). Another useful study is Harry W. Strachan's *Family and Other Business Groups: The Case of Nicaragua* (New York: Praeger, 1976). My studies, Timothy C. Brown, "Realist Revolutions: Free Trade, Open Economies, Participatory Democracy, and Their Impact on Latin American Politics," *Policy Studies Review* 15, no. 2/3 (Summer/Autumn 1998), pp. 35–51, and Brown, *The Real Contra War*, 2000, may also be of interest.
2. Brown, *The Real Contra War*, 2000.

BIBLIOGRAPHY

Alarcon Ramírez, Dariel. *"Benigno," Memorias de un Soldado Cubano; Vida y Muerte de la Revolucíon*. Barcelona, Spain: Tusquets Editores, 1997.

Ameringer, Charles D. *The Caribbean Legion: Patriots, Politicians, Soldiers of Fortune, 1946–1950*. University Park: Pennsylvania University Press, 1996.

Andrews, Christopher, and Mitrokhin, Vasili. *The Sword and the Shield: The Mitrokhin Archive and the Secret History of the KGB*. New York: Basic Books, 1999.

Barquero, Sara L. *Gobernantes de Nicaragua, 1825–1947*. Managua, Nicaragua: Publicaciones del Ministerio de Instruccion Publica y E.F., 1945.

Borge, Tómas. *La Paciente*. Mexico City: Editorial Diana, 1981.

Borge, Tomás, *La Paciente Impacientia*. Buenos Aires, Argentina: Editorial Contrapunto, 1986.

Brown, Timothy C. *Causes of Continuing Conflict in Nicaragua: A View from the Radical Middle*. Stanford: Hoover Institution Press, 1995.

————. "Realist Revolutions: Free Trade, Open Economies, Participatory Democracy, and Their Impact on Latin American Politics." *Policy Studies Review* 15, no. 2/3 (Summer/Autumn 1998): 35–51.

————. "Nahuas, Gachupines, Patriarchs and Piris: Nicaraguan History Through Highlands Peasant Eyes." *Journal of Popular Culture* (Summer 1997).

————. "Comandos of the Comarcas: The Origins of Nicaragua's Contra War." Ph.D. dissertation, New Mexico State University, 1997.

————. *The Real Contra War: Highlander Peasant Resistance in Nicaragua.* Norman: University of Oklahoma Press, 2000.

Chamorro, Pedro Joaquin. *Estírpe Sangrienta Los Somoza.* Mexico, City: Patria y Libertad, 1957.

CIAV/OAS. *Nicaragua, La Frontera del Conflicto.* Managua, Nicaragua: CIAV/OEA, 1995.

————. "Informes estadisticos de denuncias por homicidio—desmovilizados de la Resistencia y familiares." Programa de Seguimiento y Verificacíon, Managua, Nicaragua: CIAV/OEA, April 1996.

Clarrige, Dewey. *A Spy for All Seasons.* New York: Scribner's, 1997.

Colmenares, Francisco. *Petroleo y lucha de clases en Mexico, 1864–1982.* Mexico City: Ediciones El Caballito, 1986.

Del Vasto, César, *El "Ché" Guevara estuvo en Panama.* Panama City: Editorial Portobelo, 1997.

Fonseca Amador, Carlos. *Un Nicaragüense en Moscú.* Managua, Editorial Artes Graficas, 1958.

Gazetteer of Nicaragua, 3d ed. Washington, D.C.: Defense Mapping Agency, 1985.

Gould, Jeffrey, *To Die This Way: Nicaraguan Indians and the Myth of Mestisaje, 1880–1965.* Durham: University of North Carolina Press, 1998.

Hernandez Sancho, Plutarco Elías. *El FSLN Por Dentro—Relatos de un combatiente.* San Jose, Costa Rica: Trejos Hermanos, 1982.

Hodges, Donald C. *The Intellectual Foundations of the Nicaraguan Revolution.* Austin: University of Texas Press, 1986.

Informe Sobre el Trafico de Armas. San José, Costa Rica: Comision Especial, National Assembly, May 14, 1981.

Jiron, Manuel. *Quién es Quién en Nicaragua.* San José, Costa Rica: Editorial Radio Amor, 1986.

Macauley, Niell. *The Sandino Affair*. Durham, N.C.: Duke University Press, 1985.

Mendieta, Alfaro. *Oláma y Mojellónes*. Managua, Nicaragua: Impressiones CARQUI, 1992.

Morales Carazo, Jaime. *La Contra: Anatomía de una multiple traición: Bahia de Cochinos de Reagan?* Mexico City: Editorial Planeta, 1989.

Nicaraguan Biographies: A Resource Book. Washington, D.C.: United States Department of State, Special Report No. 174, January 1988.

Nolan, David. *FSLN: The Ideology of the Sandinistas and the Nicaraguan Revolution*. Coral Gables, Fla.: University of Miami Press, 1984.

Organization of American States. *La Comisión Internacionál de Apoyo y Verificacíon: La Experiencia de la OEA en Nicaragua, 1990–1997*. Washington, D.C.: OAS, 2000.

———. *Demobilizing and Integrating the Nicaraguan Resistance, 1990–1997*. Washington, D.C.: General Secretariat of the OAS, 1998.

Osorno Coleman, Salomón *[Comandante Blass]. Diario—Anos 1983–1985*, mss, private collection.

Pérez-Brignoli, Hector. *A Brief History of Central America*. Berkeley: University of California Press, 1989.

Pomáres Ordoñez, Germán. *El Danto: Algunas Correrias y Andánzas*. Managua, Nicaragua: Editora Nueva Nicaragua, 1989.

Quirk, Robert E. *Fidel Castro*. New York and London: W. W. Norton & Co., 1993.

Ramírez, Sergio. *El Pensamiento Vivo de Sandino: Selección y Notas*. Havana, Cuba: Casa de Las Americas, 1980.

———. *Adios Muchachos—Una memoria de la revolución Sandinista*. Mexico City: Aguilar, 1999.

Rojas, Marta, and Rodríguez, Mirta, eds. *Tania—The Unforgettable Guerrilla*. New York: Random House, 1971.

Somoza Garcia, Anastacio. *El Verdadero Somoza, o El Calvario de Las Segovias*. Managua, Nicaragua: Editorial y Litografia San José, 1936.

Stone (Zemurray), Samuel. *The Heritage of the Conquistadores: Ruling Classes in Central America from the Conquistadores to the Sandinistas*. Lincoln: University of Nebraska Press, 1990.

Strachan, Harry W. *Family and Other Business Groups in Economic Development: The Case of Nicaragua*. New York: Praeger, 1976.

Thomas, Hugh. *Cuba: The Pursuit of Freedom*. New York: Harper & Row Publishers, 1971.

Tórres Rivas, Edelbérto. *Crísis en el Podér en Centroamerica*. San José, Costa Rica: EDUCA, 1989.

Villanueva, Carlos. *Sandino en Yucatán: 1929–1930*. Mexico City: Secretaria de Educacion Publica, 1988.

Villega Mora, Xavier. *Petróleo, Sangre y Jusicia*. Mexico City: Editorial Relampagos, 1938.

Volpini, Federico. *Desde Managua*. Barcelona, Spain: Plaza y Janes Editores, 1987.

Wheelock, Jaime. *Nicaragua: El papel de La Vanguárdia*. Mexico City: Editorial Diana, 1989.

———. *1 Papel*. Buenos Aires: Editorial Contrapunto, 1986.

Willoughby, Malcolm F. *Rum War at Sea*. Washington, D.C.: U.S. Government Printing Office, 1964.

Wunch, James S., and Olamu, Dela. *The Failure of the Centralized States: Institutions and Governance in Africa*. Geneva: Institute for International Studies, 1995.

Index